MONOPOLISTIC
COMPETITION AND
INTERNATIONAL TRADE

MONOPOLISTIC COMPETITION AND INTERNATIONAL TRADE

Edited by
HENRYK KIERZKOWSKI

CLARENDON PRESS · OXFORD

Oxford University Press, Walton Street, Oxford OX2 6DP
Oxford New York Toronto
Delhi Bombay Calcutta Madras Karachi
Petaling Jaya Singapore Hong Kong Tokyo
Nairobi Dar es Salaam Cape Town
Melbourne Auckland
and associated companies in
Berlin Ibadan

Oxford is a trade mark of Oxford University Press

Published in the United States
by Oxford University Press, New York

First published 1984
Reprinted 1985

First Published in Paperback 1989

British Library Cataloguing in Publication Data
Monopolistic competition and international trade.
1. Monopolies
I. Kierzkowski, Henryk
338.8'2'01   HD2757.2
ISBN 0–19–828467–5
ISBN 0–19–828726–7 (Pbk)

Library of Congress Cataloging in Publication Data
Main entry under title:
Monopolistic competition and international trade.
Papers presented at a workshop at the Graduate Institute of
International Studies, Geneva, in June 1982.
Bibliography: p.
Includes index,
1. Competition, International—Congresses.   2. Commerce—
Congresses.   3. Industrial organization—Congresses.   4. Oligopolies—
Congresses.   I. Kierzkowski, Henryk.   II. Graduate Institute of
International Studies (Geneva, Switzerland)
HF1414.M66 1974   382.1'04   83–26727
ISBN 0–19–828467–5
ISBN 0–19–828726–7 (Pbk)

Printed and bound in
Great Britain by Biddles Ltd,
Guildford & King's Lynn

Acknowledgements

The conference on monopolistic competition and international trade was held at the Graduate Institute of International Studies, Geneva, in June 1982. I gratefully acknowledge the financial assistance provided by the Graduate Institute of International Studies, Nestlé and Ciba-Geigy. In addition to the authors of the papers, Max Corden, Victoria Curzon, Ronald Findlay, Jacques L'Huillier, and Frederic Pryor also participated in the meeting and I wish to thank them as well for their involvement and contributions.

HENRYK KIERZKOWSKI

Contents

viii   *Contents*

1
Introduction

Henryk Kierzkowski

International trade theory was until very recently dominated by the competitive paradigm. Monopolistic competition, fifty years after the publication of Chamberlin's book, has yet to take the place it deserves in international trade literature and teaching of the subject. To be fair, most of the trade textbooks have a chapter or two on imperfect competition; similarly most of those involved in university teaching cover the topic, time permitting, in the standard trade course, but it usually gets a 'curiosity' treatment. This situation, however, is now in the process of change.

In the last few years, several important contributions have provoked an avalanche of research on monopolistic competition and international trade. One of the earliest was the empirical book of Grubel and Lloyd (1975) which clearly demonstrated the importance of intra-industry trade between developed countries with similar factor endowments and technological know-how. The Heckscher–Ohlin model with its reliance on relative factor endowments as the basis for trade could not provide a satisfactory explanation of this phenomenon. As a result the attention of theorists has been increasingly directed towards preferences as a source of trade.

Two important theoretical contributions were made soon after the publication of the Grubel and Lloyd work. Dixit and Stiglitz (1977) have modelled situations where individuals value variety and where the production side of the economy is characterized by monopolistic rather than perfect competition. Their model has an immediate importance for international trade theory which has already been demonstrated by several authors. For example, Krugman (1979, 1980, 1981) proves that international exchange of goods can, in addition to improving allocation of resources, bring about greater variety.

An alternative approach to product variety has been presented by Lancaster (1979). In his version, products represent bundles of characteristics and every consumer has his most preferred 'package' of characteristics. This, again, gives rise to demand for variety at the aggregate level. Due to the existence of internal economies of scale, only some consumers are able to obtain their ideal product, others buy differentiated goods which only approximate their most preferred model. The characteristic approach has been applied to international trade by Lancaster (1980) and Helpman (1981) among others. It readily explains intra-industry trade by showing that no single variety of a differentiated product can be produced in more than one country. Both the Dixit–Stiglitz and Lancaster approach to product differentiation rely on the existence of increasing returns to scale and, naturally, extend the vast body of literature on international trade in homogeneous products with increasing returns to scale. These two fields coexist and reinforce each other.

Industrial organization models for closed economies have become an additional source of inspiration for researchers concerned with monopolistic competition in international trade. Market structure can by itself provide a basis for trade. One of the more interesting applications of this type has been provided by Brander (1981) who has shown that market segmentation can lead to two-way trade in the same good. This trade may be beneficial by increasing competition.

The present book offers a collection of the most recent contributions to the field of monopolistic competition in international trade. These papers which were with only a few exceptions presented at a special conference at the Graduate Institute of International Studies in Geneva in the summer of 1982 illustrate the vastness of the topic and the multitude of approaches. They also suggest new directions for research and offer a number of policy conclusions and implications.

The opening paper in this volume (Chapter 2) provides a valuable service to the profession. Its authors, James Markusen and James Melvin, attempt to look across the existing models and establish conditions for gains from trade in the world of increasing returns to scale. The failure of the gains-from-trade theorem can be traced to two sources: first, prices being in excess of marginal costs (the tangency condition); and second, non-convexities in the production structure (the convexity condition). With regard to the first condition several authors, and among them Kemp and Negishi (1970), Eaton and Ponagariya (1979), Markusen and Melvin (1981) have already demonstrated that gains from trade can be assured if the output of every good produced with increasing returns to scale technology is greater under trade than in autarky. An expansion of the industries with economies to scale is only a sufficient, but not necessary, conditions for gains from trade. Markusen and Melvin push the analysis further by arguing that the sufficient condition is somewhat weaker than previously thought. The addition of non-convexities in the production set makes the conditions for gains from trade more complex. The final contribution of the Markusen–Melvin paper consists of showing that recent monopolistic competition models often rely on a number of restrictive assumptions which guarantee that both the tangency and convexity conditions are satisfied.

In the Lancasterian world different varieties of a differentiated product are of the same quality. The choice of the preferred model of an individual does not depend on his income and consumers just happen to have different ideal types of differentiated good. This representation of consumers' preferences is a case of horizontal differentiation. Avner Shaked and John Sutton are concerned with an alternative representation of consumers' preferences. They discuss the case of vertical differentiation in their contribution to this volume (Chapter 3).

According to them, products differ in quality and consumers choose different types of a differentiated product, not so much because their tastes are different, but rather because their incomes are different. This specification of preferences harks back to the model of Linder (1961) in which the range of goods consumed in a particular country depends on the average level of income and its distribution.

In the case of horizontal differentiation, an increase in the size of the market through opening of trade tends to increase the number of products varieties which consumers can purchase. As the market expands, the number of firms producing the differentiated good increases as well and therefore the typical consumer gets a product which is closer to his ideal model. In the limit the differentiated good industry becomes atomistic. Under vertical differentiation, depending on the interaction of tastes and technology, there may be a limit to the number of firms operating in the market which is quite independent of the size of the market. As a result, the opening of trade may provoke competition which will lead to price reductions and also force firms producing low-quality goods to leave the industry. The remaining producers will, in the long run, improve the quality of their products thus further enhancing consumers' welfare.

In the best tradition of theory of product differentiation, Shaked and Sutton have increased the variety of available model specifications. In doing so they have drawn attention to the sensitivity of results to the specification of consumer choice over differentiated products. Clearly more can and should be done on vertical differentiation. It should be most useful to endogenize distribution of income and capture the interplay between model changes, commodity prices, and factor rewards. One also needs to explore further whether the 'finiteness property', i.e. the existence of an upper limit to the number of firms which can operate independently of the market size, is specific to the vertical differentiation model or whether it can be also generated under the horizontal differentiation.

Henrik Horn's paper (Chapter 4) contributes to the discussion of optimal product diversity and more precisely the relationship between the size and openness of the economy and socially optimal manifold of products. The traditional literature does not offer a consensus on this question; Hotelling (1929), for instance, argued that the market mechanism would produce too little product variety whereas Chamberlin (1933) held the opposite view. More recently, Dixit and Stiglitz (1977) and Spence (1976) came out in support of the Hotelling view, and Koenker and Perry (1981) demonstrated the importance of the assumption regarding firms' conjectures about rivals' behaviour to the question of excess diversity.

The model developed by Horn generalizes various special assumptions with regard to expected responses of competitors and also demonstrates that in a small country the unrestricted market equilibrium is likely to be characterized by excess product diversity compared with social optimum whereas in a large economy one can expect to find too little diversity. It follows then that opening of trade between similar countries is likely to reduce excessive product variety.

When the market mechanism does not produce the optimal solution, different regulatory policies may be called for. Henrik Horn considers two types of regulations – output control and structural control – and shows that their relative welfare-improving potential depends on the size of the economy, with structural regulations likely to be more efficient in large countries.

A substantial part of the literature on imperfect competition invokes the zero-profit condition in determining equilibrium. Entry, price, and output decisions are typically taken simultaneously and although a fixed production cost is often assumed to exist, it is not a sunk cost. The contestable market model offers a good description of many market situations but it is only one member of the family of monopolistic competition models. Alternative formulations seem worth studying. In contrast with the usual practice, Eaton and Kierzkowski develop a model (Chapter 5) of industrial structure where entry and price decisions are taken sequentially. A typical firm first makes a decision on whether to enter a differentiated-product industry and on the model it wishes to produce. Only at the second stage does it decide on prices and output. This sequential decision-making is judged particularly appropriate in the international trade context and it follows in the tradition of Linder (1961) and Vernon (1966).

The abandoning of the contestable market framework produces a number of new results. Pure profits can now exist in full equilibrium. Since firms select models prior to taking output and price decisions, free entry no longer leads to average-cost pricing. Firms using product selection as a means of entry deterrence and an artificial monopoly may be established by an appropriate model choice. Opening of trade may have an impact on the structure of an economy even if actual trade does not materialize. It is also no longer necessarily true that trade gives rise to greater product variety and is welfare-improving. Eaton and Kierzkowski show cases where just the opposite happens.

Frances Stewart has been interested for some time in problems faced by developing countries and her paper (Chapter 6) draws implications from the new trade theories for the South. Although the view that the Heckscher–Ohlin model is basically useless because of its reliance on unrealistic assumptions is probably held only by a small minority, the need to develop new theoretical formulations is commonly recognized by the profession. This volume, it is hoped, attests to this desire. The new models which are now emerging need not be viewed as a substitute for the Heckscher–Ohlin framework but rather as refinement thereof. This point has been forcefully made by Helpman (1981) who generalized the Heckscher–Ohlin model by introducing product differentiation and monopolistic competition. It is commendable that these new models can be directly applied to North–South trade. The following paper by Avinash Dixit is particularly useful in this respect, along with the papers of Shaked and Sutton, Krugman, and Eaton and Kierzkowski. Unfortunately, there is still a long way to go. As Stewart points out, one of the most important questions which remains unanswered concerns South–South trade.

Models of monopolistic competition can shed new light on old and much-debated questions; one of the more prominent being the supposed failure of developing countries to gain benefits from trade with developed countries. As Avinash Dixit points out, this failure has been often associated with the alleged monopoly power of the North. The debate has however suffered from the lack of a formal model of trade under imperfect competition between developed and developing countries and Dixit proposes, in Chapter 7, to fill this gap.

In the Dixit model, the North and the South produce non-traded goods under constant returns to scale. In addition, the developing countries produce an intermediate product (again with constant returns) which is then used to produce differentiated goods in the developed countries. In this kind of framework the question of losses and gains from trade cannot be reduced to terms of trade changes for account has to be taken of the extent to which growth affects the variety of the differentiated products available to the consumers in the North as well as in the South (whose consumption patterns are allowed in the model to differ).

Growth in the developed countries, identified in this one-factor framework with an expansion of the labour force, improves the commodity and also the double-factoral terms of trade of the developing countries. In addition, it also increases product variety. When the developing countries grow, terms of trade turn against them; however, this process may be accompanied by greater product diversity. Dixit establishes the precise condition under which the variety effect can dominate the terms of trade effect resulting from the LDCs growth. He also shows possible applications of the model to questions such as technological progress and tariffs.

In the classic paradigm of international trade, capital movements resulting from private decisions based on profit maximization usually lead to social welfare maximization as well. This coincidence of social and private welfare stems from marginal-cost pricing which underlies equilibrium in a competitive economy. The marginal-cost pricing goes by the board as soon as the economic system operates under increasing returns to scale. If free entry is assured, prices will reflect average, rather than marginal, costs. If under imperfect competition an inflow of one unit of foreign capital no longer increases the gross domestic product by the market rate of return, can private capital flows still be expected to be socially beneficial? This is the question raised and answered by Elhanan Helpman and Assaf Razin in Chapter 8.

The model developed in Helpman (1981) can be readily applied to welfare analysis of capital movements. In addition to the traditional channels through which capital flows affect a country's economic well-being, two new influences come into play: first, changes in the scale of operation of the average firm; and second, changes in product diversity. The significance of the latter effect is self-explanatory. As far as the former is concerned, Helpman and Razin show in a very elegant way that with economies of scale a unit capital inflow increases the gross domestic product by more (less) than the market rental rate if it provokes an increase (decrease) of the individual firm's size. It should be pointed out that the variety and size effect need not work in the same direction. Given the general results established by Helpman and Razin, one can readily construct cases where investing and host countries can suffer a welfare loss from private capital movements. This analysis, then, carries an important policy implication.

Several contributions to this volume deal with different aspects of commercial policy. Kelvin Lancaster takes up (Chapter 9) an important problem of the relationship between product differentiation (the number of goods produced) and product variety (the number of goods consumed). In a closed economy the two must be the same. When international trade is allowed to take place, the average country tends to produce a smaller number of goods than is consumed by its domestic residents.

To what extent will product differentiation and product variety change when a country imposes a non-prohibitive tariff? It turns out that the result depends on the arrangement of goods along the taste spectrum (represented by a line). One can distinguish the 'interleaved' case where products of two countries alternate in specification and the 'split' case where all the domestic producers are situated, say, to the left of a point on the taste spectrum, and the foreign producers are to the right of that point. Lancaster shows that a tariff reduces the degree of product differentiation in the split case. One can see how the latter result comes about. When a domestic firm faces foreign, rather than domestic, producers in the adjacent markets, tariff protection increases its monopoly power and hence profits. Excess profits attract new entrants to the differentiated product industry who offer consumers new models which were not produced under free trade. Lancaster advances a number of reasons why the interleaved case is more appropriate and recognizes that the arrangement of the firms on the spectrum should be endogenously determined. Indeed, this issue is investigated in depth in the next contribution to this volume.

The paper by Bruce Lyons (Chapter 10) follows the neo-Hotelling–Lancaster tradition of the treatment of differentiated products. It shows how equilibrium with flexible locations (along the product spectrum) will be established. The general result is that the most profitable location of products is Lancaster's interleaving arrangement with alternate products produced in each country. This may be seen as the location which minimizes the firm's transport costs while maximizing entry deterrence.

Against this background, multinational firms have an incentive to develop in such a way that they can price and space optimally both along the spectrum and geographically. One would expect firms to specialize along segments of the spectrum, but with each firm producing in two countries. This result gets reinforced when producers are concerned with problems such as tariffs and the bargaining power of trade unions. Multi-product firms also benefit by being able to effectively 'threaten' to remain immobile even when fixed costs are not fully sunk into specific locations. This makes for an alternative entry barrier and positive long-run profits.

In a profession as divided as economics, one of the very few proposals which can claim almost universal support is that, generally, speaking, protection is not a sound policy. This kind of conclusion should not be expected to be well received by the business community. Indeed it is not; the average businessman continues to assert that protection may not only offer advantages in the home market but in foreign markets as well. This persistent divergence of opinion between those who do and those who teach may be partly due to a different perception of what the real world is like. Paul Krugman has explicitly set out (Chapter 11) to provide a model which would render the protectionist argument more sensible. Instead of perfect competition and constant returns to scale, he assumes that markets are oligopolistic and segmented and production can be characterized by internal economies of scale. Using a multi-market Curnot model, Krugman shows how protection of the domestic market can allow a country to achieve economies of scale and, as a result, become more competitive in unprotected markets. Import protection can thus serve as an instrument of export promotion policy. A similar result follows in a dynamic setting with costs reductions based either on R & D investments or some learning-by-doing process.

If markets are imperfectly competitive it may happen that the existing firms earn pure profits. That policy intervention may be justified under imperfect competition has been recognized previously by numerous authors. James Brander and Barbara Spencer develop the argument further and show (Chapter 12) how a tariff can be applied to shift profits from foreign to domestic firms. A domestic producer following Curnot duopoly strategy always profits from tariff protection. Welfare of the home country may improve as well but as Corden (1974) pointed out, and Brander and Spencer amplify, a subsidy rather than a tariff may be the optimum policy. The two authors offer an ingenious explanation why tariff liberalization has tended to be multilateral rather than unilateral. They also show that a positive tariff may be required to maximize the world welfare but that such a tariff would be generally lower than the non-cooperatively selected tariffs.

One of the obvious and very useful applications of the theories of monopolistic competition and product differentiation is in the field of economic integration. None-the-less, the theory of customs unions has concentrated on homogeneous products and remained silent on product differentiation and intra-industry trade. Similarly, the problem of scale economies has received less attention than the importance of the subject suggests.

The contribution of Wilfred Ethier and Henrik Horn is to incorporate product differentiation and intra-industry trade as well as scale economies and imperfect competition into the customs unions theory (Chapter 13). In addition, they also modify the traditional framework by analysing (i) small, rather than large, tariff changes, and (ii) changes in trade patterns which result from tariff units on goods that are traded between member countries but not with the outside world. Their concern with the latter points leads to two general propositions, namely, that preferential trade is better than free trade and that preferential trade is better than a customs union. Having included four major modifications in the traditional theory of customs unions, Ethier and Horn then show how changes in internal and external tariffs affect product variety, commodity prices, terms of trade, and welfare.

Given the highly mathematical and abstract character of the papers contained in this volume it is quite a challenge to chart a path from theory to empirical research. David Greenaway has written a very useful paper delineating the difficulties facing empirical investigations of trade in differentiated products (Chapter 14).

Some measure of product differentiation is needed to obtain a clearer picture of this type of trade and its determinants. Greenaway argues that three types of differentiation should be distinguished: (1) horizontal differentiation of the Lancasterian kind; (ii) vertical or quality differentiation; and (iii) technological differentiation in the Vernon sense. So far two alternative approaches have been developed: first, the application of a number of proxies for product differentiation such as the Hufbauer index, advertising intensity, and census classification; and second, the use of the recorded intra-industry trade as a measure of trade in differentiated goods. Greenaway gives a critical assessment of these measures and offers suggestions for their improvement.

REFERENCES

Brander, J. (1981), 'Intra-Industry Trade in Identical Commodities', *Journal of International Economics*, 11, 1–14.

Chamberlin, E. (1933), *The Theory of Monopolistic Competition* (Cambridge, Mass.: Harvard University Press).

Corden, W. M. (1974), *Trade Policy and Economic Welfare* (Oxford: Oxford University Press).

Dixit, A. and Stiglitz, J. (1977), 'Monopolistic Competition and Optimum Product Variety', *American Economic Review*, 67, 297–308.

Eaton, J. and Ponagariya, A. (1979), 'Gains from Trade under Variable Returns to Scale, Commodity Taxation, Tariffs and Factor Market Distortions', *Journal of International Economics*, 9, 481–501.

Grubel, H. and Lloyd, P. (1975), *Intra-Industry Trade: The Theory and Measurement of International Trade in Differentiated Products* (London: Macmillan).

Helpman, E. (1981), 'International Trade in the Presence of Product Differentiations, Economies of Scale and Monopolistic Competition: A Chamberlin-

Heckscher-Ohlin Approach', *Journal of International Economics*, 11, 305–40.

Hotelling, H. (1929), 'Stability in Competition', *Economic Journal*, 34, 41–57.

Kemp, M. and Negishi, T. (1970), 'Variable Returns to Scale, Commodity Taxes, Factor Market Distortions, and Implications for Trade Gains', *Swedish Journal of Economics*, 72, 1–11.

Koenker, R. and Perry, M. (1981). 'Product Differentiations, Monopolistic Competition, and Public Policy', *Bell Journal of Economics*, 12, No. 1, 217–31.

Krugman, P. (1979), 'Increasing Returns, Monopolistic Competition, and International Trade', *Journal of International Economics*, 9, 469–79.

Krugman, P. (1980), 'Scale Economies, Product Differentiation, and the Pattern of Trade', *American Economic Review*, 70, 950–9.

Krugman, P. (1981), 'Intra-industry Specialization and the Gains from Trade', *Journal of Political Economy*, 89, 959–73.

Lancaster, R. (1979), *Variety, Equity and Efficiency* (New York: Columbia University Press).

Lancaster, R. (1980), 'Intra-industry Trade under Perfect Monopolistic Competition', *Journal of International Economics*, 10, 151–75.

Linder, S. B. (1961), *An Essay on Trade and Transformation* (New York: Wiley).

Markusen, J. and Melvin, J. (1981), 'Trade, Factor Prices, and Gains from Trade with Increasing Returns to Scale', *Canadian Journal of Economics*, 14, 450–69.

Spence, A. M. (1976), 'Product Selection, Fixed Costs, and Monopolistic Competition', *Review of Economic Studies*, 43, 217–35.

Vernon, R. (1966), 'International Investment and International Trade in the Product Cycle', *Quarterly Journal of Economics*, 80, 190–207.

2

The Gains-from-Trade Theorem with Increasing Returns to Scale

James R. Markusen and James R. Melvin*

1. INTRODUCTION

We have in recent years seen a strong interest in incorporating returns to scale into international trade models. Since Helpman (1984) has surveyed and synthesized many of the relevant contributions, we will not repeat a literature review here, but rather simply note that a number of quite different approaches have been explored. One category of analysis, based on models with homogeneous products, can be subdivided into models with economies of scale external to the firm and models with internal economies.[1] Subject to correctly incorporating the externality-induced distortions, the former models can make use of competitive general equilibrium analysis. The latter models rely either on partial equilibrium analysis based on classical duopoly theory, or attempt to develop simple general equilibrium analyses which can be more easily related to traditional trade theory. A second category of analysis is based on models with differentiated goods and makes use of recent developments in the theory of monopolistic competition.[2]

In attempting to formulate a theory of the gains from trade in the presence of increasing returns to scale (IRS), it strikes us that there exist two problems. First, do there exist common underlying features in the classes of models just mentioned such that a unified approach to the gains from trade (GFT) might be developed? Second, many of the recent papers as surveyed by Helpman rely on very specific assumptions and functional forms. We should therefore enquire whether or not there exist reasonably general sufficient conditions under which GFT will be assured, or whether it appears that restrictive assumptions are in fact necessary to generate such conditions.[3]

The purpose of this paper is to address both issues and to offer some tentative conclusions about each question. Specifics of the paper are as follows. Section 2 reviews the GFT theorem and offers a simple but useful dichotomy between alternative sources of breakdowns in the theorem (losses from trade). We will refer to these two sources as failures of the 'tangency condition' and the 'convexity condition' and will suggest that they are features that all of the models discussed above have in common. The convexity condition relates to the structure of IRS technologies while the tangency condition relates to economic pricing behaviour. We will argue that for both analytical reasons and conceptual reasons these two factors deserve separate attention.

Section 3 reviews the possibility of losses from trade due to the failure of the tangency condition and shows that fairly simple (at least on a conceptual level) restrictions are sufficient to ensure GFT. We shall also argue that these conditions have a fairly intuitive interpretation in terms of 'industry rationalization' that makes them seem less restrictive and improbable than they appear to be from a purely technical perspective.

Section 4 analyses the possibility of losses from trade due to failures of the convexity condition and argues that existing analyses are much less complete than in the case of the tangency condition. We are able to show that the same expansion of *all* IRS industries that ensures GFT in the presence of non-tangencies remains sufficient when there are non-convexities as well. This argument is contained in Helpman (1984) and implicitly in Kemp (1969) and we add to their findings by noting that the result does not rely on any special functional forms or on average-cost pricing. We note further that in the presence of non-convexities, this expansion effect is sometimes necessary as well as sufficient for GFT. On the other hand, we argue that the same weighted change in the outputs of IRS goods which is sufficient for GFT in the convex case is not sufficient in the case of non-convexities. Thus non-convexities do complicate the conditions when some IRS goods expand and others contract.

Section 5 presents a discussion of recent monopolistic competition models in light of the results of the previous section. We show how some of the restrictive assumptions used in that literature ensure that both the tangency and convexity problems are avoided and demonstrate how the weakening of some of these assumptions may lead to losses from trade. Section 6 applies the analysis of the tangency condition to a multinational enterprise model and shows how a simple modification of that condition allows the GFT inequality to be expressed in terms of the distribution of profits.

In summary, the paper shows that the restrictions needed for GFT in the presence of IRS reduce to a fairly simple analytical condition. Further effort may well result in more robust sufficient conditions for the non-convex case. Yet even this would not be entirely satisfactory since the analysis does not show the circumstances in which the relevant conditions will or will not be satisfied in actual trading equilibria. Much further work is needed in this area.

2. THE GAINS-FROM-TRADE THEOREM

The following notation will be used throughout the paper. X_i will denote the production of good i and C_i will denote the consumption of good i. Superscripts f and a will indicate free trade and autarky values, respectively. p_i will denote the price of good i. Since the focus here is on technology, we will simply assume that welfare can be represented by a set of community indifference curves, and let U stand for the level of national welfare or utility. $e(p, U)$ will be the expenditure function; that is, $e(p, U)$ gives the minimum expenditure necessary at prices p to attain utility level U.

The gains-from-trade theorem as advanced in international trade is almost elegant in its simplicity. It states that subject to certain restrictions on technology and pricing discussed below, the value of the free trade production bundle at free trade prices is greater than or equal to the value of any other feasible production bundle (e.g. the autarky bundle) at those free trade prices. This proposition is given by

$$\Sigma p_i^f X_i^f \geqslant \Sigma p_i^f X_i^a. \tag{2.1}$$

Only a few additional equations are needed. These are the autarky market-clearing equations and the free trade balance-of-payments condition:

$$X_i^a = C_i^a; \qquad \Sigma p_i^f X_i^f = \Sigma p_i^f C_i^f. \tag{2.2}$$

Substituting (2.2) into (2.1) we have

$$\Sigma p_i^f C_i^f \geqslant \Sigma p_i^f C_i^a. \tag{2.3}$$

Since C^f was chosen when C^a was available, the free trade consumption bundle is 'revealed preferred' to the autarky consumption bundle. Below we will argue that the analysis is perfectly applicable to situations in which the number of goods produced and consumed changes between the two equilibria.

Since the right-hand side of (2.3) generally exceeds the minimum expenditure necessary at p^f to attain U^a, (2.3) in turn implies

$$e(p^f, U^f) \geqslant e(p^f, U^a), \quad \text{implying that } U^f \geqslant U^a. \tag{2.4}$$

The theorem is illustrated in the two-good case in Fig. 2.1 where F is the free trade production point and A is the autarky production/consumption point.

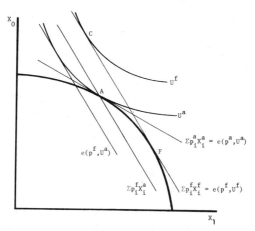

Fig. 2.1

The value of F at p^f exceeds the value of A at p^f which in turn exceeds $e(p^f, U^a)$ if there is some elasticity of substitution in consumption as shown.

In order for equation (2.1) and the theorem to be valid, the free trade price vector (p^f) must form a separating hyperplane to the production set and the upper contour set of the utility function.[4] The price plane (price line in Fig. 2.1) must not 'cut' the production frontier at any point and no portion of the price plane may lie interior to the production set. If any portion of the price plane lies strictly interior to the production set, equation (2.1) will not hold since we will always be able to find a feasible X whose value at p^f exceeds $p^f X^f$.

Two conditions are sufficient for the separating hyperplane condition to hold. First, the free trade price plane must not cut the production frontier at the free trade production point. Let $T(X_0, \ldots, X_n) = 0$ be the transformation function specifying the production frontier. Assuming that T is differentiable, this condition requires that p^f be tangent to T at any interior solution, or more generally, that $p_i^f / p_j^f = T_i^f / T_j^f$ for all $X_i^f, X_j^f > 0$ $(T_i = \partial T / \partial X_i)$. Corner solutions modify the requirement to $p_i^f / p_j^f \leqslant T_i^f / T_j^f$ for $X_i = 0$, $X_j > 0$. We will refer to these restrictions as the 'tangency condition' even though 'tangency' is not an entirely appropriate term for corner solutions. Subject to certain other restrictions, the tangency condition will be satisfied by marginal-cost pricing.

Second, the production set must be convex so that tangency ensures that the price plane does indeed form a separating hyperplane. This will be referred to as the 'convexity condition'. As is well known from general equilibrium theory, the convexity condition will be satisfied if technology has non-increasing returns plus other restrictions such as distortion-free factor markets.

The final important point is that the GFT theorem can be interpreted such that it does not require that every good available in autarky be available in free trade or vice versa. Let i in equations (2.1), (2.2), and (2.3) index all of the goods that could be produced in the economy. Let p_i^f be the demand price for X_i at the free trade equilibrium (i.e. the actual price of X_i if X_i is produced at home or abroad or the price that consumers would be willing to pay for one unit if X_i is not available in free trade). If free trade production evaluated at these prices forms a separating hyperplane to the production set then equation (2.1) continues to hold. The balance-of-payments equation in (2.2) holds as well since for any good not available in free trade $X_i^f = C_i^f = 0$. The right- and left-hand sides of the balance-of-payments constraint thus continue to give the values of actual production and consumption. Equation (2.3) then remains valid under this expanded interpretation. This will be relevant below in connection with monopolistic competition.

3. THE TANGENCY CONDITION

Given convex production possibilities, the absence of factor market distortions etc., the value of production at a particular set of prices is maximized by marginal-cost pricing. This is embodied in the usual marginal-cost pricing rule for economic efficiency. For our purposes, marginal costs form the 'tangent' to the production surface ($MC_i/MC_j = T_i/T_j = -\,dX_j/dX_i$) and thus form a separating hyperplane at the free trade production point. Let i index all goods that could be produced and p_i^f the demand prices as per the previous section. Given convexity, we have

$$\Sigma\,(MC_i^f)X_i^f \;\geqslant\; \Sigma\,(MC_i^f)X_i^a. \tag{2.5}$$

Some of the X_i^f can, of course, be zero. Marginal-cost pricing implies

$$p_i^f \;=\; MC_i^f \text{ if } X_i^f > 0; \quad p_i^f \;\leqslant\; MC_i^f \text{ if } X_i^f = 0. \tag{2.6}$$

Equations (2.5) and (2.6) together give us

$$\Sigma\,p_i^f X_i^f \;=\; \Sigma\,(MC_i^f)X_i^f \geqslant \Sigma\,(MC_i^f)X_i^a \geqslant \Sigma\,p_i^f X_i^a, \tag{2.7}$$

which satisfies the condition in equation (2.1).

It is well known that marginal-cost pricing is not a characteristic of goods produced with any of the types of returns to scale mentioned in the introduction to the paper. Regardless of whether there are: (i) homogeneous products with external economies; (ii) homogeneous products with internal economies; or (iii) differentiated products with monopolistic competition, prices will exceed marginal costs for these goods. This must always be the case since in all categories marginal-cost pricing would imply negative profits. (In category (i), prices equal firm marginal costs and industry average costs, but these costs are more than industry marginal costs which form the relevant measure.)

Let w_i^f be the 'wedge' between p_i^f and MC_i^f expressed in an *ad valorem* fashion so that $p_i^f(1 - w_i^f) = MC_i^f$ for all $X_i^f > 0$. For any of the types of returns to scale just mentioned, we know that $0 < w_i^f < 1$ ($p_i > MC_i$) in equilibrium. In the case of pure monopoly or monopolistic competition, for example, $w_i^f = 1/\eta_i$ where η_i is the elasticity of demand for X_i. $w_i^f = 0$ of course for competitive industries producing goods with constant returns. The case of external diseconomies ($w_i^f < 0$) has been dealt with by Eaton and Panagariya (1979) and Helpman (1984) and will not be treated here.

If $X_i^f = 0$, the definition of w_i^f is a bit more arbitrary. With $X_i^f = 0$, it must, however, be the case that $p_i^f \leqslant AC_i^f$ where AC denotes average cost evaluated in the neighbourhood of $X_i = 0$ (AC may go to infinity as X_i approaches zero). Therefore define w_i^f for $X_i^f = 0$ as $(1 - w_i^f) = MC_i^f/AC_i^f$ so that we have $p_i^f(1 - w_i^f) \leqslant AC_i^f(1 - w_i^f) = MC_i^f$. w_i^f will thus continue to equal zero for constant returns to scale (CRS) goods and will lie between 0 and 1 for increasing returns to scale (IRS) goods. Equation (26) becomes

$$p_i^f(1 - w_i^f) \;=\; MC_i^f \text{ if } X_i^f > 0; \quad p_i^f(1 - w_i^f) \;\leqslant\; MC_i^f \text{ if } X_i^f = 0. \tag{2.8}$$

Now assume that the convexity condition is satisfied such that equation (2.5) continues to hold.[5] Using (2.8) and (2.5) the present equivalent of equation (2.1) is therefore

$$\Sigma\, p_i^f(1 - w_i^f)X_i^f \geqslant \Sigma\, p_i^f(1 - w_i^f)X_i^a. \tag{2.9}$$

Equation (2.1) is of course simply a special case of (2.9) in which the w_i are identically zero. Equations (2.2) above remain unchanged and substituting (2.2) into (2.9) gives us

$$\Sigma\, p_i^f C_i^f \geqslant \Sigma\, p_i^f C_i^a + \Sigma\, p_i^f w_i^f (X_i^f - X_i^a). \tag{2.10}$$

Equation (2.10) gives us a condition which can be found in various forms in Kemp and Negishi (1970), Eaton and Panagariya (1979), Markusen and Melvin (1981), Markusen (1981), and Helpman (1984). A sufficient condition for gains from trade is that trade lead to an increase in the output of every good produced with increasing returns (i.e. if $w_i > 0$, then $X_i^f > X_i^a$).

Figures 2.2, 2.3, and 2.4 display the possibilities. In these figures and throughout the paper, it is assumed that X_1 is produced with IRS and X_0 with CRS unless otherwise indicated ($0 < w_1 < 1$ and $w_0 = 0$). Thus the price ratio p_1^f/p_0^f is steeper than the slope of the production frontier at the free trade production point F. Point A in each figure continues to represent the autarky equilibrium. Equation (2.9) holds in each of Figs. 2.2, 2.3, and 2.4 as shown.

Figure 2.2 shows the result of equation (2.10) that gains from trade must occur when trade expands production of the IRS good. Figure 2.3 shows the result that losses may occur when trade leads to a contraction of the IRS industry. Figure 2.4 emphasizes that expansion of the IRS industry is sufficient but not necessary by showing a case in which welfare increases despite a contraction in X_1.

It should be noted from equation (2.10) that a weighted increase in production of the IRS goods is sufficient for GFT, where the weights are $p_i w_i = (p_i - MC_i)$. It can be argued that such an increase is perhaps not at all unlikely in practice. Ignoring for the moment the $p_i w_i$ weights in (2.10) and differences in industry size, what is required is that trade have a certain 'rationalizing' effect on the IRS industries. By this we mean that the proportion of the output of the IRS

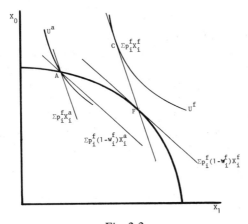

Fig. 2.2

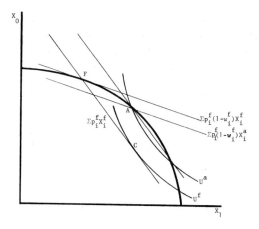

Fig. 2.3

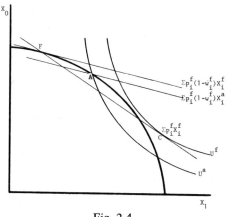

Fig. 2.4

production eliminated by trade is less than the proportional increase in the output of the surviving IRS industries. Such an outcome is reasonable if, for example, trade does not decrease the total domestic resources devoted to the IRS industries. With the same total resources, the lower average costs of the remaining industries due to larger free trade production will tend to outweigh the loss of the other industries. A rigorous statement of the sufficient conditions is postponed to Section 5 on monopolistic competition.

4. THE CONVEXITY CONDITION

The fact that with IRS the production set may be non-convex (the production frontier may be convex to the origin) is probably well known and does not deserve extensive comment here. In the absence of strong factor-intensity effects, production frontiers can be everywhere convex as in Figs. 2.5, 2.6, and 2.7. Stronger factor-intensity effects can lead to complex outcomes with alternating convex and concave segments (Kemp, 1969; Markusen and Melvin, 1981; Section 7 below).

GFT analyses in the presence of non-convexities contain a certain irony in that there is more potential for gains from trade yet also more things that can go wrong relative to the case of convex production possibilities. Figure 2.5 suggests some of the things that can go right while Figs. 2.6 and 2.7 suggest some of the things that can go wrong.

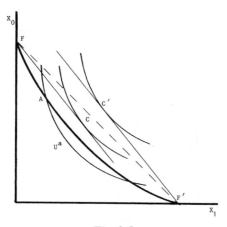

Fig. 2.5

Figure 2.5 shows the same two-good problem we have been using but with a convex production frontier (X_1 has IRS, X_0 has CRS). Note first that specialization in either good may produce gains at a given price ratio (Melvin, 1969). This in turn implies, of course, that specialization in the IRS good is not necessary. Second, note that GFT may occur even if trade decreases the price of the export good relative to autarky (e.g. specializing in X_1 at F' leads to gains even though ($p_1^f/p_0^f < p_1^a/p_0^a$). Third, the chord connecting F and F' forms a portion of the boundary of the convex hull of the production set. Note that GFT may occur even if consumption occurs at a point like C interior to this convex hull, a point which will be relevant later in connection with monopolistic competition.

Figure 2.6 illustrates the fact that in general expansion of an IRS good may not be sufficient for GFT. Note from Fig. 2.6 that with non-specialization, equation (2.9) now becomes

$$\Sigma\, p_i^f(1 - w_i^f)X_i^f \leqslant \Sigma\, p_i^f(1 - w_i^f)X_i^a, \qquad (2.11)$$

that is, the direction of the inequality in (2.9) is reversed. The present equivalent of (2.10) becomes

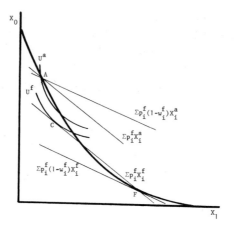

Fig. 2.6

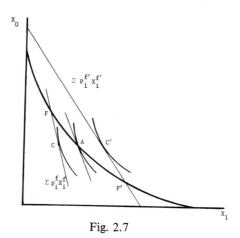

Fig. 2.7

$$\Sigma\, p_i^f C_i^f \leqslant \Sigma\, p_i^f C_i^a + \Sigma\, p_i^f w_i^f (X_i^f - X_i^a). \tag{2.12}$$

It can be shown, however, that non-negative profit restrictions will ensure that expansion of all IRS industries is still sufficient for GFT. If X_0 is a CRS good in Fig. 2.6, the situation shown cannot occur. We can show that if the output of the IRS good expands, then the situation must be shown in Fig. 2.7, where the value of production at F' exceeds the value at prices p^f of any other bundle with a smaller output of X_1. The proof proceeds as follows. Gains will occur if

$$\Sigma\, p_i^f X_i^f \geqslant \Sigma\, p_i^f X_i^a. \tag{2.13}$$

Let r_i and R_{ij} denote the price of resource i and the quantity of the ith resource used in the production of the jth good respectively. From each side of equation (2.13) we can subtract the value of the total resource endowment at free trade prices: $\Sigma\Sigma r_i^f R_{ij} = \Sigma r_i^f R_i$. For the moment, assume that we have only two goods (X_0, X_1) as shown in Figs. 2.5, 2.6, and 2.7. Suppose also that there are only two resources (R_1, R_2). Equation (2.13) can be written as

$$(p_1^f X_1^f - \Sigma r_i^f R_{i1}^f) + (p_0^f X_0^f - \Sigma r_i^f R_{i0}^f) \geqslant (p_1^f X_1^a - \Sigma r_i^f R_{i1}^a) + (p_0^f X_0^a - \Sigma r_i^f R_{i0}^a).$$
(2.14)

Sufficient conditions for this inequality to hold are that

$$(p_1^f - \Sigma r_i^f R_{i1}^f / X_1^f) X_1^f \geqslant (p_1^f - \Sigma r_i^f R_{i1}^a / X_1^a) X_1^a$$
(2.15)

and

$$(p_0^f - \Sigma r_i^f R_{i0}^f / X_0^f) X_0^f \geqslant (p_0^f - \Sigma r_i^f R_{i0}^a / X_0^a) X_0^a.$$
(2.16)

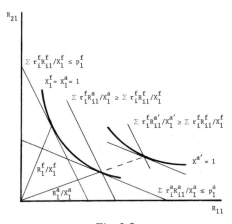

Fig. 2.8

These inequalities can be analysed using Fig. 2.8. Suppose that X_1 is a CRS industry in which case the unit isoquant is given by $X_1^f = X_1^a = 1$ in Fig. 2.8. R_1^f / X_1^f and R_1^a / X_1^a give the cost-minimizing unit input vectors at factor prices r^f and r^a respectively. As is clear from Fig. 2.8, the costs of the autarky unit inputs at r^f exceed the costs of the free trade unit inputs at r^f. With reference to equation (2.15), we have

$$(p_1^f - \Sigma r_i^f R_{i1}^f / X_1^f) \geqslant (p_1^f - \Sigma r_i^f R_{i1}^a / X_1^a).$$
(2.17)

If the left-hand side of (2.17) is zero due to average-cost pricing in the CRS industry, then the right-hand side is non-positive. Thus for any CRS industry, the left-hand side of (2.15) or (2.16) exceeds the right-hand side and the inequalities hold.

For IRS industries, the left-hand side of (2.17) may be positive (free trade profits are positive) and more to the point, the unit isoquant is in a different position for the two equilibria. If $X_1^f > X_1^a$, then the X_1^a unit isoquant lies further from the origin as in Fig. 2.8 where $X^{a'} = 1$ denotes its new position. With $X_1^f > X_1^a$ equation (2.17) remains valid (illustrated in Fig. 2.8) as does equation (2.15).

Thus despite non-convexities, expansion of the IRS sectors remains sufficient for gains from trade. Note especially that this result is robust with respect to the following: (i) we can add any number of goods and factors to the analysis, (ii) average-cost pricing in the IRS sectors is not required, (iii) no special functional forms are needed for the result, and (iv) the production frontier may have any number of concave and convex segments.

Unfortunately, it is not true that the same weighted change in the IRS industries that was sufficient for GFT in the convex case is sufficient here. Suppose in Fig. 2.6 that both X_1 and X_0 have IRS but that at A and F $w_1 > w_0$ so that the price ratio continues to cut the frontier in the direction shown. In this case, the situation shown in Fig. 2.6 cannot be ruled out. Algebraically, equation (2.16) need not hold and thus (2.13) need not hold. With IRS in X_0, the unit cost of X_0^a at r^f may in fact be less than the unit cost of X_0^f at r^f since the unit isoquant for X_0^a lies closer to the origin. With $X_0^a > X_0^f$ this would be sufficient for (2.16) not to hold. Thus the price ratio through F could possibly pass below A in Fig. 2.6 and we would have

$$\Sigma p_i^f X_i^f < \Sigma p_i^f X_i^a \quad \text{or} \quad \frac{p_1^f}{p_0^f} < \frac{X_0^a - X_0^f}{X_1^f - X_1^a}. \tag{2.18}$$

With both industries characterized by IRS, we noted following equation (2.10) above that $\Sigma p_i^f w_i^f (X_i^f - X_i^a) > 0$ is sufficient for gains. In the present case, this requires

$$\frac{p_1^f w_1^f}{p_0^f w_0^f} > \frac{X_0^a - X_0^f}{X_1^f - X_1^a}. \tag{2.19}$$

But our example in Fig. 2.6 is constructed under the assumption that $w_1^f > w_0^f$. Thus (2.18) and (2.19) may be consistent. GFT are not realized despite the fact that the weighted increase condition of equation (2.10) is satisfied. Such a result would, of course, be consistent with our equation (2.12).

In Section 7 below, we present an example in which (2.19) and (2.18) are consistent, thus proving that the IRS expansion condition of equation (2.10) is not sufficient for GFT in the presence of non-convexities. This example does rely on some restrictive assumptions such as no factor-intensity effects. On the other hand, the example does not rely on non-specialization and well-behaved functional forms are used as well as average-cost pricing.

It may be tempting to argue that a trading equilibrium such as that in Fig. 2.6 is not a global maximum. It would seem that at p^f the economy should specialize in either X_0 or X_1. This approach has pitfalls as well. While we should surely be able to show that profits at p^f would be greater at one or both specialized production points, it does not follow that p^f could be the price at such an equilibrium except in the very special case where the country is a price-taker on world markets. In a two-country model it is quite possible that an equilibrium such as that shown in Fig. 2.6 is the only one possible, as can easily be demonstrated by an offer curve or a reaction curve diagram. Specifically, a movement toward specialization in X_1 beginning at F in Fig. 2.6 should drive down the price of X_1 (and vice versa for moving toward specialization in X_0). If marginal revenue falls faster than marginal cost in such a movement, F is indeed a global profit maximum.

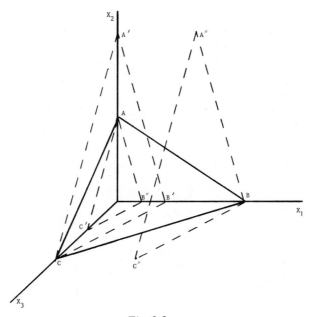

Fig. 2.9

This general problem is illustrated in Fig. 2.9 where it is assumed that the plane ABC represents a portion of the convex hull of the production set. The dotted triangles represent the price plane drawn through alternative points of specialization and thus represent alternative consumption possibilities sets. At these prices, specializing in X_2 is the worst alternative, X_3 the next worst, and X_1 clearly the best. The point is that with a non-convex production set, the economy could indeed get stuck at a production point like A or C. For reasons noted in the previous paragraph, A or C could indeed be a profit maximum. When they are not, a second problem arises with respect to whether or not free entry will ensure that the economy moves to the optimal pattern of specialization. Further discussion of this point is postponed until the following section.

5. AN APPLICATION TO MONOPOLISTIC COMPETITION

Recent monopolistic competition models have moved the discussion of returns to scale into an interesting new area (Krugman, 1979, 1980; Lancaster, 1980, Helpman, 1981). But as noted by Helpman (1984), little has been done in the way of formulating a theory of the GFT in the presence of monopolistic competition. The purpose of this section is to show that the theory of the previous several sections is in fact widely applicable to monopolistic competition as well.

In Sections 2 and 3 above, we argued that the general theory is applicable to situations in which the number of goods produced and consumed changes between the free trade and autarky equilibria. An important source of GFT as emphasized by the above-mentioned authors is changes in the number of goods available for consumption. Let us therefore examine the IRS production expansion condition given in equations (2.10) and (2.12) in light of recent monopolistic competition models. (Recall that we demonstrated that this condition is generally not sufficient for GFT in the presence of non-convexities.) For simplicity, we will for the moment adopt the assumptions of Krugman (1979) and others that all differentiated products are perfectly symmetric in production and consumption such that all goods produced are produced in the same amount at the same price. If there is no other class of IRS goods, the IRS expansion condition becomes

$$\Sigma\, p_i^f w_i^f (X_i^f - X_i^a) \;=\; q^f w^f (n^f X^f - n^a X^a) \geqslant 0, \qquad (2.20)$$

where q^f and w^f are the price and inverse demand elasticity of a representative differentiated good, respectively. n^i and X^i are the number of varieties produced at equilibrium i and the amount of a representative good produced at that equilibrium. The right-hand term in (2.20) can be rearranged as follows:

$$(n^f X^f - n^a X^a) \;=\; (X^f/X^a - n^a/n^f)(n^f X^a). \qquad (2.21)$$

The expansion condition is therefore satisfied if $X^f/X^a \geqslant n^a/n^f$, an inequality which does hold in Krugman's model. In Krugman's case, trade rationalizes production, with each country producing larger amounts of each of fewer varieties in the post-trade equilibrium (the number of varieties consumed, of course, increases). The fact that $X^f/X^a > n^a/n^f > 1$ follows from two factors: (i) Since there are only differentiated products, total resources allocated to these goods is unaffected by trade; (ii) with IRS, the amount of the representative good produced must expand more than in proportion to the number of varieties lost by virtue of the lower average cost of larger production (total resources held constant). Note, finally, that in this model the IRS expansion condition is sufficient for GFT. With the w_i's equal and only IRS goods produced, the common w^f can be factored out of (2.20) and (2.20) is reduced to equation (2.1).

Now consider the convexity condition, again using Krugman's (1979) model. Krugman uses a simple one-factor model in which each good requires an initial lump sum of labour and can thereafter be produced at constant marginal cost.

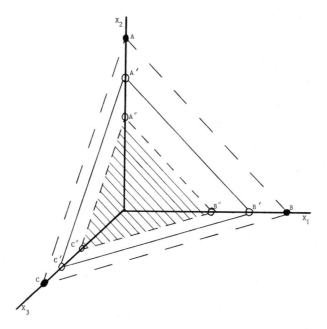

Fig. 2.10

The resulting production set is illustrated in Fig. 2.10 for a three-dimensional sub-space of the infinite-dimensional space of possible varieties.

If the economy produces only one good, it can be at any of points A, B, or C in Fig. 2.10. If two goods are produced, a lump sum of resources is lost in fixed costs, so that the economy 'drops down' toward the origin and produces somewhere on the boundary of the triangle A′B′C′, vertices excluded. If three goods are produced, another lump of resources is used up and the economy produces in the interior of the planar surface bounded by the triangle A″B″C″. Figure 2.10 helps to illustrate the trade-off between scale economies and product diversity.

The production set in Fig. 2.10 is quite obviously non-convex. How then are GFT guaranteed in Krugman's analysis? We maintain that GFT probably rely on a number of restrictive assumptions. The first is that there are infinitely many perfectly symmetric goods that can be produced all with identical production functions. The second is that all consumers have identical additive utility functions which treat all commodities symmetrically. The third is the usual monopolistic competition assumption about entry. This implies that firms will enter whenever prices of existing products exceed average costs, thereby guaranteeing average-cost pricing. A final assumption is that only differentiated goods are produced which ensures the expansion effects mentioned in (2.20) and (2.21) above. The first three assumptions guarantee that all goods produced trade for the same price. More to the point, the assumptions collectively guarantee that the price plane will lie on the convex hull of the production set (if this is still appropriate terminology) in the sub-space of goods produced and consumed.

Suppose for example that in autarky the economy produces X_1 and X_2 in Fig. 2.10. Production and consumption thus take place on the line segment $A'B'$. Suppose with trade the economy reduces the number of varieties produced to one and increases the number consumed to three as per the above results. The Krugman assumptions imply that whichever variety is produced, the price plane coincides with the plane defined by ABC in Fig. 2.10. The price plane thus forms a supporting hyperplane and GFT are assured.

Several restrictive features of the assumptions used here have already been discussed by Dixit and Norman (1980) and Eaton and Kierzkowski (1984). They show that under somewhat different assumptions trade may not increase product variety and free entry may not be sufficient to induce average-cost pricing. The Eaton–Kierzkowski result in particular is important in emphasizing that average-cost pricing should not be automatically assumed, but rather that the equilibrium-pricing configuration should be derived from underlying behavioural assumptions.

We will confine our comments to the role of the symmetry assumptions used above. Consider briefly the production side and retain for the moment the symmetry assumptions on the demand side. If there are different technologies for different goods then price ratios will not in general equal ratios of marginal costs. For goods X_i and X_j, the equilibrium conditions give us

$$\frac{p_i(1 - 1/\eta_i)}{p_j(1 - 1/\eta_j)} = \frac{MC_i}{MC_j}. \tag{2.22}$$

Let us retain all of Krugman's assumptions except let the constant marginal costs be related by $MC_i > MC_j$. Figure 2.10 continues to be perfectly applicable except that the chords such as $A'B'$ and $B'C'$ will now have different slopes (equal to MC_i/MC_j). If the fixed costs are in a similar ratio across goods, then these marginal costs define a plane coincident with $A'B'C'$ as well.

If $(p_i/p_j) = (MC_i/MC_j)$ in (2.22), it must be the case that $\eta_i = \eta_j$, but this can only occur if $X_i = X_j$ and $p_i = p_j$ due to the demand assumptions. Thus the equilibrium in (2.22) cannot be characterized by $(p_i/p_j) = (MC_i/MC_j)$ and the price plane will not lie on the convex hull of the production sub-space in Fig. 2.10.

A similar problem occurs with respect to consumption. Suppose we now retain all of Krugman's production assumptions but make goods non-symmetric in demand ($MC_i/MC_j = 1$). For $(p_i/p_j) = (MC_i/MC_j)$ in (2.22) we must have $\eta_i = \eta_j$ and $p_i = p_j$. But if i is the preferred good, $p_i = p_j$ must imply $X_i > X_j$. Given the structure of technology, however, $X_i > X_j$ and $p_i = p_j$ must imply that profits in i exceed profits in j. Depending on the behavioural assumptions adopted, this will generally not be an equilibrium (e.g. average-cost pricing).

Referring back to Fig. 2.9, let the plane ABC correspond to ABC in Fig. 2.10.

The above analysis implies that with asymmetries in production and/or consumption, the price plane will generally not coincide with ABC. The equilibrium prices could look something like the dotted triangle in Fig. 2.9. Identical countries will enjoy different welfare levels and some countries may suffer losses depending upon the pattern of specialization.

6. AN APPLICATION TO THE MULTINATIONAL ENTERPRISE

The purpose of this section is to show briefly how the tangency condition can be expressed in terms of profits when returns to scale are internal to the firm and then show how this result is helpful in analysing GFT in the presence of multi-national enterprises (MNE). Suppose for simplicity that the production set is convex despite IRS in sector X_1. The only other good, X_0, is produced with CRS by a competitive industry. We know then that

$$p_0^f = MC_0^f \quad \text{and} \quad p_1^f(1 - w_1^f) = MC_1^f, \; w_1^f = 1/\eta_1^f.$$

Equation (2.10) above then becomes

$$\Sigma p_i^f C_i^f \geqslant \Sigma p_i^f C_i^a + p_1^f w_1^f (X_1^f - X_1^a)$$
$$= \Sigma p_i^f C_i^a + (p_1^f - MC_1^f)(X_1^f - X_1^a). \tag{2.23}$$

But with IRS in X_1, $MC_1 \leqslant AC_1$. Thus if X_1 expands with trade, (2.23) can be rewritten as

$$\Sigma p_i^f C_i^f \geqslant \Sigma p_i^f C_i^a + (p_1^f - AC_1^f)(X_1^f - X_1^a)$$
$$= \Sigma p_i^f C_i^a + (\pi_1^f - \pi_1^{af}), \tag{2.24}$$

where π_1^f denotes profits at the free trade equilibrium and π_1^{af} denotes profits at the autarky output at free trade prices. Equation (2.24) states that there will be GFT if free trade profits at p^f exceed autarky profits at p^f (subject also of course to $X_1^f > X_1^a$).

The geometry of the situation is illustrated in Fig. 2.11. Using X_0 as numeraire, I^f gives total income while I_r^f gives income of the domestic resource owners. The difference between I^f and I_r^f thus constitutes monopoly profits. I_r^f will lie somewhere between I^f and the tangent at F depending on the strength of the IRS and the possibilities of entry.

By itself, equation (2.24) adds little since it is only true when $X_1^f > X_1^a$ and we know that is sufficient for GFT in any case. But there are situations in which this formulation is very useful. Figure 2.12 applies this analysis to a simple MNE problem (Markusen, 1984). Suppose that the economy initially produces at A realizing an income of I^a at p^f. Suppose instead that a MNE controls the X_1 sector by virtue of superior technology. This technology expands production possibilities for X_1 and MNE production is assumed to occur at point F (satisfying our restriction that $X_1^f > X_1^a$). Income is now higher at I^f. But if the MNE is entirely foreign-owned and profits are repatriated, domestic citizens could end

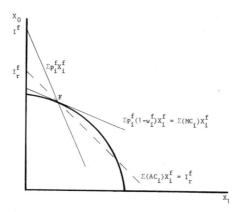

Fig. 2.11

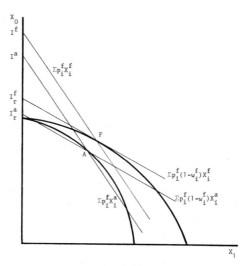

Fig. 2.12

up with an income as low as I_r^f, corresponding to the lower bound case in Fig. 2.11 where $MC_1 = AC_1$. Domestic factor owners do gain in this case ($I_r^f > I_r^a$) but total domestic income is lower due to the fact that profits which would have accrued to domestic entrepreneurs now go to foreigners.

Let π^* denote profits repatriated by the MNE. The balance-of-payments constraint (2.2) above now becomes $\Sigma p_i^f X_i^f - \pi^* = \Sigma p_i^f C_i^f$. Substitution will give us a new equivalent to (2.24):

$$\Sigma p_i^f C_i^f \geqslant \Sigma p_i^f C_i^a + (\pi^f - \pi^{af} - \pi^*) \qquad (2.25)$$

so that GFT are assured if $(\pi^f - \pi^{af} - \pi^*) \geqslant 0$. A simple rule is easily derived from this equation: if the host country can retain a share of the MNE profits $(\pi^f - \pi^*)$ that is at least equal to the profits that would have been earned by a domestic monopolist in the absence of MNE activity (π^{af}) and the NME expands production, then GFT are assured.

7. AN ALGEBRAIC EXAMPLE OF NON-CONVEXITIES

The shape of the production surface is determined by the interaction of factor-intensity effects (which tend to make the surface concave to the origin) with IRS effects (which tend to make the surface convex to the origin). The purpose of this section is to present an example of how these effects interact to determine the shape of the frontier.

Assume that there are two goods (X, Y), produced from two factors (K, L) in inelastic supply. X is characterized by multiplicatively separable external economies (Herberg and Kemp, 1969; Markusen and Melvin, 1981; Helpman, 1984) while Y is characterized by CRS. Production functions are CES and are given by

$$X = (X^T)(aL_x^{-\beta} + bK_x^{-\beta})^{-1/\beta} \qquad Y = (cL_y^{-\gamma} + dK_y^{-\gamma})^{-1/\gamma}$$

$$-1 \leqslant \beta, \qquad \gamma < \infty; \qquad 0 < T < 1. \tag{2.26}$$

Let $p = p_x/p_y$ and $\omega = w/r$ (i.e. ω equals the wage/rental ratio). Herberg and Kemp's results together with Markusen and Melvin's results give the following relationship:

$$\frac{dp}{p} \bigg/ \frac{d\omega}{\omega} + T \frac{dX}{X} \bigg/ \frac{d\omega}{\omega} = \frac{1}{1 + k_x/\omega} - \frac{1}{1 + k_y/\omega},$$

$$k_x = K_x/L_x, \qquad k_y = K_y/L_y. \tag{2.27}$$

Assume throughout that X is labour intensive so that $k_x < k_y$. If there were CRS in X $(T = 0)$, then $(dp/p)/(d\omega/\omega) > 0$ and the relative price of X and the wage/rental ratio rise together. Since $dX/d\omega > 0$ this in turn implies that $dX/dp > 0$ or that the supply price of X rises with output. Since the supply price is related to the marginal rate of transformation (MRT) by $p(1 - T) = \text{MRT}$, this in turn implies that the MRT rises with X and the production frontier is concave. But when $T > 0$, $(dp/p)/(d\omega/\omega)$ could be negative and the production frontier convex.

The outcome turns out to depend very much on the elasticities of substitution in production, given by σ_x and σ_y.

$$\sigma_x \frac{d\omega}{\omega} = \frac{dk_x}{k_x} = \frac{dK_x}{K_x} - \frac{dL_x}{L_x}; \qquad \sigma_x = \frac{1}{1 + \beta}; \qquad \omega = \frac{a}{b} \left(\frac{K_x}{L_x}\right)^{\beta+1} = \frac{c}{d} \left(\frac{K_y}{L_y}\right)^{\gamma+1}. \tag{2.28}$$

Differentiating the production function for X, dividing through by X, and substituting for dK_x/K_x from (2.28), we have

$$(1 - T)\frac{\mathrm{d}X}{X} = \frac{aL^{-\beta}}{aL^{-\beta} + bK^{-\beta}}\frac{\mathrm{d}L_x}{L_x} + \frac{bK^{-\beta}}{aL^{-\beta} + bK^{-\beta}}\frac{\mathrm{d}K_x}{K_x};$$

$$(1 - T)\frac{\mathrm{d}X}{X}\bigg/\frac{\mathrm{d}\omega}{\omega} = \frac{\mathrm{d}L_x}{L_x}\bigg/\frac{\mathrm{d}\omega}{\omega} + \frac{bK_x^{-\beta}}{aL_x^{-\beta} + bK_x^{-\beta}}\sigma_x$$

$$= \frac{\mathrm{d}L_x}{L_x}\bigg/\frac{\mathrm{d}\omega}{\omega} + \sigma_x\left[\frac{a}{b}\left(\frac{L_x}{K_x}\right)^{-\beta} + 1\right]^{-1}. \qquad (2.29)$$

Since L_x/K_x falls with an increase in X, the second term on the right-hand side of the second line of (2.29) increases with X if $\beta < 0$ ($\sigma_x > 1$), falls with X if $\beta > 0$ ($\sigma_x < 1$), and remains constant with X in the special case of unitary elasticity of substitution (the Cobb–Douglas case). Turning to the first term on the right-hand side of (2.29), we note from (2.28) that this can be written as

$$\frac{\mathrm{d}L_x}{L_x}\bigg/\frac{\mathrm{d}\omega}{\omega} = \sigma_x\left[\frac{\mathrm{d}K_x}{K_x}\bigg/\frac{\mathrm{d}L_x}{L_x} - 1\right]^{-1}. \qquad (2.30)$$

Total differentiation of ω in (2.28) will show that

$$\frac{\mathrm{d}K_x}{K_x}\bigg/\frac{\mathrm{d}L_x}{L_x} = \frac{s + r(k_y/k_x)}{s + r} > 1 \qquad \begin{array}{l} s = (\beta + 1)(a/b) \\[4pt] r = (\gamma + 1)(c/d)(L_x/L_y)(k_y^\gamma/k_x^\beta). \end{array} \qquad (2.31)$$

It can be shown that the value of (2.31) will fall with increases in X provided that k_y/k_x increases with X. It follows from (2.28) and a corresponding equation for Y that this will occur if and only if $\sigma_x < \sigma_y$. Given this restriction, (2.31) falls with X implying in turn that (2.30) falls with X. Given the discussion following equation (2.29), it then follows that $\sigma_x \leq 1$ and $\sigma_x < \sigma_y$ is sufficient for $(\mathrm{d}X/X)/(\mathrm{d}\omega/\omega)$ to fall monotonically with X.

Finally, note with reference to the right-hand side of (2.27) that k_x/ω decreases with X if and only if $\sigma_x < 1$. Similar comments apply to k_y/ω. Thus sufficient conditions for the right-hand side of (2.27) to be non-decreasing in X are that $\sigma_x \leq 1$ and $\sigma_y \geq 1$. Note that the right-hand side of (2.27) is constant when $\sigma_x = \sigma_y = 1$. In total, we have

$$\frac{\mathrm{d}p}{p}\bigg/\frac{\mathrm{d}\omega}{\omega} \text{ rises monotonically with } X \text{ if } \sigma_x \leq 1 \text{ and } \sigma_y \geq 1. \qquad (2.32)$$

Since Kemp has shown that (2.27) must be negative in the neighbourhood of $X = 0$ (i.e. the production possibility curve must be convex in the neighbourhood of $X = 0$), this implies that the production-possibility curve has at most one inflection point and that it cannot be everywhere concave. More specifically, the Kemp result allows us to state unambiguously where the concave and convex segments of the production-possibility curve occur. When it does exist under the restrictions noted on σ_x and σ_y, the concave section necessarily occurs at high levels of X production.

What this amounts to is the fact that the elasticities of substitution play an important role in determining the relative strengths of the factor-intensity and IRS effects. With σ_x small and σ_y large, the factor intensity effect becomes relatively stronger as the output of X increases. With σ_x large and/or σ_y small more complex outcomes can occur. We have for example generated by computer simulation the case in which there are convex segments at each end of the frontier with a concave segment in the middle.

The functional forms in (2.26) can be used to show that the IRS expansion condition of equation (2.10) is not sufficient for GFT in the presence of non-convexities as noted in Section 5. Suppose that two goods, X_0 and X_1, are both characterized by IRS so that $T_0, T_1 > 0$. Assume that the production functions are given by

$$X_0 = (X_0^{T_0})F(L_0, K_0), \quad X_1 = (X_1^{T_1})F(L_1, K_1) \tag{2.33}$$

where the F's are identical so that there are no factor-intensity effects and the contract curve is the diagonal of the factor box. The production frontier is clearly convex to the origin throughout. Let $\alpha = F(\bar{L}, \bar{K}) = (\bar{X}_i/\bar{X}_i^{T_i})$ where $\bar{L}$ and $\bar{K}$ are the total endowments of L and K and $\bar{X}_i$ is the maximum production of X_i. Finally, assume that the economy specializes in X_1. The results of Markusen and Melvin (1981) will show that the supply/price ratio is given by $(p_1/p_0 = X_0^{T_0}/X_1^{T_1})$. Thus, strictly speaking, the minimum value of p_1/p_0 consistent with specialization in X_1 approaches zero which would guarantee losses from trade. But lest we be accused of creating a pathological case by focusing on a local maximum, let $X_0^{T_0} = 1$ so that $(p_1/p_0) = (1/X_1^{T_1})$ at $X_1 = \bar{X}_1$. For the parameter values used below, this supply/price ratio will imply that $p_0 < AC_0$ over most of the production frontier even if prices remained constant after moving away from $\bar{X}_1$. If demand is relatively inelastic, $(X_1 = \bar{X}_1, X_0 = 0)$ will indeed be a global profit maximum at these prices. In any case, we have

$$p_1/p_0 = (1/\bar{X}^{T_1}) = (\alpha/\bar{X}_1) = (\alpha/\alpha^{T_1^*}) = \alpha^{1-T_1^*}, \tag{2.34}$$

where $T_i^* = 1/(1 - T_i) > 1$. The slope of the chord connecting the ends of the production frontier is on the other hand given by

$$(\bar{X}_0/\bar{X}_1) = \alpha^{T_0^* - T_1^*}. \tag{2.35}$$

Thus for $\alpha > 1$, we have

$$p_1/p_0 < (\bar{X}_0/\bar{X}_1) \text{ or } (p_1/p_0)(\alpha^{T_0^* - 1}) = (\bar{X}_0/\bar{X}_1). \tag{2.36}$$

The price ratio through $\bar{X}_1$ lies below the chord $\bar{X}_0/\bar{X}_1$ and must cut the production frontier, implying that GFT are not assured. (Note that with CRS in $X_0(T_0^* = 1)$, the price ratio equals the slope of the chord, a special result due to the absence of factor intensity effects. Positive factor intensity effects ensure that p^f exceeds the slope of the chord, as demonstrated in Section 5 for CRS in X_0.)

Let the relevant parameters take on the following values: $\alpha = 1.5$; $T_0 = 0.5$

(or $T_0^* = 2$); $T_1 = 0.9$. From the second equation in (2.36), we then have $(p_1/p_0)(1.5) = (\bar{X}_0/\bar{X}_1)$. Since $p_i(1 - T_i) \leqslant MC_i$ as noted above, the IRS expansion condition in (2.10) could be expressed as

$$(p_1/p_0)(T_1/T_0) \geqslant (\bar{X}_0/\bar{X}_1) \quad \text{since } (\bar{X}_0/\bar{X}_1) \geqslant (X_0^a/(\bar{X}_1 - X_1^a)). \quad (2.37)$$

Since $T_1/T_0 = 1.8$, we have

$$(p_1/p_0)(T_1/T_0) = (p_1/p_0)(1.8) > (p_1/p_0)(1.5) = (\bar{X}_0/\bar{X}_1). \quad (2.38)$$

Thus the IRS expansion condition holds, but the production inequality $\Sigma p_i^f X_i^f \geqslant \Sigma p_i^f X_i^a$ does not follow. For at least some bundles X^a near $X_1 = 0$ we must have $\Sigma p_i^f X_i^f < \Sigma p_i^f X_i^a$.

8. SUMMARY AND CONCLUSIONS

The primary purpose of this paper was to look for a unified approach to the gains from trade in the presence of increasing returns that could be applicable across a wide range of models. These models include analyses based on (i) homogeneous goods with external economies, (ii) homogeneous goods with internal economies, and (iii) differentiated products produced in a setting of monopolistic competition. We argued that in all three cases a failure to realize GFT could occur for the same two reasons. First, in all cases, the IRS goods are priced above marginal cost and thus the price plane may cut the production surface at the free trade production point. We referred to this as a failure of the 'tangency' condition. Second, IRS may imply that the production set is non-convex and thus even if the tangency condition is satisfied, the price plane may not form a separating hyperplane to the production set. This was referred to as a failure of the convexity condition. The tangency condition relates to economic pricing behaviour while the convexity condition relates to the structure of technology.

With respect to the tangency condition, results (generally well known) show that losses from trade may occur if trade contracts the IRS industries. The intuition is fairly straightforward. With prices greater than marginal costs in autarky, the economy is already under-producing the IRS goods. If trade reduces production further, the economy may be moving away rather than towards its optimal production mix. We suggested that a sufficient condition for GFT is that trade have a certain rationalizing effect on production. This is a rather crude notion to the effect that surviving industries expand output more than in proportion to the number of IRS industries lost due to the opening of trade. We argued that this is in fact a reasonable outcome (although hard to define rigorously) provided that trade does not decrease the total resources devoted to the IRS industries.

Non-convexities present a more difficult problem. On the one hand, we are able to show that the same expansion of all IRS industries that is sufficient for

GFT in the convex case continues to be sufficient in the presence of non-convexities. Further, this result does not rely on restrictive functional forms, specialization in production, or on average-cost pricing in the IRS industries. On the other hand, the weighted increase in the outputs of the IRS industries that is sufficient in the convex case is no longer sufficient with non-convexities. We are thus still without a sufficient condition for GFT in the realistic case in which trade expands some IRS industries and contracts others. Further work which exploits profit restrictions, stability conditions, and restrictions on oligopolistic behaviour may help to produce such conditions.

Section 5 emphasized the applicability of these results to recent monopolistic competition models and noted how some of the very restrictive assumptions used in that literature imply that both the tangency condition and the convexity condition are satisfied. These assumptions include (i) symmetry assumptions which ensure that price ratios equal ratios of marginal costs, and (ii) free entry that results in average-cost pricing. Together these assumptions imply that the price plane will not cut the convex hull of the production set (i.e. the price plane is a separating hyperplane).

Section 6 showed how the tangency condition can be expressed in terms of profits in addition to the more usual formulation in terms of output levels. This turns out to be quite useful in analysing the gains from trade in the presence of multinational enterprises and allows the GFT condition to be expressed in terms of restrictions on profit repatriation by the MNE.

NOTES

*The authors would like to thank Mark Bagnoli and Ignatius Horstmann for helpful discussions.
1.   For treatments of external economies, see for example Jones (1968), Herberg and Kemp (1969), Melvin (1969), Kemp (1969), Kemp and Negishi (1970), Eaton and Panagariya (1979), Markusen and Melvin (1981), and Panagariya (1981). Markusen (1981) treats internal economies with homogeneous products. As noted, see Helpman (1984) for an excellent survey of these contributions. One type of external economy which will not be treated here is 'international external economies' (Ethier, 1979) in which returns to scale depend on the total world output of a good.
2.   Recent monopolistic competition and product differentiation models include Helpman (1981), Krugman (1979, 1980), Lancaster (1980), and Ethier (1982).
3.   These assumptions as discussed below include specific functional forms for production and utility functions, symmetry assumptions, free entry, average-cost pricing and so forth.
4.   In general the gains from trade theorem cannot be proved if either producer or consumer prices differ from p^f (or from each other). Our concern in this paper is with ways in which production conditions can cause the breakdown of

the theorem, and so hereafter it will always be assumed that the upper contour sets of the utility function are convex and that consumers are free to maximize subject only to p^f. Thus such things as distortionary consumption taxes are ruled out.

5.   Herberg and Kemp (1969) show that for a special type of technology, the production frontier must be convex in the neighbourhood of zero production of an IRS good. This technology relies on a separable externality effect and 'Heckscher–Ohlin' technology (all factors used in the production of each good). This convex segment need not occur for example with a specific factors technology.

REFERENCES

Dixit, A. and Norman, V. (1980), *Theory of International Trade* (Cambridge, England: Cambridge University Press).

Eaton, J. and Panagariya, A. (1979), 'Gains from Trade under Variable Returns to Scale, Commodity Taxation, Tariffs and Factor Market Distortions', *Journal of International Economics*, 9, 481–501.

Eaton, J. and Kierzkowski, H. (1984), 'Oligopolistic Competition, Product Variety, and International Trade', this volume.

Ethier, W. (1979), 'Internationally Decreasing Costs and World Trade', *Journal of International Economics*, 9, 1–24.

Ethier, W. (1982), 'National and International Returns to Scale in the Modern Theory of International Trade', *American Economic Review*, 72, 389–405.

Helpman, E. (1981), 'International Trade in the Presence of Product Differentiation, Economies of Scale and Monopolistic Competition: A Chamberlin-Heckscher-Ohlin Approach', *Journal of International Economics*, 11, 305–40.

Helpman, E. (1984). 'Increasing Returns, Imperfect Markets, and Trade Theory', in R. Jones and P. Kenen (eds.), *Handbook of International Economics* (Amsterdam: North-Holland), forthcoming.

Herberg, H. and Kemp, M. (1969), 'Some Implications of Variable Returns to Scale', *Canadian Journal of Economics*, 2, 403–15.

Jones, R. (1968), 'Variable Returns to Scale in General Equilibrium Theory', *International Economic Review*, 9, 261–72.

Kemp, M. (1969), *The Pure Theory of International Trade and Investment* (New Jersey: Prentice Hall).

Kemp, M. and Negishi, T. (1970), 'Variable Returns to Scale, Commodity Taxes, Factor Market Distortions, and Implications for Trade Gains', *Swedish Journal of Economics*, 72, 1–11.

Krugman, P. (1979), 'Increasing Returns, Monopolistic Competition, and International Trade', *Journal of International Economics*, 9, 469–79.

Krugman, P. (1980), 'Scale Economies, Product Differentiation, and the Pattern of Trade', *American Economic Review*, 70, 950–9.

Lancaster, K. (1980), 'Intra-Industry Trade under Perfect Monopolistic Competition', *Journal of International Economics*, 10, 151–75.

Markusen, J. (1981), 'Trade and the Gains from Trade with Imperfect Competition', *Journal of International Economics*, 11, 531–51.

Markusen, J. (1984), 'Multinationals, Multi-Plant Economics, and the Gains from Trade', *Journal of International Economics*, 14, forthcoming.

Markusen, J. and Melvin, J. (1981), 'Trade, Factor Prices, and Gains from Trade with Increasing Returns to Scale', *Canadian Journal of Economics*, 14, 450–69.

Melvin, J. (1969), 'Increasing Returns to Scale as a Determinant of Trade', *Canadian Journal of Economics*, 2, 389–402.

Panagariya, A. (1981), 'Variable Returns to Scale and Patterns of Specialization', *American Economic Review*, 71, 221–30.

3

Natural Oligopolies
and International Trade *

Avner Shaked and John Sutton

1. INTRODUCTION

Until very recently, a serious imbalance was evident between the large and active empirical literature on intra-industry trade, and the fragmentary theoretical foundations which served as an underpinning for such studies (Grubel and Lloyd, 1975). The two-way flow of 'similar' products, which such trade involves, suggests of course some kind of model of product differentiation in which firms in each economy produce competing 'varieties' of some good. The analysis of trade then centres around two questions: suppose two initially separated economies are joined via free trade:

(i) the short run: keeping product specifications fixed, how will competition affect consumer welfare?

(ii) the long run: here, we allow firms to choose their product specifications in an optimal manner in each of these environments. The focus of interest now lies both in the differences in the range of products on offer, and their respective prices – and so on the impact of trade on consumer welfare.[1]

The answers to these question turn out to be rather sensitive to the underlying model of consumer choice over differentiated products. The most familiar model derives from Hotelling's classic 'location' paradigm. Here, we imagine consumers distributed 'along a line', and rival firms first choose their respective locations, and thereafter compete in price.

Now, interpreting the firm's location as its product specification, and the consumer's position on the line as his most preferred specification, we have a one-dimensional model of product differentiation. Indeed, it is natural to see it, as Lancaster (1979) suggests, as the simplest case of his 'characteristics' approach.

The answers to the questions we just posed, within this framework, are straightforward. In the short run, the typical consumer enjoys a welfare gain, in that he consumes a product which is 'closer' to him, at a lower price. In the long run, the greater extent of the market results in a finer net of product varieties being produced, and so the same result again follows. Indeed, as the extent of the market increases the number of firms rises indefinitely, so that the market becomes increasingly atomistic.

Now this outcome reflects the central features of such a 'locational' paradigm: were all sellers to set the same price, then each firm would enjoy a positive market share — consisting of those consumers 'closest' to him. Lancaster (1979) has suggested the label 'horizontal differentiation' for this case.

In the present paper we will be concerned with the alternative case in which products differ in 'quality'; here, were rival goods offered at the same price then all consumers would prefer the same, 'highest quality', product. In this 'vertical differentiation' case, we imagine an industry in which R & D expenditure allows a firm to produce a 'better' product, as it were.

This 'vertical differentiation' case has been studied in a recent sequence of papers[2] by J. Jaskold Gabszewicz, J.-F. Thisse, and the present authors. Within this 'vertical differentiation' paradigm, the increase in the extent of the market is not necessarily associated with an increasingly large number of firms. Two quite different cases arise, depending on the interplay between technology and tastes.

The situation in which *unit variable costs* rise steeply with quality, we have elsewhere labelled the 'Chamberlinian' case. Here, industry equilibrium is reminiscent of the familiar 'location' paradigm: a fall in the level of fixed costs, or an extension of the market, is associated with a rise in the number of product varieties on offer, and we can converge to a 'zero-profit' equilibrium as the industry becomes more atomistic — in the spirit of the familiar 'limit theorems' of monopolistic competition. In respect of trade, the answers to the questions we posed earlier again mirror those for the 'horizontal' differentiation case.

The other case to be considered is that in which unit variable cost does not rise steeply with quality — this case is likely to be relevant in situations where the main burden of quality improvement falls on fixed (R & D) costs, rather than increases in labour and raw material inputs. (The simplest case arises where variable costs are zero, as in the illustration we employ below.) In this case, it turns out that an upper bound exists to the number of firms which can survive with positive market shares, and prices in excess of unit variable cost, at a Nash equilibrium in prices (the 'finiteness' property). We denote this latter situation, the 'natural oligopoly' *case.*

Here, the answers to the questions posed earlier are radically different.

In the short run, joining economies via trade is associated in general with the exit of (low-quality) producers, and a fall in the prices of the various products on offer, with a consequent gain in consumer welfare.

In the long run, on the other hand, precisely as a result of the 'finiteness' property, which ensures that the greater extent of the market is not associated with any increase in the equilibrium number of firms, it follows that those firms which survive enjoy greater marginal returns to (R & D) expenditure on quality improvement — so that the 'combined economy' created by trade enjoys higher quality products — and the resulting impact on prices is such that consumer welfare is enhanced.

It is worth stressing the fundamental nature of the basic ('finiteness') property which leads to these results. This is most clearly seen by thinking in terms of the 'limit theorems' which characterize the horizontal differentiation case: here, a rise in the extent of the market produces an increasingly 'atomistic' industry, and so convergence to a zero-profits equilibrium. In the 'natural oligopoly' case, no such outcome is possible — a change in the size of the market has no effect on the equilibrium number of firms — it impinges only on the range of products (qualities) which they offer, and on their respective prices.

2. THE EQUILIBRIUM CONCEPT

We aim to address ourselves both to the problems of the short run, where product qualities are taken as given, and to the long run, where they are determined endogenously. This is facilitated by our characterization of market equilibrium, in terms of a three-stage game, as follows. In the first stage, firms decide whether or not to enter the industry; in the second, they choose their respective qualities, and in the third, their respective prices. This three-stage process is intended to capture the notion that the price can in practice be varied at will, but a change in the quality of a product involves a period of research and development activity, while entry to the industry involves, again, a prior decision on the part of the firm.

When the third stage is reached, therefore, each firm is aware of the number of competing firms present, and the qualities of their representative products. We then characterize equilibrium in this final stage as a Nash equilibrium in prices; in other words, we seek a set of prices, such that each firm, given the prices chosen by its competitors, is setting a profit maximizing price.

In this problem, then, the qualities chosen by the various firms are fixed; and so we may find the pay-offs (profits) of each firm, as a function of these parameters. But this allows us, therefore, to define another game, pertaining to the second stage of our process, in which firms choose their respective qualities. The pay-off functions of this game are defined as the levels of profit which will be achieved in the third stage, these profit levels being specified as a function of the qualities chosen by the various firms at the second stage. Again we seek a Nash equilibrium in this game.

This procedure defines a perfect equilibrium in the two-stage game (choice of quality, choice of price). Continuing in a similar manner, we may incorporate the entry decision of firms as a prior stage, and so characterize market equilibrium in a three-stage game.

A (pure) *strategy* in this game takes on of two forms: (i) 'Don't Enter', or (ii) 'Enter, choose quality (as a function of the number of firms who have entered), and choose price (as a function of the *quality* choices made by rival firms in the preceding stage).'

The equilibrium we have described consists of a set of strategies which have the following property: suppose all firms follow these strategies up to any stage. Then the remaining parts of the firms' strategies constitute a Nash equilibrium in the sub-game which remains.

This equilibrium concept is known as a perfect equilibrium (Selten, 1975).

A perfect equilibrium, then, is a set of strategies possessing the important feature, that, whatever the history of events prior to a certain stage, the remaining parts of the firms' strategies form a Nash equilibrium in the remaining sub-game. The importance of this feature is that it rules out non-credible threats, in the following sense: suppose a firm was to announce an intention of offering a high-quality product at a low price in an attempt to deter entry — it might be the case however that it would not in fact be profitable for the firm to carry out that threat, once a rival firm had actually entered. Then such a threat would not be credible.

Now the problem with using a Nash equilibrium in our present context is that many such equilibria exist, and these will, in general, embody such non-credible threats. The advantage of the perfect equilibrium concept is that it excludes such candidates.

Finally, we remark on the roles played by variable costs, and by fixed costs, respectively, in this model. The fundamental 'finiteness' property adduced earlier is a property of *price equilibrium*; only variable costs enter the pricing decision, all fixed costs incurred in choosing the firm's level of quality being sunk costs. It is for this reason that the requirement for 'finiteness' takes the form of a condition on the relationship between unit variable cost and quality.

Fixed costs, on the other hand, enter at the 'quality choice' stage of the process, being a function of the level of quality chosen by firms. The relationship between fixed costs and quality thus affects the configuration of qualities offered on the market at equilibrium. Whether they affect the equilibrium number of firms, however, depends on whether the variable cost — quality relationship leads to the 'Chamberlinian' case — where fixed costs do indeed affect the number of firms — or in the 'natural oligopoly' case — where fixed costs have no effect[3] on the number of firms which can coexist at equilibrium.

In the remaining sections of the paper, then, we will proceed by first describing the final stage of this game; taking product qualities as given, we consider price competition. This allows us to illustrate the short-run impact of trade. Then, we return to an examination of the full, three-stage, equilibrium — and so proceed to a description of the impact of trade in the long run.

3. PRICE COMPETITION AND THE 'FINITENESS' PROPERTY

We will be concerned throughout with a situation in which consumers choose *between* alternative products, buying either one, or another (or possibly none) of the qualities on offer, at prevailing prices.

We also assume that consumers differ from one another in their willingness to pay for a higher-quality product — so that at some set of prices, firms can partition the market between them. The simplest framework in which to do this, is one in which consumers are identical in tastes, but differ in income, and where richer consumers are willing to pay more for a higher-quality product. In this case the market is partitioned in a straightforward manner: the top-quality product on offer is clearly bought by all consumers above some critical income level; the second highest quality by consumers in some income band stretching down from this critical level, and so on. The marginal consumer, lying on the boundary of these two income bands, is indifferent between buying the higher quality product at its (higher) equilibrium price, or buying the second highest quality instead.

The manner in which the 'finiteness' property arises, is as follows: competition between 'high-quality' products drives their prices down to a level at which not even the poorest consumer would prefer to buy certain lower-quality products at any price sufficient to cover unit variable cost.

We may illustrate this mechanism, by appeal to a simple example:

Let a number n of firms, indexed by k, each sell a single product of some quality level u_k at price p_k. Suppose they all have zero (variable) cost.

They sell to a number of consumers who differ in income; the distribution of incomes is described by a uniform density taking the value s on some support $[a, b]$, where $a > 0$. Here, s is a measure of the size of the economy. All consumers have the same utility function, as follows: a consumer of income t derives utility

$$u_k \cdot (t - p_k)$$

from consuming one unit of product k, and spending his remaining income $(t - p_k)$ on 'other things'. (We label products in increasing order of quality.) Otherwise, in buying none of these alternative goods, he achieves a utility level

$$u_0 \cdot t.$$

Consider a consumer who is indifferent between consuming good $k - 1$ at price p_{k-1} or good k at price p_k. Then

$$u_k \cdot (t - p_k) = u_{k-1} \cdot (t - p_{k-1}). \tag{3.1}$$

This implicitly defines an income level which we label t_k. Figure 3.1 illustrates equation (3.1); the level of utility achieved by consuming good $k - 1$, with $t_k - p_{k-1}$ units of income remaining, coincides with that achieved by consuming good k with income $t_k - p_k$ remaining.

The horizontal distance between the lines $U = u_k \cdot t$ and $U = u_{k-1} \cdot t$ thus represents the consumer's willingness to pay for a given quality improvement; and Fig. 3.1 illustrates the assumption which we invoke on the utility function: that this willingness to pay is increasing in income — reflecting the idea that the marginal utility of the 'residual good' is diminishing.

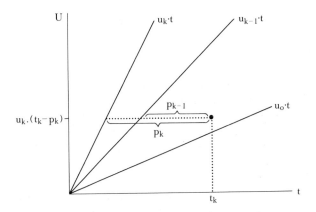

Fig. 3.1. Consumer preferences

Now this means that consumers of income greater than t_k will strictly prefer good k at price p_k, to good $k-1$ at price p_{k-1}; and so we may partition consumers into the respective market shares of successive firms. The sales of firm n are thus $s \cdot (b - t_n)$, those of firm $n-1$ become $s \cdot (t_n - t_{n-1})$, and so on.

Now, from this, it is easy to write down the demand schedule faced by any firm, which will depend both on the qualities, and the prices, offered by its neighbours.

As an illustration, consider the demand schedule faced by firm n, which offers the top-quality product.

Suppose, to begin with, that its neighbour offers a product of quality u_{n-1} at price zero. Now the richest consumer, of income b, will be willing to pay some positive price in order to consume good n, rather than good $(n-1)$, and this determines the vertical intercept of our demand schedule (Fig. 3.2). As poorer consumers are willing to pay less, demand increases as price falls, until that price is reached which the poorest consumer is just willing to pay for good n, rather than consume good $(n-1)$ at price zero. At that price, demand equals $(b-a)$, and the top-quality product covers the market. Finally, notice that this demand schedule, if extended, will intersect the horizontal axis at a demand level equal to b – this corresponds quite simply to the fact tha a consumer of income zero is willing to pay price zero for good n, rather than $(n-1)$. It is easily shown that this demand schedule, moreover, is linear.

Now if the lower-quality firm $(n-1)$ instead sets some positive price, then the demand schedule of firm n shifts upwards, and, if extended, it cuts the horizontal axis at a demand level greater than b.

Now the profit (revenue) maximizing choice of price for a firm facing a linear demand schedule is that which corresponds to a sales level equal to half that given by the horizontal intercept of the demand schedule. Hence, if

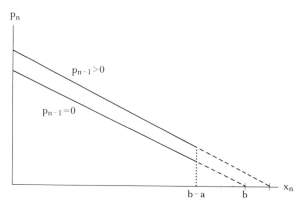

Fig. 3.2

$(b-a)<\frac{1}{2}b$ it follows that firm n will set a price so low that it covers the market (a corner solution), and so firm $(n-1)$ has a zero market share. This condition can be re-expressed as $a>b/2$; it requires that the range of incomes be sufficiently narrow.

Now if the range of incomes is broader, so that $a<b/2$, it can be shown that firm n will not cover the market. However, if $a>b/4$, then the market will be covered by the *two* top firms; price competition between these two will drive their prices down to a level where even the poorest consumer will prefer to buy product 2 at its equilibrium price rather than consume a product of quality u_3 even at price zero.

It may be shown, in general, then, that the number of firms which survive is bounded, and this bound depends in general on the pattern of income distribution, and consumer tastes. It is independent, however, of the qualities of the various products offered by rival firms.

Leaving our example, then, we proceed to a general *definition*: we remarked earlier that the criterion for the finiteness property depends only on the relationship between unit variable cost, c, and product quality, u. We say that a cost curve $c(u)$ defined on some domain $[u_0, \bar{u}]$ satisfies the *finiteness property* if there exists a bound B, independent of the qualities of the products offered, to the number of firms which can coexist with positive market shares, and prices exceeding unit variable cost, at a Nash equilibrium in prices.

In Shaked and Sutton (1983), we develop a condition on $c(u)$ which is necessary and sufficient for this *finiteness property* to hold. In order to illustrate the nature of this condition, it is helpful to begin by recalling the case of horizontal product differentiation, based on the 'location' paradigm. Consider a number of firms located at different points, each with the same, constant level of unit variable cost. Here, an infinite number of firms may coexist, for we can always introduce a new entrant between two existing firms, without precipitating the exit of either. All firms will, at equilibrium, enjoy a positive

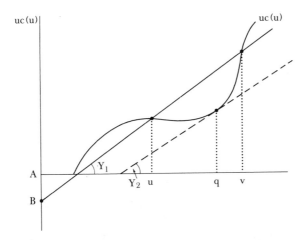

Fig. 3.3

market share consisting of certain 'nearby' consumers — no firm can be driven out of the market, for it can always achieve positive profits when its neighbours set any prices sufficient to cover their variable costs.

Now returning to the 'vertical differentiation' case, consider a hypothetical situation in which a number of products are offered at a price equal to their respective levels of unit variable cost. (The relevance of this case lies in the fact that some firms may not be able to achieve positive sales at a price which covers variable cost, and it is this which limits the number of firms surviving at equilibrium.)

As before, suppose a consumer with income t purchases one unit of a product of quality u, at price $c(u)$, thereby achieving utility $u \cdot (t - c(u))$. Figure 3.3 shows the function $uc(u)$. Take a line of slope Y_1 through the point $(u, uc(u))$. Then the vertical intercept AB, which equals $u(Y - c(u))$, represents the utility attained by a consumer of income Y_1 in purchasing a product of quality u at price $c(u)$. Again referring to Fig. 3.3, the consumer of income Y_1 is indifferent between u at price $c(u)$ and v at price $c(v)$. Finally, we illustrate the optimal quality choice for a consumer of income Y_2, who can purchase any quality at unit variable cost, as the point of tangency q (chosen to maximize the associated intercept).

We are now in a position to identify a fundamental dichotomy: let consumer incomes lie in some range $[a, b]$ and suppose unit variable cost rises only slowly with quality. Then, if two products are made available at unit variable cost, all consumers will agree in preferring the higher-quality product, i.e. all consumers rank the products in the same order. On the other hand, consider the cost function shown in Fig. 3.4; here, we illustrate an example in which $uc(u)$ is convex. (No requirement on the convexity of $uc(u)$ is used in the analysis; it

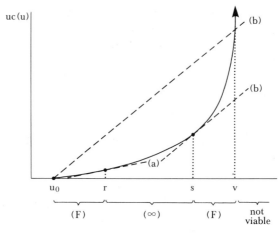

Fig. 3.4

merely offers a very simple illustration here.) We identify two points of tangency *r* and *s* where the slope of the curve coincides with our extreme income values *a* and *b*. Here, if any set of products lying in the interval below *r* is made availabe at unit variable cost, all consumers will agree in ranking them in increasing order of quality; and for a set of qualities drawn from the interval above *s*, and sold at unit variable cost, consumers will agree in ranking them in decreasing order of quality. Above *v*, no product is viable: all consumers prefer u_0 to any good in the range, at a price covering variable cost. In the intermediate quality range, however, consumers will differ in their ranking of products, at unit variable cost. Now this is reminiscent of the 'location' paradigm noted above, and the property just alluded to continues to hold good here — an unbounded number of firms may coexist with positive market shares and prices exceeding unit variable cost, at equilibrium.

Now, in this 'location-like' situation, the manner in which an arbitrarily large number of firms may be entered, is straightforward: for, within a certain interval, we can always insert an additional firm (product) *between* two existing firms, without precipitating the exit of any other firm.

A second, and quite distinct, kind of situation may arise, however, which is also consistent with the coexistence of an unbounded number of competing firms. While many sub-cases of this possibility arise, all are quite analogous, and a clear illustration of the mechanism involved is provided by the following example. Suppose costs were zero; and suppose further that the range of incomes extends downwards to zero. In this case, an unbounded number of products may be entered: for no product can have zero profits at equilibrium unless some higher-quality product sells for price zero (remember the consumer of income zero is indifferent between all products are price zero, so any product can otherwise find some positive price at which it can earn positive profits). But it now suffices to notice that the highest-quality product in the sequence will *not* be sold at price zero; for clearly there exists some price at which it can earn positive profits.

Hence in this situation, an infinite number of products may again be entered — but now, the method by which they are entered is by introducing new products of successively lower quality at the end of the existing range.

What characterizes this situation, and all analogous sub-cases, is the presence of a consumer — here the consumer of income zero — who is (locally) indifferent between alternative products, at unit variable cost (i.e. the derivative of his utility score with respect to product quality is zero).

The condition which we develop for finiteness in Shaked and Sutton (1983) is designed to exclude these two types of situation. Where that condition is satisfied, all consumers will be agreed in ranking the products in the same strict order, at unit variable cost. When this is so, it follows that one firm could set a price which would drive the remaining firms out of the market. This will not in general occur at equilibrium, as we emphasized in our example above. However, *there will exist an upper bound independent of product qualities, to the number of firms which can coexist with positive market shares and prices exceeding unit variable cost, at a Nash equilibrium in prices.*

We have already noted that the case which is likely to be of practical relevance here relates to those 'high technology' industries where the main burden of quality improvement falls on fixed (R & D) costs, rather than on any improvements in labour and raw material inputs, so that unit variable costs rise only slowly with quality. (The condition clearly admits a second possibility however, where unit variable costs rise so quickly with quality that all consumers rank products in decreasing order of quality, when all are offered at unit variable cost.)

Finally, we emphasize the mechanism through which the result comes about: whatever the set of products entered, competition between certain 'surviving' products drives their prices down to a level where every consumer prefers either to make no purchase, or to buy one of these surviving goods at its equilibrium price, rather than switch to any of the excluded products, *at any price sufficient to cover unit variable cost.*

4. THE IMPACT OF TRADE I: THE SHORT RUN

We now proceed to consider the short-run impact of trade, in an industry of the 'natural oligopoly' type.

We first note that the bound B to the number of products which can coexist at a Nash equilibrium in prices is *independent of the size of the economy*; an increase in the extent of the market merely shifts the demand schedule faced by all firms proportionately, raising sales and profits but leaving equilibrium prices unchanged.[4]

Now this implies that the number of firms will in general be *reduced* in consequence of the introduction of trade — in the most extreme case, consider two economies identical in all respects, except possibly size. Then each may support up to some number B of firms initially; joining the economies via trade then implies the exit[5] of certain firms in the combined economy, since at most B will remain in all.

We now turn to the case where the economies are different. This case has been examined in Jaskold Gabszewicz *et al.* (1981a). There, we consider two economies which differ in respect of the distribution of income. We show how, according as the economies are more 'dissimilar', the combined economy can support a larger number of firms — but as the distributions of income become closer, the number of firms which can coexist in the combined economy is reduced.

The mechanism through which this occurs, as we emphasized above, involves a fall in the prices of 'surviving' products. It follows immediately that trade is welfare improving, in so far as *all* consumers are made better off, via this fall in the level of prices.

5. QUALITY CHOICE AND THE EQUILIBRIUM CONFIGURATION OF PRODUCTS

We now turn to the question of how in a natural oligopoly, the various firms choose their respective qualities. Here we follow Shaked and Sutton (1982a, b).

As mentioned in Section 2 above, we invoke the notion of a perfect equilibrium in a three stage game.

Returning to the example introduced earlier (Section 3), we assume variable costs are zero, and we let the range of income distribution be such that $\frac{1}{4}b < a < \frac{1}{2}b$, so that $B = 2$. It can in fact be shown, that, for any choice of qualities, *exactly* two firms now survive with positive market shares, at (price) equilibrium (Shaked and Sutton, 1982a).

We now suppose that each of a number of potential entrants is free to choose any quality $u \in [u_0, \bar{u}]$ by incurring some fixed cost $F(u) > 0$. To ensure the existence of equilibrium, we require some (rather strong) convexity conditions on $F(u)$.

We first analyse the final stage of the game. As described above, we seek a Nash equilibrium in prices, taking the various firms' quality choices as given. This allows us to write down the profits attained by each firm, as a function of the set of qualities offered both by itself, and by its rivals. These functions now constitute the pay-off functions for the game in which firms choose their qualities.

Suppose, firstly, that two firms have entered. Then the equilibrium configuration of qualities is illustrated in Fig. 3.5. Given a choice of u_1 by firm 1, we show the revenue function $s \cdot R^2(u_1, u)$ of firm 2 as a function of the quality

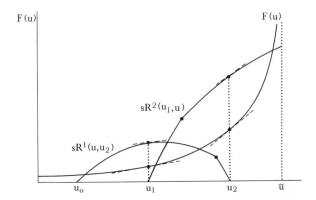

Fig. 3.5. The equilibrium configuration of products

u which it chooses. The notation here reflects the fact that the revenue attained is proportional to the size s of the economy. If it chooses $u = u_1$, then its pay-off is zero (our model here reduces to a Bertrand duopoly model, the products of the two firms being identical). If, on the other hand, it chooses $u > u_1$, revenue is greater. A necessary condition for equilibrium is that the slope of the revenue function coincides with the slope of the cost function; this condition defines u_2, in Fig. 3.5, as the 'optimal reply from above' to u_1.

Similary, given a choice of u_2 by firm 2, we define the revenue $s \cdot R^1(u, u_2)$ of firm 1 as a function of the quality u which it chooses. This function takes the value zero at $u = u_2$; as u falls, revenue rises, reflecting the relaxation of price competition which accompanies a widening of the gap between the two qualities – but now a second effect operates, in that the fall in the quality of product 1 means a decline in consumers' willingness to pay for 1, given any quality–price combination offered by firm 2. This effect in fact dominates, eventually, and the revenue of firm 1 then declines as u falls further.

We define the 'optimal reply from below' to u_2 as that point, u_1, at which the slopes of the revenue function coincides with the slope of the cost curve.

For (u_1, u_2) with $u_1 < u_2$, to be a Nash equilibrium, we further require that given u_2, firm 1 achieves a higher profit from a choice of $u_1 < u_2$, that it can obtain by choosing any quality $u > u_2$ (i.e. it prefers not to 'jump above' u_2); and that u_2 similarly prefers not to 'jump below' u_1.

It can in fact be shown that, at least for s sufficiently large, there exists a unique equilibrium point (u_1, u_2).

All this refers to the case where exactly two firms enter; suppose, however, that $k > 2$ firms enter. It can be shown that, for any Nash equilibrium in this 'quality choice' sub-game, at least $k - 2$ firms earn negative profits (we assume that $F(u) > 0$ everywhere).

Now this allows an analysis of the complete, three-stage, game. Here, it can be shown that (i) no perfect equilibrium exists[6] in which more than two firms enter, and (ii) for s sufficiently large, there exists a perfect equilibrium in which exactly two firms enter; they choose, respectively, the qualities u_1 and u_2 which we identified above; and they both earn positive profits at equilibrium.

Part (i) of this result follows directly from our observation that, if $k > 2$ firms enter, then at least $(k - 2)$ of them earn negative profits. For, given the strategies chosen by its rivals, it must be the case that at least one firm is using a strategy which yields a negative pay-off — while it could achieve a pay-off of zero by not entering.

The idea underlying part (ii) of the results is that we can find a set of strategies for firms, all but two of which take the form 'Don't Enter'; and these are such that if any of the non-entrant firms decided instead to enter, then it will have a negative pay-off in the resulting game. (The nature of this result is rather subtle, and depends in an important way on the precise nature of the perfect equilibrium concept. For a detailed explanation, the reader is referred to the proof of Theorem 1 in Shaked and Sutton (1982b).

6. THE IMPACT OF TRADE: THE LONG RUN

We now turn to the question of how international trade will impinge on industries of this kind in the long run.

We consider two separate economies, identical in all parameters, except possibly their sizes, s and s', and we pose the standard 'comparative statics' question: we compare the vector of products which would appear in a combined economy of size $(s + s')$, with the vector of products which would appear in an economy of size s, and in an economy of size s', respectively.[7]

Our exercise thus reduces to an examination of the effect of the size parameter s in the one-economy model just described.

To see its effect, we remark firstly on the characterization of the equilibrium configuration of products in the model. In Fig. 3.5, we illustrated how, given u_1, the quality u_2 is determined as the point where the slope of the cost function coincides with the slope of the revenue function $s \cdot R^2(u_1, u)$, describing the revenue of firm 2 as a function of its quality u, given the choice u_1 by firm 1; and similarly for u_1.

Now the effect of raising s here is to shift upwards the two families of revenue schedules $s \cdot R^2(u_1, u)$ and $s \cdot R^1(u, u_2)$. Thus, for any u_1, the revenue function $R^2(u_1, u)$ is steeper, at any u; and conversely. Thus the marginal returns for a given increase in R & D expenditure increases with the extent of the market. It can be shown,[8] consequently, that the new quality pair $(\tilde{u}_1, \tilde{u}_2)$ for the enlarged market, is higher, in the sense that $\tilde{u}_1 > u_1$ and $\tilde{u}_2 > u_2$.

In order to obtain an unambiguous welfare result, here, one further restriction is required: that $\bar{u}$ be 'close' to u_0 — this corresponds to the fairly natural restriction that consumers spend only a small fraction of their incomes on the products of this industry.

In these circumstances, the reaction of prices is such that *all* consumers are made better off.

(It is worth emphasizing, perhaps, that this is an extremely strong result.[9] For, in the case of differentiated products, we would not normally anticipate such an outcome: for certain consumers may be relatively 'lucky' in the original configuration, enjoying access to a product very close to their most preferred specification, but not so 'lucky' in the new configuration; some average (consumer surplus) must be taken (see Lancaster, 1979, 1980).

What we wish to emphasize here, however, is the novelty of the mechanism through which trade enhances welfare: the finiteness property limits the number of firms which can coexist at equilibrium − and it is precisely this limitation which ensures that those firms which do remain will enjoy enhanced economies of scale, in the sense that the marginal returns to a given level of R & D expenditure are greater, as the extent of the market is increased.

7. EXTENSIONS

We have described here a very simple, and special, model; the results however are quite robust and may be relaxed in a number of directions.

First, the special form of the utility function cited above does not play a critical role, and our results may be extended to a wider class of functions. (For a full treatment of existence, and finiteness, in the zero cost case, see Jaskold Gabszewicz *et al.* (1981b).)

Second, the assumption that consumers be identical can be relaxed, once some ranking of consumers in order of their willingness to pay is available.

Finally, an extension of central importance is to the case of multi-product firms: common experience suggests a paucity of producers in many industries, but a proliferation of product varieties. We stress, therefore, that the finiteness property is a property of the number of *firms*, not of products. It is the *competition* between rival firms which causes the fall in prices which excludes further entry. If we allow firms to produce a number of, or even an interval (continuum) of products, a bound still exists to the number of independent producers who can coexist at equilibrium.

8. CONCLUSIONS

It has long been felt that one of the most significant areas through which gains from trade are achieved in practice is by way of the enhanced economies of scale which derive from the extension of the market. (See for example the introductory remarks in Krugman (1979).) Within the familiar paradigm of 'horizontal' product differentiation, however, what tends to happen as a result of trade is that a wider range of products becomes available, but the typical firm operates at a similar scale to that which holds under autarky.[10] Thus the gains from trade which occur in this setting are of a kind which emanate from an increase in product variety — the 'city lights' effect identified by Krugman.

The present paper has been concerned with exploring a context in which the gains from trade seem likely to be much more dramatic than this.

We have been concerned here with 'vertical' differentiation (quality). We have pointed out that market equilibrium in this context may take two quite different forms. The first is analogous to the usual 'Chamberlinian' structure familiar from the horizontal differentiation case. Our focus of interest here, however, lies in the second possibility. This will arise in those industries where unit variable cost rises slowly, relative to consumers' willingness to pay, as quality is improved. Such a possibility is likely to be associated with those industries where the main burden of quality improvement falls on fixed (R & D) costs, rather than on any increases in labour and raw material inputs.

In such circumstances, the number of firms which can coexist at a Nash equilibrium in prices is limited; we have labelled this case a 'natural oligopoly'. The fact that only a bounded number of firms can coexist carries strong implications for the impact of international trade in industries of this kind. Bringing together economies which are initially separated, by introducing free trade, here implies the *exit* of a number of firms — and it is precisely because of this exit that the remaining firms now enjoy enhanced economies of scale.

In the short run, this leads to a welfare gain in that consumers now enjoy higher-quality products at lower prices.

In the long run, however, the gains from trade emanate from the fact that, precisely because the number of firms is reduced, those firms which survive enjoy greater marginal returns to R & D expenditure on quality improvement. The effect of trade is to raise the qualities of the products provided on the market; moreover, the concomitant impact on prices is such that consumers benefit: indeed, under certain restrictions we have shown that, even though we are here in a 'second best' world, the opening of trade makes *all* consumers better off.

NOTES

*   Our thanks are due to the International Centre for Economics and Related Disciplines at LSE for financial support.
1.   In dealing with differentiated products, trade will take place even between identical economies, so that the obvious case to consider is that in which identical economies are linked by trade — so the opening of free trade is analytically equivalent to a rise in the size of an economy (an increase in the extent of the market).
2.   Jaskold Gabszewicz and Thisse (1980), Shaked and Sutton (1982a, b; 1983), Jaskold Gabszewicz *et al.* (1981a, b).

3. Of course, if fixed costs are sufficiently large, they may further limit the number of firms.
4. Marginal costs are assumed to be constant as output changes.
5. Strictly, if the products are distinct. A number of firms producing identical products may coexist with positive market shares, and prices equal to unit variable cost (here equal to zero).
6. We confine ourselves to pure strategies at the entry stage.
7. Thus, we avoid the analysis of the transition path to this configuration, consequent on the opening of trade.
8. So long as the economies are sufficiently large, so that a unique equilibrium is guaranteed in each.
9. It should further be noted, therefore, that if the restriction that consumers spend only a small fraction of their incomes on the good in qeustion is relaxed, then it is possible to construct an example in which those consumers with incomes close to the level which forms the boundary between the two market shares, experience a fall in welfare.
10. This applies not only to the Lancaster model, but also to the Dixit–Stiglitz (1977) model explored by Krugman (1979).

REFERENCES

Dixit, A. K. and Stiglitz, J. E. (1977), 'Monopolistic Competition and Optimum Product Diversity', *American Economic Review*, 67, pp. 297–308.

Grubel, H. G. and Lloyd, P. J. (1975), *Intra-Industry Trade* (London: Macmillan).

Jaskold Gabszewicz, J. and Thisse, J.-F. (1980), 'Entry (and Exit) in a Differentiated Industry', *Journal of Economic Theory*, 22, pp. 327–38.

Jaskold Gabszewicz, J., Shaked, A., Sutton, J. and Thisse, J.-F. (1981a), 'International Trade in Differentiated Products', *International Economic Review*, 22, pp. 527–35.

Jaskold Gabszewicz, J., Shaked, A., Sutton, J. and Thisse, J.-F. (1981b), 'Price Competition among Differentiated Products: A detailed study of a Nash Equilibrium', ICERD Discussion Paper No. 37, London School of Economics.

Krugman, P. (1979), 'Increasing Returns, Monopolistic Competition and International Trade', *Journal of International Economics*, 9, pp. 469–79.

Lancaster, K. (1979), *Variety, Equity and Efficiency* (New York: Columbia University Press).

Lancaster, K. (1980), 'Intra Industry Trade Under Perfect Monopolistic Competition', *Journal of International Economics*, 10, pp. 151–76.

Selten, R. (1975), 'Re-examination of the Perfectness Concept for Equilibrium Points in Extensive Games', *International Journal of Game Theory*, 4, pp. 25–55.

Shaked, A. and Sutton, J. (1983), 'Natural Oligopolies', *Econometrica*, 51 pp. 1469–83.

Shaked, A. and Sutton, J. (1982a), 'Relaxing Price Competition through Product
    Differentiation', *Review of Economic Studies*, 49, pp. 3–13.
Shaked, A. and Sutton, J. (1982b), 'Natural Oligopolies and the Gains from
    Trade', ICERD Discussion Paper No. 51, London School of Economics.

4

Product Diversity, Trade and Welfare[*]

Henrik Horn

1. INTRODUCTION

Does a market economy yield brand proliferation in excess of what is socially desirable? Or, put differently, is the profit signal appropriate in establishing the socially optimal diversification and output of each product? This question has been debated for at least half a century. Chamberlin (1933), for instance, argued that firms will operate with excess capacity, and that there will be excessive product differentiation in a monopolistically competitive market equilibrium, as compared to a perfectly competitive one. This was conventional wisdom for fifty years, although some economists, e.g. Hotelling (1929), expressed other views. In the mid-seventies two influencial papers, Spence (1976), and Dixit and Stiglitz (1977), challenged the wisdom of this belief in arguing that the market equilibrium instead exhibits too *little* diversity, relative to a first-best social optimum.[1] These two papers also considered ways of regulating the market equilibrium when the first-best policy is not available, and properties of these second-best equilibria. Dixit and Stiglitz (1977) concluded that a second-best optimum where each firm's output volume is regulated, is identical to the market equilibrium. Spence (1976) also showed this, and in addition found that this type of regulation is less efficient in raising social welfare than one that regulates the number of firms.

Koenker and Perry (1981) presented a framework within which some new light is shed on the questions mentioned above. Their answers to these questions depend, in particular, on the degree to which there are increasing returns to scale, and on firms' conjectures about rivals' responses.

The present paper considers these problems in a framework similar to that of Koenker and Perry (1981) but from another point of view: it analyses whether changes in the *size* of the economy, as measured by its factor endowment, affect the relation between the market equilibrium, and first- or second-best optima. It will be shown that size indeed is crucial to the probability of excess diversity and the relative efficiency of different second-best policies, as long as the perceived elasticity of demand for a differentiated good is not confined to being constant. This change in the scale of factor endowments is interpreted as the result of the opening up of international trade between economies that are scaled replices of one another. An alternative view would be a growing, closed economy interpretation where we compare different steady states. A by-product of our analysis is that we will analytically derive some of the results that Koenker and Perry (1981) obtained with numerical simulation techniques.

Our analysis based on a one-factor, two-sector general equilibrium model, with a demand side representation that is by now common, particulary in the theory of international trade in differentiated products. We express our variables of interest as functions of the factor endowment and compare different equilibria for various sizes of this endowment. Following Koenker and Perry (1981) we make different assumptions about the individual firm's conjectures regarding competitors' strategies, and about its share of the market, than do the authors referred to above. Chamberlin (1933), as well as Dixit and Stiglitz (1977), assume that firms behave in a Cournot or Bertrand fashion, and that the individual firm is of negligible size relative to the market. Spence (1976) makes the analogous assumption that each firm expects the rest of the industry to accommodate any marginal change the firm undertakes in its supply. Here, on the other hand, we do not restrict conjectures to either of these types, but allow in this respect for a more general treatment. The important difference is that the individual firm's perceived elasticity of demand is no longer constant.[2]

The model and the resulting equilibria, owing to particular assumptions chosen, are characterized by strong symmetry. However, these special assumptions simplify the analysis considerably, and it is hoped that they can be justified on the ground that we are not presently interested in biases in product selection.[3] But it deserves to be emphasized that by assuming consumers have identical preferences many essential aspects of product differentiation are not captured.[4] We believe, however, that our analysis deals with phenomena that are much more general than our special assumption would seem to imply.

Our analytical framework stands in the following relation to the previous literature. Just as in Dixit and Stiglitz (1977), we rely on a two-sector general equilibrium model, as opposed to Spence's (1976), and Koenker and Perry's (1981), partial equilibrium analysis with neglected income effects. Dixit and Stiglitz (1977), and Koenker and Perry (1981), assume a fixed cost and a constant marginal cost technology, whereas in Spence (1976), and also here, there is a more general representation of the technology in the industry of particular interest. Preferences are more general in Spence (1976), and in Dixit and Stiglitz (1977), than they are here or in Koenker and Perry (1981). Conjectures about competitors' responses are the same here as in Koenker and Perry (1981); they include the other two papers' assumptions as special cases. In other words, on the production side the assumptions are equally or less restrictive, and on the demand side equally or more restrictive, than in the other three studies.

The paper is structured as follows. In the next section the model is presented in detail, and demand functions are derived, as well as the equations that define the market equilibrium. Section 3 solves the problem facing the planner of finding the first-best social optimum. The market equilibrium and the unrestricted social optimum are compared in Section 4 for various sizes of the economy. Section 5 compares two non-first best regulatory policies. Finally, Section 6 offers a summary and some concluding remarks.

2. THE MARKET EQUILIBRIUM

Envision and economy which produces goods in two sectors, X and Y, using the same mobile factor of production L, which we refer to as 'labour'. One sector, industry Y, is supposed to represent 'the rest of the economy'.[5] In this crude characterization it produces a homogeneous good under constant returns to scale, and the good is sold on a perfectly competitive market. The condition for profit maximiation and industry equilibrium in sector Y is therefore simply that price equals unit cost, i.e.

$$p_y = a_y w, \tag{4.1}$$

where p_y and w are the prices of the output and of labour, respectively, and where a_y is the (constant) requirement of labour per unit of output. In what follows w is the numeraire, set at unity. We assume furthermore, for convenience, a unitary labour requirement, so that $p_y = 1$.

The industry of prime interest is industry X. It consists of n firms each producing only one variant of good X, and each being the sole producer of that particular specification.[6] Due to product differentiation on the demand side, each producer enjoys some monopoly power. There are economies of scale at the firm level, and hence there will only be a limited number of firms active in a zero-profit equilibrium, where each firm maximizes its profit given its conjectures about competitors' strategies.[7]

The technology of any firm i ($i = 1, \ldots, n$) can be represented by the same cost function f, which for each output level x_i gives the minimum requirement of labour l_i. We assume that the economies of scale are eventually exhausted, at some finite output volume. Let us define a measure of the degree of economies of scale as

$$\theta(x_i) \equiv \frac{f'(x_i)}{f(x_i)/x_i}, \tag{4.2}$$

i.e. marginal over average cost. Our assumptions about the returns to scale can then more exactly be stated as

$$0 < \theta(x_i) < 1 \quad \text{for } 0 < x_i < \bar{x}, \tag{4.3a}$$

$$\theta(x_i) \geqslant 1 \quad \text{for } x_i \geqslant \bar{x}, \tag{4.3b}$$

and

$$\theta'(x_i) > 0 \quad \text{for } x_i > 0, \tag{4.3c}$$

for some finite $\bar{x}$.

Firm i's profit is

$$\pi_i = p_i x_i - f(x_i) \tag{4.4}$$

and the first-order condition for profit maximiation with respect to output is

$$p_i \left(1 - \frac{1}{\epsilon_i}\right) = f'(x_i), \tag{4.5}$$

where ϵ_i is the price elasticity of demand for good i.[8]

Of prime interest in the subsequent analysis are the properties of the elasticity of demand ϵ_i. To derive an expression for this elasticity we have to specify the demand side. We will assume that the representative consumer's preferences can be represented by a two-stage Cobb–Douglas–CES utility function

$$u = \left(\sum_{j=1}^{n} x_j^{\beta}\right)^{\alpha/\beta} Y^{(1-\alpha)} \quad \text{where } 0 < \alpha < 1 \text{ and } 0 < \beta < 1, \tag{4.6}$$

and where Y denotes the amount of good Y consumed and n is the number of products in existence. This representation resembles the general equilibrium representations used by Dixit and Stiglitz (1977), although they alternatively allowed for a more general formulation in the upper or lower stages, and the partial equilibrium representations employed by Spence (1976) and by Koenker and Perry (1981). In standard fashion, the consumer maximizes utility subject to a budget constraint. If I is total income the demand functions become

$$p_i = \frac{x_i^{\beta-1}}{\sum_j x_j^{\beta}} \alpha I \quad \text{and} \quad p_y = \frac{(1-\alpha)I}{Y}, \tag{4.7)(4.8}$$

when written on implicit form.

Let us now revert to the elasticity of demand as perceived of by a typical firm i. From (4.7) we derive

$$-\frac{1}{\epsilon_i} = \beta - 1 - \frac{x_i}{z} \frac{dz_i}{dx_i}, \tag{4.9}$$

where $z \equiv \sum_{i=1}^{n} x_i^{\beta}$, and where

$$\frac{x_i}{z} \frac{dz_i}{dx_i} = \frac{\beta x_i}{z} \left(x_i^{\beta-1} + \sum_{j \neq i} x_j^{\beta-1} \frac{dx_j}{dx_i}\right). \tag{4.10}$$

The elasticity of demand for firm i can, as (4.9) shows, be thought of as consisting of two parts. One is the direct effect when the industry's total output volume (as measured by z) remains unchanged, and the second is the effect of the induced change in this volume. In Spence (1976) and in Dixit and Stiglitz (1977) it is assumed that the latter effect – the expression in (4.10) – is equal to zero.[9,10] The implication of this is of course that the elasticity of demand is equal to $1/(1 - \beta)$, i.e. it is invariant both to the number of competing products and to the amount in which the different varieties are consumed. This assumption obviously facilitates the ensuing comparative statics, and might

therefore be defended, if the question at issue so permits. It might also be justified if one believes that it is actually a good description of the industry's product space, i.e. that the entry of new varieties does not make it more 'crowded'.
This, of course, is contradictory to the basic idea of locational models of product choice and, we would argue, to our usual perceptions of the product spaces
of most differentiated products.[11]

We will, following Koenker and Perry (1981), assume that each firm's conjectural derivative can be approximated by

$$\frac{\mathrm{d}x_j}{\mathrm{d}x_i} = \frac{\delta}{n-1}, \quad \forall j \neq i, \tag{4.11}$$

with $\delta \geqslant -1$. $\Sigma_{j \neq i}(\mathrm{d}x_j/\mathrm{d}x_i) = \delta$ is hence the total response by all other firms
conjectured by the oligopolist. If all firms entertain Cournot conjectures, i.e.
no response by the rest of the industry, $\delta = 0$. If the rest of the industry accommodates any change in firm i's quantity, δ would be -1. Our purpose is to
analyse not only economies where n is very large (as studied by Dixit and
Stiglitz (1977)), but also those in which there are fewer firms. Since Cournot
conjectures are often argued to be unreasonable for smaller markets, it seems
desirable to allow for other types of behaviour. All the subsequent results are
qualitatively similar for all values of $\delta > -1$; hence including Cournot conjectures as a special case.

To facilitate the subsequent analysis we make an additional assumption
concerning firms' conjectures: we assume that $(1 + \delta)/n$ goes to zero as n goes to
infinity. A sufficient, although not necessary condition for this to be true, is that
$\mathrm{d}\delta/\mathrm{d}n < 0$, i.e. that the more firms there are in the market, the less a firm's conjectured response from each individual competitor for a given change in the
firm's output volume (see Appendix 1). This indeed seems reasonable for
positive values of the conjectural derivative, but is less attractive for negative
values. A general sufficient condition is that the elasticity of δ with respect to n
is negative (positive) for positive (negative) δ.

Since the assumptions we have made imply complete symmetry on both
sides of the market, a potential equilibrium is a symmetric one where all firms
produce the same quantity x, and sell at the same price p. All the different
types of equilibria that are treated below are symmetric in this way, and the
symmetry allows us to rewrite (4.9) for the representative firm as

$$-\frac{1}{\epsilon} = \beta\left(1 - \frac{(1+\delta)}{n}\right) - 1. \tag{4.12}$$

The first-order condition for profit maximization is therefore

$$p\beta\left(1 - \frac{1+\delta}{n}\right) = f'(x). \tag{4.13}$$

For marginal revenue to be positive it is required that $n > \delta + 1$, which is henceforth assumed. As usual we also have for the market equilibrium an industry equilibrium condition which states that profits are zero

$$px = f(x). \tag{4.14}$$

Finally we require that labour and goods markets are in equilibrium, respectively[12]

$$nf(x) + Y = L, \tag{4.15}$$

$$pnx = \alpha I, \tag{4.16}$$

and

$$Y = (1 - \alpha) I. \tag{4.17}$$

We are now able to characterize the market equilibrium E. (4.13)–(4.17) constitute, due to Walras's Law, four independent equations that suffice to determine n, x, Y, p. Equations (4.13) and (4.14) imply

$$\beta \left(1 - \frac{1 + \delta}{n^e} \right) = \theta(x^e), \tag{4.18}$$

where superscript e denotes market equilibrium values.[13] Since we have assumed that θ is a monotonic function of x, it is invertible. Our quantities of primary interest are then

$$x^e = \theta^{-1} \left[\beta \left(1 - \frac{(1 + \delta)}{n^e} \right) \right], \tag{4.19}$$

and, due to (4.15) and (4.17),

$$n^e = \frac{\alpha I}{f(x^e)}. \tag{4.20a}$$

But since we have zero profits in both sectors in E, all income is factor income, and therefore

$$n^e = \frac{\alpha L}{f(x^e)}. \tag{4.20}$$

Subsequently we will refer to L as the 'size' of the economy. We assume that households are identical in all respect, and that the supply of labour is fixed for each. Increasing the size of the economy is hence equivalent to increasing the number of workers-households. It is clear from (4.19) and (4.20) that both x^e and n^e are affected by the size of L.

To interpret the increase in size as the opening up of frictionless international trade should not cause any problem, since with identical technologies and preferences, factor price equalization will occur.[14] Due to the symmetry of the demand side each producer faces the same elasticity of demand regardless of the location of production. With n^e in (4.19) now denoting the number of products in the world, each producer chooses the same total output x^e, and therefore receives the same price p^e. The zero-profit conditions then assure that factor prices equalize, and since the trading economies are scaled replicas of one another there will be no net trade, although there is intra-industry trade in differentiated products.[15]

Let us explore the relation between the equilibrium output volume per firm and the size of the economy. Industry and firm equilibrium requires that $\theta(x^e) = 1 - (1/\epsilon)$. The maximum value that ϵ can take on is $1/(1 - \beta)$, which occurs when n^e is infinitely large.[16] Therefore the maximum value for $\theta(x^e)$ is β, and as $\beta \leqslant 1$ no firm will ever operate 'to the right' of its minimum average cost. Now, if we use (4.20) to substitute for n^e in (4.18) we get

$$\frac{\beta - \theta(x^e)}{f(x^e)} = \frac{\beta(1 + \delta)}{\alpha L}, \tag{4.21}$$

and hence, since minimum average cost by assumption is at a finite x^e,

$$x^e \rightarrow \theta^{-1}(\beta) \quad \text{as} \quad L \rightarrow \infty. \tag{4.22}$$

3. THE UNRESTRICTED SOCIAL OPTIMUM

In order to determine whether or not there is excess diversity in the market equilibrium, we obviously need to know what the optimal allocation is. It is as usually possible to think of several different concepts of optimality, depending on how the set of feasible allocations is restricted. In this section we will consider what will be referred to as an *unrestricted* social optimum *U*. This is the allocation that a planner would choose to maximize the representative consumer's utility *B*, subject only to given preferences, technology, and endowments. In the international trade interpretation the planner hence decides on the optimal world allocation. The optimum is unrestricted in the sense that the planner is free to set both the number of firms, and their output volumes. We will in the next section also consider a couple of optima where the planner is constrained to the use of just one of these instruments.

The symmetry of preferences and technology allows us to formulate the planner's problem as

$$\max_{n, x, Y} B = n^{\alpha/\beta} x^\alpha Y^{1-\alpha}, \tag{4.23}$$

$$\text{s.t.} \begin{cases} l = f(x), & \text{and} & \tag{4.24a} \\ n\,l + Y = L, & \tag{4.24b} \end{cases}$$

or

$$\max_{n, x} B = n^{\alpha/\beta} x^\alpha (L - nf(x))^{1-\alpha}. \tag{4.25}$$

First-order conditions are (letting superscript *u* denote the unrestricted optimum)

$$n^u = \frac{\alpha L}{f(x^u)} [(1 - \alpha)\beta + \alpha]^{-1}, \tag{4.26}$$

and, when we take (4.26) into account,

$$x^u = \theta^{-1}(\beta). \tag{4.27}$$

This result, that the optimal firm size is independent of the size of the economy, can be interpreted as follows. The marginal rate of substitution in consumption between n and x is $\beta n/x$, whereas the marginal rate of transformation between the two is $\theta(x)n/x$. Hence, due to the economies of scale the MRT changes at a different rate the MRS when x changes, and therefore only one particular x can be optimal.[17]

4. A COMPARISON OF THE MARKET EQUILIBRIUM AND THE SOCIAL OPTIMUM

We are now in a position to compare the allocation in the market equilibrium with that in the social optimum. It is immediate from (4.19) and (4.27) that since θ is increasing in x, and since $0 \leqslant (1 + \delta)/n < 1$, it will generally be the case that

$$x^e < x^u, \tag{4.28}$$

that is, firm size in the market equilibrium will be less than what is socially optimal. The result obtained by Spence (1976), and by Dixit and Stiglitz (1977), that these are equal, is hence a special case that arises when $(1 + \delta)/n = 0$. It is also clear that the closer the representative firm's conjecture is to that its competitors seek a market share solution, the more pronounced is the inequality (4.28).[18]

Let us now turn to the question of diversity: (4.20), (4.26), and (4.27) give

$$\frac{n^e}{n^u} = \frac{f(\theta^{-1}(\beta))[(1 - \alpha)\beta + \alpha]}{f(x^e)}. \tag{4.29}$$

We first note that, for x^e sufficiently close to, though not necessarily equal to, $\theta^{-1}(\beta)(= x^u)$, the ratio on the RHS is less than unity. Since x^e converges towards x^u when L grows infinitely, it seems that Spence's (1976), and Dixit and Stiglitz (1977), assertion that there is too lite diversity in the market equilibrium, is most likely to be valid for the very large economy. On the other hand, with x^e small enough, i.e. for the sufficiently small economy the opposite will prevail, at least if the fixed-cost element is small.[19] That is, it is also possible that the market equilibrium implies an excess diversity relative to the social optimum. This possibility was demonstrated by Koenker and Perry (1981) in their numerical analysis, and by Lancaster (1980). To repeat, what is shown here is that, given the degree of product differentiation and economies of scale, and given firms' conjectures about competitors' strategies, *excess diversity in the market equilibrium is more likely the smaller the economy's factor endowment,* and that *it is the large economy that is likely to have too little diversity.* Furthermore, *there exists some finite size of the economy $\tilde{L}$, for which the number of firms in the market equilibrium is equal to that in the first-best optimum.*

Not only the market equilibrium, but also the reference point – the unrestricted social optimum – is influenced by the factor endowment. We will consider the relation between utility levels in the two allocations in more detail below. But it is clear that there is a gain from trade that derives from the increase in product variety it brings about, regardless of whether or not a country's autarky factor endowment is smaller or larger than $\tilde{L}$. But comparing $n^e(L)$ with $n^u(L)$ we see that it is possible that consumers in a country that face excess diversity in autarky, will after trade is opened up find themselves living on a world with more, but now too little, diversity, in both cases relative to the respective first-best optimum. Trade may in this way actually *increase* the relative divergence between the market equilibrium and the social optimum in terms of product variety.

One way of interpreting these results is the following. Each firm's perceived elasticity of demand increases as the economy becomes larger through increased competition from entering firms. With a fixed budget share for differentiated goods, and an increasing output of each, the number of product varieties must increase proportionally *less* than the size of the economy, i.e. n^e is strictly concave in L. Two conflicting forces influence whether there is excess diversity in the market equilibrium. One is that the X-industry uses more resources in the social optimum than in the market equilibrium. This is clear from a comparison of (4.20) and (4.26):

$$n^e f(x^e) = \alpha L \qquad (4.20)$$

$$n^u f(x^u) = [\alpha(1-\beta) + \beta]^{-1} \alpha L, \qquad (4.26)$$

where $[\alpha(1-\beta) + \beta]^{-1} > 1$. This tends to make $n^u > n^e$. On the other hand, as $x^e < x^u$, less resources are devoted to the production of each variant in the market equilibrium, then in the social optimum. Since these resources can be used to produce additional specifications, there is also a tendency for $n^e > n^u$. The smaller the economy, the lower the equilibrium elasticity of demand, and the larger the difference between x^e and x^u. Hence for L sufficiently small n^e exceeds n^u, whereas the opposite prevails when L is sufficiently large, and at $\tilde{L}$ these forces are just balancing each other.

The market equilibrium E, and the unrestricted social optimum U are shown in Fig. 4.1 in (n, x)-space. ZP is the zero-profit locus and $PM(\delta_1)$ and $PM(\delta_2)$ are two profit-maximizing loci where $\delta_2 > \delta_1$. The 'elliptic' contours around U are iso-benefit contours. Whether n^u is larger or small than n^e obviously depends on the size of δ. But, as depicted in Figs. 4.2 and 4.3, country size also matters.

Consider next consumer utility levels. Per capita utility is higher the larger

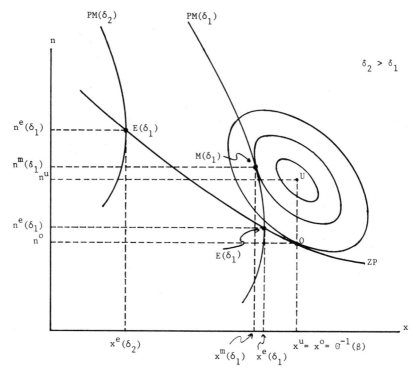

Fig. 4.1

the economy regardless of whether it is a market economy or not. This gain from trade stems from the fact that in the larger economy each consumer can consume less of each specification, but more different types of goods, *without* incurring any higher average costs. Per capita utility in the market economy is of course in most cases lower than in the social optimum. But what happens when the economy grows infinitely large? As we saw above $x^e \to x^u$, and hence we have

$$\frac{(B^e/L)}{(B^u/L)} \to \frac{[\alpha(1-\beta) + \beta]^{(\alpha/\beta)+1-\alpha}}{\beta^{1-\alpha}} \quad \text{when } L \to \infty. \qquad (4.30)$$

The limit value is less than unity for β less than unity, and therefore, *the per capita utility level in the market equilibrium will generally* not *converge towards the level in the corresponding social optimum. But, it is shown in Appendix 3 that the RHS is increasing in β, and hence the less differentiated products are, the less will be the difference between the two per capita utility levels be.* The opening up of international trade thus in this sense reduces, even though it usually does not completely eliminate, the scope for regulation of the market economy.

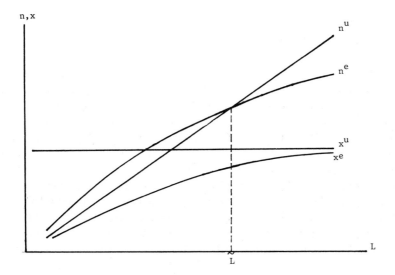

Fig. 4.2

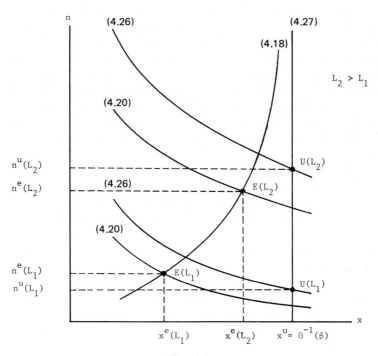

Fig. 4.3

5. A COMPARISON OF TWO CONSTRAINED OPTIMA

In the unrestricted social optimum treated above, the planner was free to choose both the representative firm's output volume and the number of producers in the differentiated goods industry. Let us now assume that our planner is less omnipotent in that just one of these instruments is available at a time. Consider first a regulatory policy that aims at controlling the *size* of the representative firm, while the profit potential determines the number of firms active in the market, just as in the market equilibrium. This can be called a *behavioural regulation* since we do not allow the firms to act in the way they would otherwise do. The planner's problem is hence to choose only x and leave n free to vary, so as to maximize the benefit function (4.25) subject to the zero-profit condition (4.14) and the market demand function (4.16). Since free entry and exit will eliminate all profits, factor services will constitute the only source of income, just as in the market equilibrium. The solution to the maximization problem is the constrained equilibrium O, with the following solution:[20]

$$x^o = \theta^{-1}(\beta), \tag{4.31}$$

$$n^o = \frac{\alpha L}{f(x^0)}. \tag{4.32}$$

As demonstrated also by other authors the planner will choose the same output volume when restricted to the behavioural regulation as would prevail in the unrestricted social optimum. If we compare (4.32) to the corresponding equations (4.20), and (4.26), it is immediate that the number of firms in the social optimum that is restricted to behavioural regulation is *less* than *both* what is socially fully optimal, *and* what will prevail in the market equilibrium. But the welfare level is of course in between these two allocations.

A comparison of (4.31)–(4.32) and (4.19)–(4.20) shows why Dixit and Stiglitz (1977) had a case where the market equilibrium is identical to the social optimum where only output per firm can be regulated: they assume that $(1 + \delta)/n = 0$, implying $x^o = x^e$ and $n^o = n^e$. Therefore, once again, the results of Dixit and Stiglitz (1977) are valid for the very large economy, but not necessarily for smaller economies.

The restricted social optimum O is shown in Fig. 4.1. Due to the zero-profit restriction it obviously has to be located along the ZP locus, at the point of tangency with the highest iso-benefit contour.

Let us now consider whether the efficiency of the behavioural regulation in increasing welfare is dependent on the size of the economy. If we measure the efficiency of the regulatory policy by the relative increase in welfare it brings about, and if we take the market equilibrium as a basis, our measure is

$$\mu(L) \equiv \frac{B^o(L) - B^e(L)}{B^e(L)} = \frac{B^o(L)}{B^e(L)} - 1. \tag{4.33}$$

From the expressions above we have that

$$\frac{B^o(L)}{B^e(L)} = \left[\frac{f(x^e)^{1/\beta}x^o}{f(x^o)^{1/\beta}x^e}\right]^\alpha. \tag{4.34}$$

Since x^o is determined by β, and since

$$\frac{\mathrm{d}}{\mathrm{d}x^e}(f(x^e)\,x^e) > 0 \quad \text{and} \quad \frac{\mathrm{d}x^e(L)}{\mathrm{d}L} > 0, \tag{4.35}$$

B^o/B^e must be decreasing in L. This implies that

$$\frac{\mathrm{d}\mu(L)}{\mathrm{d}L} < 0, \tag{4.36}$$

i.e. *the behavioural regulation is in relative terms more efficient the smaller the economy.* This is intuitively appealing when we recall the result that the output quantity which is established in the market equilibrium approaches what is socially desirable as the economy grows. Hence, it seems natural that the scope for this type of policy shrinks as the economy gets larger.

Another type of regulatory policy is *structural* regulation which aims at controlling the *number* of firms in the market, while leaving to the individual firm to set its quantity at a profit maximizing level. The planner's problem is hence to maximize benefits (4.25), subject to the first-order condition for profit maximization (4.13), and the market demand function (4.16). The solution is depicted graphically as the point M in Fig. 4.1, for the case where $\delta = \delta_1$. An algebraic solution in the form presented above is hard to derive since the constraint is an implicit function on a somewhat complicated form. Nevertheless, some conclusions can be drawn concerning the efficiency of this regulatory policy. We recall that for low values of L, we have $n^e > n^u$, whereas for L larger than $\tilde{L}$ we have $n^e < n^u$ (see Fig. 4.2). It is therefore immediate that *at $\tilde{L}$ there is nothing to be gained from structural regulation.* But *the more the size of the economy differs from $\tilde{L}$ the more scope there is for this policy.*

A direct comparison of the efficiency of the two policies for various L is difficult as we have not derived the optimal n and x for the structural regulation. But as the structural policy is pointless at $\tilde{L}$, the behavioural policy must clearly be superior for this size. Since the market equilibrium output volume converges towards the social first best volume when L grows larger than $\tilde{L}$, and simultaneously the number of firms in the market equilibrium falls relative to what is socially optimal, we can make the following statements:
There exists a $\bar{L} > \tilde{L}$ such that for $L > \bar{L}$ the structural regulation is the most fruitful one. There will also be a $\underline{L} < \tilde{L}$ such that for $\underline{L} \leq L \leq \bar{L}$ the behavioural regulation must yield a higher benefit level. For $L < \underline{L}$ it is indetermiate which policy performs best.[21]

6. SUMMARY AND CONCLUDING REMARKS

We have shown that, as the size of the economy increases through the opening up of international trade, or through growth in the factor endowment:

(i) output per firm in the market equilibrium approach the first-best optimum;

(ii) the number of firms in the market equilibrium changes gradually from being in excess to being too few, as compared to the unrestricted social optimum;

(iii) the scope for a regulatory policy that aims at controlling the firms' behaviour decreases;

(iv) the welfare-improving potential of an entry-controlling policy is first reduced and thereafter increased; and that

(v) welfare in the market equilibrium will generally not approach the welfare levels of the unrestricted social optimum, but will, in the limit, converge towards a level that is negatively correlated with the degree of product differentiation.

Finally, due to (iii) and (iv), when we compare the efficiency of the two regulatory policies

(vi) all possible sizes of the economy can be divided into three mutually exclusive intervals. In the highest, structural regulation is most efficient, in the middle interval behavioural regulation is preferred, whereas for the lowest region the result is ambiguous.

A conceptual difference between this paper and most of the earlier literature is that we allow for situations where firms believe that their actions will influence the actions of others; that is, where the perceived cross elasticity of demand is different from that when firms hold Cournot conjectures, and where firms' market shares are not close to zero.

That firms take into account how their actions affect others makes the framework suitable for the analysis of other cases than Chamberlin's (1933), and Dixit and Stiglitz's (1977), 'large group' industry. It seems that their models are most suitable for the analysis of large economies. On the one hand, they assume that there are *many* firms active in the industry, so as to motivate, for example, Bertrand conjectures. On the other they require that the industry is well defined, and possible to distinguish from the rest of the economy. The second point seems to require that the elasticity of substitution between different variants of the differentiated good is high, to make products similar from the consumers' point of view. But the higher this elasticity, the larger the size of the representative firm, and hence the *lower* the number of firms in equilibrium. The number of firms will be larger again if the industry constitutes a large proportion of the economy, but this probably runs contrary to our attempt at making a clear distinction between the industry and the rest of the economy.

A way out is hence to assume that the economy is large. For cases other than this, however, the framework presented here should have some merit.

APPENDIX

1 : A CONDITION FOR $d((1 + \delta)/n)/dn < 0$

$$\frac{d}{dn}\left(\frac{1+\delta}{n}\right) = \frac{1}{n}\frac{d\delta}{dn} - \frac{1+\delta}{n^2}$$

$$= \frac{\delta}{n^2}\left(\frac{n}{\delta}\frac{d\delta}{dn} - \frac{1+\delta}{\delta}\right).$$

Since $\delta \geqslant -1$, we have that

$$\frac{d}{dn}\left(\frac{1+\delta}{n}\right) < 0$$

if   (i) $\dfrac{d\delta}{dn} < 0$,

or if (ii) $\dfrac{d\delta}{dn}\dfrac{n}{\delta} < 0$ (> 0) for $\delta > 0$ (< 0).

2 : $\tau(x^u) \geqslant 0$ IS SUFFICIENT TO FULFIL THE SECOND ORDER CONDITION

For $B = n^{\alpha/\beta}x^\alpha(L - nf(x))^{1-\alpha}$ we have that

$$\frac{\partial^2 B}{\partial n^2} = -B(\cdot)\left[\frac{\alpha}{\beta}\frac{1}{n^2} + (1-\alpha)\frac{f(x)^2}{(L-nf(x))^2}\right], \qquad (4.A1)$$

$$\frac{\partial^2 B}{\partial x^2} = -B(\cdot)\frac{\alpha}{x^2}\left[\frac{1}{1-\alpha} + \tau\right], \qquad (4.A2)$$

$$\frac{\partial^2 B}{\partial x \partial n} = -B(\cdot)\frac{\alpha}{xn}\left(1 + \frac{\alpha}{\beta(1-\alpha)}\right). \qquad (4.A3)$$

A sufficient condition for the function to have a local maximum at (x^u, n^u) is that the Hessian is negatively definite at this point, i.e.

$$\frac{\partial^2 B}{\partial n^2}\frac{\partial^2 B}{\partial x^2} - \left[\frac{\partial^2 B}{\partial x \partial n}\right]^2 > 0. \qquad (4.A4)$$

(4.A1)–(4.A3) inserted in (4.A4) gives after some manipulations the condition

$$\tau(x^u) > -(1-\beta). \qquad (4.A5)$$

3 : THE LIMIT VALUE FOR $(B^e/L)/(B^u/L)$

If we take the logarithm of the limit value in (4.30) we get

$$\left(\frac{\alpha}{\beta} + 1 - \alpha\right) \ln \left(\alpha(1 - \beta) + \beta\right) - (1 - \alpha) \ln \beta.$$

Differentiating with respect to β yields

$$-\frac{\alpha}{\beta^2} \ln \left(\alpha(1 - \beta) + \beta\right) + \left(\frac{\alpha}{\beta} + 1 - \alpha\right)\frac{1 - \alpha}{(\alpha(1 - \beta) + \beta)} - \frac{(1 - \alpha)}{\beta}$$

$$= -\frac{\alpha}{\beta^2} \ln \left(\alpha(1 - \beta) + \beta\right) > 0.$$

So the limit value is hence increasing in β.

When β attains its maximum value unity in (4.30)

$$\frac{(B^e/L)}{(B^u/L)} \to 1.$$

NOTES

*   Thanks are due to James Markusen, Torsten Persson, and Lars E. O. Svensson for valuable discussions. They also, together with Avinash Dixit, Wilfred Ethier, Harry Flam, and Carl Hamilton, provided comments on earlier drafts, as did participants in seminars of the Stockholm Theory Workshop and at the Institute for International Economic Studies. I am also grateful to Sholeh Blom, Caroline Burton, and Edda Liljenroth for typing and editorial assistance, and to Humanistisk Samhällsvetenskapliga Forskningsrådet for financial support.
1.   We refer to the sections of the two papers where a CES utility index for the differentiated goods is employed.
2.   Spence (1976), and Dixit and Stiglitz (1977), also consider cases where the elasticity of demand is not confined to being constant, but then this is due to other formulations of the preferences over the differentiated goods, rather than this supply side phenomenon.
3.   Such biases are studied in Spence (1976).
4.   Locational models as those used by Hotelling (1929) and Lancaster (1979) attempt to capture some of these aspects.
5. L might be thought of as the total endowment of good Y, $\bar{Y}$ the amount consumed and $L - \bar{Y}$ the amount that is transformed into X goods. In particular, as suggested by Dixit and Stiglitz, we can interpret the economy's factor endowment as the time at the disposal of the consumers. If each individual has a fixed amount of time available, L will be number of consumers, and good Y might be interpreted as leisure.
6.   There are generally, in a model such as this, incentives for firms to gain control over other firms in order to co-ordinate output decisions, but this is not dealth with here.

7.   All co-operative solutions are assumed away.

8.   The second-order condition is that the elasticity of marginal cost exceeds that of marginal revenue, i.e.

$$-\frac{1}{\epsilon_i} + \frac{1}{(\epsilon_i - 1)} \frac{x_i}{\epsilon_i} \frac{d\epsilon_i}{dx_i} < \frac{x_i f''(x_i)}{f'(x_i)} \equiv \tau(x_i).$$

$\tau(x_i)$ and $\theta(x_i)$ are related in the following way

$$\frac{x_i \theta'(x_i)}{\theta(x_i)} = 1 - \theta(x_i) + \tau(x_i).$$

9.   However, cf. note 1.

10. Dixit and Norman (1980) motivate this with, first, that firms hold Cournot conjectures and hence $dx_j/dx_i = 0$ for all $j \neq i$, and second, that the firm under study is assumed to be small relative to the market and therefore $\beta x_i^\beta / \Sigma_j x_j^\beta$ is approximately zero. The same approximation is done in Dixit and Stiglitz (1977), but with Bertrand-type conjectures.

11. For a discussion of this issue see Pettengill (1979), and Dixit and Stiglitz (1979).

12. n is henceforth treated as a real variable, although it should be an integer.

13. The second-order condition can be written as

$$\eta(x^e) = \frac{x^e \, \theta'(x^e)}{\theta(x^e)} > -\frac{1}{n^e - 1} \delta + \frac{f'(x^e)}{p^e}$$

or, in a zero-profit equilibrium,

$$\eta(x^e) > -\frac{1}{n^e - 1}(\delta + \theta(x^e)).$$

14. See e.g. Dixit and Norman (1980), or Helpman (1981), for an explicit treatment of the international equilibrium.

15. Net trade is the net exchange of differentiated goods for food.

16. Lancaster (1980) calculates an intra-group elasticity of demand with this property, using the same demand representation.

17. It is shown in Appendix 2 that a sufficient, although not necessary, condition for B to have a local maximum at (n^u, x^u) is that $x^u f''(x^u)/f'(x^u) > -(1 - \beta)$; so the marginal cost might hence be decreasing in the output volume at the equilibrium point.

18. That is, each individual firm strives to keep its share of the market, implying $dx_j/dx_i = x_j/x_i = \delta/n - 1$, or by symmetry that $\delta = n - 1$. As we assumed that $n > \delta + 1$ above, we hence only allow conjectures to be *close* to that of a market share behaviour. (This restriction would not be necessary with non-constant budget shares for the two types of goods.)

19. Fixed costs must be small to allow for a sufficiently small $f(x^e)$.

20. A sufficient second-order condition is that $\eta = 0$.

21. We can distinguish additional unambiguous intervals, if we allow ourselves to completely ignore the integer problem. If $L < \tilde{L}$, and $L \to 0+$, then $n^e \to n^u+$, whereas x^e diverges more and more from x^u. There will therefore be an

additional interval $(0, \underline{L})$ in which behavioural regulation is more efficient. We hence have two possibilities: Either $\underline{L} > L$, in which case behavioural regulation is preferable for all $L \leqslant \bar{L}$, whereas structural regulation has a larger welfare improving potential for $L > \bar{L}$. Alternatively, $\underline{L} < \bar{L}$, in which case the sequence of preferable second-best policies is, starting at $L = 0$: behavioural, structural, behavioural, structural.

REFERENCES

Chamberlin, E. H. (1933), *The Theory of Monopolistic Competition*, (Cambridge, Mass.: Harvard University Press).

Dixit, A. and Norman, N. (1980), *Theory of International Trade* (Cambridge, England: Cambridge University Press).

Dixit, A. and Stiglitz, J. (1977), 'Monopolistic Competition and Optimum Product Diversity', *American Economic Review*, 67(3), 297–308.

Dixit, A. and Stiglitz, J. (1979), 'Monopolistic Competition and Optimum Product Diversity: Reply', *American Economic Review*, 69(5), 961–3.

Helpman, E. (1981), 'International Trade in the Presence of Product Differentiation, Economies of Scale and Monopolistic Competition: A Chamberlin–Heckscher–Ohlin Approach', *Journal of International Economics*, II, 305–40.

Hotelling, H. (1929), 'Stability in Competition', *Economic Journal*, 34 41–57.

Koenker, R. and Perry, M. (1981), 'Product Differentiation, Monopolistic Competition, and Public Policy', *Bell Journal of Economics*, 12(1), 217–31.

Lancaster, K. (1979), *Variety, Equity and Efficiency* (New York: Columbia University Press).

Lancaster, K. (1980), 'Pettengill versus Dixit–Stiglitz: A Third Party Intervention', Discussion Paper No. 54, Dept. of Economics, Columbia University.

Pettengill, J. (1979), 'Monopolistic Competition and Optimum Product Diversity: Comment', *American Economic Review*, 69(5), 957–60.

Spence, A. M. (1976), 'Product Selection, Fixed Costs, and Monopolistic Competition', *Review of Economic Studies*, 43(2), 217–35.

5
Oligopolistic Competition, Product Variety, and International Trade

Jonathan Eaton and Henryk Kierzkowski

1. INTRODUCTION

International trade theorists have looked increasingly to preferences, rather than to differences in technologies and factor endowments, as explanations of international trade. This focus has its more immediate origins in the observations about trade of Linder (1961), Vernon (1966), and Grubel and Lloyd (1975), in particular, their findings that trade in manufactures is most intense between countries with similar factor endowments and technologies, and frequently involves the two-way exchange of commodities in the same commodity classification. Two other areas that have received attention from trade theorists are the theory of international trade under conditions of imperfect competition and under conditions of increasing returns to scale. These three developments have not been independent. Explanations of trade based on taste differences and which account for two-way trade have been based on non-competitive assumptions and upon an assumption of increasing returns to scale.

One reason for the recent activity in the three areas is that the theory of industrial organization has provided a number of new models of market behaviour. Krugman (1979, 1980, 1981), Feenstra and Judd (1982), Helpman (1981), Brander (1981), and Brander and Krugman (1983), among others, have applied these models to problems in international trade. All models dealing with imperfect competition, either in the closed or open economy context, incorporate an increasing returns-to-scale technology. The first five of the papers cited assume that in equilibrium profits are driven to zero. The zero-profit condition plays a central role in the recent literature on imperfect competition and product differentiation; it determines the equilibrium number of firms and the consequent product variety.[1]

Using a zero-profit condition to determine equilibrium requires two assumptions about the nature of the process whereby entry is determined: first, firms enter taking the prices of existing firms as given. To quote Baumol (1982), 'potential entrants find it appropriate to evaluate the profitability of entry in terms of the incumbent firms' pre-entry prices' (p. 4). A second (and related) assumption is that any fixed cost of entry is not a *sunk* cost that is incurred sequentially and irreversibly *before* the pricing decision take place. Spence (1977) and Grossman (1981) discuss the importance of this distinction for market equilibrium.

Because entry and price decisions are typically taken sequentially rather than simultaneously, the contestable market model seems inappropriate to many market situations. This observation served as motivation for development of an alternative industrial structure in Eaton and Kierzkowski (1982). In our model firms first decide which model of a differentiated product to produce and only later make price and output decisions. Pure profits can be sustained even in equilibrium. When entry and model-choice decisions are made prior to other economic decisions, the choice of model becomes an instrument for protecting a firm's profits through entry deterrence.

In this paper we apply our model of industrial structure and product variety to an open economy. As a result we are able to make a number of predictions about the effects of trade both in the short and long run which appear quite new. The mere possibility of trade can influence the economic structure of a country even if actual trade does not take place. We also show that trade may *reduce* rather than increase product variety, and we provide examples of trade leading to a Pareto-inferior outcome.

2. AN OVERVIEW OF THE MODEL

We begin with a description of the consumer choices in our model. Following the recent literature on trade in differentiated products, especially Krugman (1979, 1980, 1981), Lancaster (1980), and Helpman (1981), it is assumed that there are only two basic commodities available for consumption. One of these commodities, good A, is homogeneous while the other, good B, is differentiated. The differentiated good contains a characteristic Z which assumes a value in R^1.

We use Lancaster's (1971) formulation to characterize demand for the differentiated commodity. Each consumer i has an ideal model of good B which can be characterized by a parameter θ_i. An individual will purchase an alternative model which deviates from the ideal if the price of the alternative is sufficiently lower. We use the following utility function throughout the paper:[2]

$$V(Y, p_i, \theta_i, Z_i) = \max [Y - p_i - |\theta_i - Z_i|, Y - \bar{p}], \qquad (5.1)$$

where Z_i stands for the model consumed by an individual i; p_i is the price of the differentiated good; and Y denotes the individual's income. The utility function (5.1) has the following characteristics: At most one unit of the differentiated good will be bought. The maximum price which an individual i is willing to pay for it is p provided that the available model corresponds exactly to θ_i. This price falls linearly with the distance $|\theta_i - Z_i|$. When the price for all available differentiated products exceeds $\bar{p} - |\theta_i - Z_i|$, the consumer will spend his entire income on the homogeneous good A.

Turning to the supply side of the model, the production of good B is characterized by increasing returns to scale. The total cost of producing x units of the differentiated good is $K + xc$, where c is a constant marginal cost and K represents a fixed cost.[3] In contrast with much of the recent literature we assume that a firm incurs the fixed cost when it chooses a model to produce, before it decides on the level of output and price. Entry and price decisions are thus taken sequentially rather than simultaneously.

It seems that this is an appropriate assumption to make in models designed to deal with international trade. A number of authors, most notably Linder and Vernon, have argued that production is typically first developed for a domestic market. Trade takes place at a later stage of the product cycle, long after firms selected their models and incurred fixed costs. The upshot of this assumption is that pure profits can exist even in full equilibrium. This will allow us to establish a number of results which differ from those arrived at by Krugman, Lancaster, and Helpman, among others.

Although the differentiated product is produced under increasing returns to scale, the homogeneous good is produced at constant returns to scale. As before, labour is the only factor of production. The A industry is perfectly competitive and it takes one unit of labour to produce one unit of A. Choosing commodity A as a numeraire sets the wage rate equal to unity.

The homogeneous good plays a secondary, or a back-up role in the model. At the micro level, it allows a consumer to spend income when he does not purchase B. From the macro point of view, commodity A serves as a balancing item when international trade in the differentiated good takes place. Having thus introduced the homogeneous good, we can now bar it from further analysis.

The discussion of market equilibrium will be carried out in two stages. In the tradition of dynamic programming, the second stage is considered first. We start off with output and price decisions, taking entry and location decisions as given. We then analyse how a firm(s) selects a model, correctly taking into account subsequent price decisions and their impact on profits. Three cases are discussed.

2.1. One Type of Consumer, One Firm

The easiest case to consider is one in which there are n consumers each having the same model, θ_1. At most one producer operates in the market. As we show elsewhere (Eaton and Kierzkowski, 1982) Bertrand price competition among *more than one firm* for sales in this market will drive price to the marginal cost of at least one firm. This firm will consequently not receive revenues sufficient to cover the fixed cost K. Anticipating this outcome, the firm would have chosen not to enter.

Let the single firm's model embody characteristic Z_1. The maximum price it can charge is $\bar{p} - |\theta_1 - Z_1|$. For an established firm to cover current cost requires, then, that

$$|\theta_1 - Z_1| < \bar{p} - c. \tag{5.2}$$

For the firm to cover fixed costs as well requires that

$$(\bar{p} - |\theta_1 - Z_1| - c)\, n_1 \geqslant K. \tag{5.3}$$

2.2. Two Types of Consumer, One Firm

When there are two types of consumers, n_1 with θ_1 as the ideal model and n_2 with ideal model θ_2, then the firm producing model Z_1 must decide whether (i) not to produce at all; or (ii) to sell to just one type of consumer, the ones whose ideal is closer to Z_1 (say θ_1), and charge $\bar{p} - |\theta_1 - Z_1|$, earning a current profit

$$(\bar{p} - |\theta_1 - Z_1| - c)\, n_1 - K; \tag{5.4}$$

or (iii) sell to both types of consumers, charging $\bar{p} - |\theta_2 - Z_2| - c$, and earning a current profit

$$(\bar{p} - |\theta_2 - Z_1| - c)\,(n_1 + n_2) - K. \tag{5.5}$$

If $\bar{p} - |\theta_1 - Z_1| < c$ no production at all will take place. We assume that price discrimination is not possible. Assuming this is not the case, choice (ii) or (iii) will be made as

$$(\bar{p} - c)\,(1 - \lambda) \gtrless |Z_1 - \theta_2| - |Z_1 - \theta_1|\,\lambda, \tag{5.6}$$

where $\lambda \equiv n_1/(n_1 + n_2)$, the proportion of consumers in the large market. Selling to the broader set of consumers, option (iii), yields higher profits when $\bar{p} - c$ is high, λ is low, and the distance between Z_1 and θ_2 is not substantially greater than between Z_1 and θ_1.

2.3. Two Types of Consumer; Two Firms

It has already been shown that with only one type of consumer, one can expect to see at most one firm in the differentiated-product industry. With two types of consumers there may be zero, one or two (but not more than two) firms.

With two firms having established products, a duopoly situation emerges. The standard Nash–Cournot solution yields a continuum of equilibria while, for a wide range of parameter values, the standard Nash–Bertrand solutions yield no equilibrium. We consequently propose a modified version of the equilibrium as an appropriate solution. More specifically, it is assumed that when a firm considers price reductions it makes the Nash assumption that the other firm's price will remain unchanged.[4] In contemplating price increases, however, each producer will anticipate that his decision will cause the competing firm to lower its price unless the competitor is charging a monopoly price in his 'natural' market. The 'natural' market for the firm producing model Z_1 consists of type-1 consumers and for the firm producing model Z_2 type-2 consumers. (By assumption $|\theta_1 - Z_1| < |\theta_1 - Z_2|$.)

Application of the semi-reactive Bertrand equilibrium will typically result in firm 1 producing for type-1 consumers and firm 2 producing for type-2 consumers. This can be demonstrated by first determining a set of prices that will protect each firm's market and then showing that no other prices can be sustained.

Suppose that firm 2 wants to prevent firm 1 from invading its 'natural' market. To accomplish this goal it has to set a price that will make firm 1 uninterested in competing for both markets. This price can be obtained from the equation:

$$[p_2 - (Z_2 - Z_1) - c_1](n_1 + n_2) = (p_1 - c_1) n_1. \tag{5.7}$$

If firm 2 wanted to compete for both markets it would have to sell at a price slightly below p_2, but then the left-hand side of equation (5.7) would be smaller than the right-hand side. Thus the p_2 for which firm 1's profits from selling to both markets are smaller than from selling to its own market is:

$$p_2 = \lambda p_1 + (1 - \lambda) c_1 + Z_2 - Z_1, \tag{5.8}$$

where, recall, $\lambda = n_1/(n_1 + n_2)$ is the relative size of the first model.

Take in turn firm 1 and suppose that it wants to keep market 1 for itself. By a similar argument it can be established that the price which will do the trick is:

$$p_1 = (1 - \lambda) p_2 + \lambda c_2 + Z_2 - Z_1. \tag{5.9}$$

Equations (5.8) and (5.9) constitute two reaction functions and can be readily represented in Fig. 5.1. For equilibrium to exist firm 2's reaction function must be flatter than that of firm 1, to the south-east of point E. This will always be the case. Prices p_1^* and p_2^* denote the threshold prices for firm 1 and 2 respectively and they constitute a semi-reactive Bertrand equilibrium. Solving (5.8) and (5.9) gives, for the equilibrium values of p_1 and p_2:

$$p_1^* = \frac{(1 - \lambda)^2 c_1 + \lambda c_2 + (2 - \lambda)(Z_2 - Z_1)}{1 - \lambda + \lambda^2}, \tag{5.10}$$

$$p_2^* = \frac{\lambda^2 c_2 + (1 - \lambda) c_1 + (1 + \lambda)(Z_2 - Z_1)}{1 - \lambda + \lambda^2}. \tag{5.11}$$

Given the behavioural assumptions, lowering p_1 below p_1^* cannot increase the profit of the first producer. Likewise the second producer has nothing to gain from selling at a price below p_2^*. If prices were initially below p_1^* and p_2^*, competition among the firms would bring them back to equilibrium at E. What remains to be shown is that neither producer will try to set the price *above* the threshold level.

The two reaction functions have been derived for a policy of selling only to one market and protecting it from invasion by a competitor. Suppose that being at equilibrium point E firm 1 contemplates a price increase. With $p_1 > p_1^*$ firm 2 would be tempted to change its policy and go after both markets. To

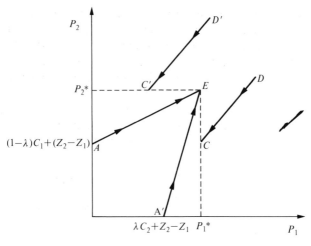

Fig. 5.1

this end it would *lower* p_2. If this were to happen the entire market would be dominated by one seller, firm 2. Since firm 1 correctly anticipates the reaction of firm 2, it will not increase its price above p_1^*. By a similar argument it can be demonstrated that firm 2 will not try to sell at $p_2 > p_2^*$.

The conjecture on the part of each firm that if it raises its price slightly from the equilibrium, the other firm will lower its price, while if it lowers its price slightly the other firm will not respond, is correct. The actual behaviour of the market will not contradict the beliefs held by the participants. The semi-reactive Bertrand equilibrium is thus based on conjectures that are locally correct, unlike the Nash–Bertrand and Nash–Cournot equilibria.[5]

Having discussed determination of equilibrium prices and output, we can now address the problem of entry and product choice. How many firms will there be in the differentiated-product industry and which models will they select to produce? To keep the discussion as short as possible we briefly review the results established in Eaton and Kierzkowski (1982).

We assume that the process of entry is governed by two rules.[6] First, entry and model choice are determined prior to price and output decisions. Second, entry occurs sequentially rather than simultaneously and each entrant takes the model choice of firms already established as given and expects other potential entrants to behave in the same fashion. It can then be shown that in a market with two classes of consumers there will be at most two producers. If a third firm decided to enter at least one firm would be making losses.

Although there may be at most two firms it may also happen that there will be only one firm or none at all. No entry will occur when both $(\bar{p} - c) n_1 - K$ and $(\bar{p} - (\theta_2 + \theta_1)/2 - c)(n_1 + n_2) - K$ are negative. Neither selling to one market nor to both markets would cover costs of production.

When either c or K are suitably small or $\bar{p}$, n_1, and n_2 are suitably large, there will be room for at least one producer. The first firm to enter must determine whether it can locate in such a way as to prevent further entry. If the firm is in a position to keep at bay potential competitors, the questions arises whether it is profitable to do so. Finally, when the firm is alone in the market it must decide whether to sell to one or both types of consumers.

If the market is very small and K very high, the first entrant's location will not be affected by the threat of further entry. Continuing to assume $n_1 \geqslant n_2$ it will choose to establish a model $Z_1 = (\theta_1 + \theta_2)/2$ or $Z_1 = \theta_1$ as

$$\left(\bar{p} - \frac{\theta_1 + \theta_2}{2} - c\right)(n_1 + n_2) \gtreqless (\bar{p} - c)\, n_1. \tag{5.12}$$

Selling to both types of consumers is more likely to be profitable when n_2 is near n_1, θ_1 and θ_2 are similar, and $\bar{p} - c$ is large.

When the market is sufficiently large or K sufficiently low, the first entrant will not be able to establish $Z_1 = (\theta_1 + \theta_2)/2$ or $Z_1 = \theta_1$ without inviting further entry. In the first case a second entrant might establish $Z_2 = \theta_1$ and in the second $Z_2 = \theta_2$ and earn positive profits. However, by biasing its model choice the first entrant may be able to deter further entry. In the first case it might choose Z_1 between θ_1 and $(\theta_1 + \theta_2)/2$ to make profits negative for any firm that established $Z_2 = \theta_1$. In the second case it might establish Z_1 away from θ_1 in the direction of θ_2 to insure that a firm establishing $Z_2 = \theta_2$ would sustain a loss. In this second case the first entrant would nevertheless not make sales to type-2 consumers in the second stage. Thus the first entrant's model choice can be affected by its entry deterrence behaviour.

When it is either impossible or unprofitable to block further entry, the first entrant must decide where to locate. The first firm will choose either θ_1 or θ_2 depending whether n_1 is larger or smaller than n_2. The second entrant will then choose the other market's ideal as its model. Thus two producers can maximize their profits from selling to their 'natural' markets. At the same time, being far apart does not create a danger of further entry for there is no room for another firm no matter what the distance between θ_2 and θ_1.

3. INTERNATIONAL TRADE AND DIFFERENTIATED PRODUCTS

We now consider the implications of the opening of trade between two countries in the context of the industrial structure discussed in the previous section. Each country is assumed to have at least one, but usually two, types of consumers. The differentiated good can be produced in either country but not necessarily at the same cost. This section investigates how international trade affects prices and the variety of traded goods and the welfare of different economic agents.

We distinguish the impact effects of the opening of trade from the long-run effects. In the first case we assume that the number of producers and the models produced are determined by pre-trade conditions. The long-run effects are those which occur when the number of entrants and their models have adjusted to the post-trade situation. One can imagine an intermediate situation in which firms make entry and model-choice decisions in closed economies anticipating that trade will occur at some future period. For example, long-lasting tariff negotiations or discussions of joining, say, the European Economic Community may exert some impact on the industrial structure of the countries concerned even before the negotiations are concluded and their results implemented.

3.1. The Effects of Trade on Impact

We have discussed how equilibrium in the closed economy can be characterized by a number of possible configurations of producers when two types of consumers exist. First, there may be zero, one, or at most two producers. Second, the number of possible cases is further increased by the fact that when there is only one firm it may not serve all customers. In order to prevent the discussion from becoming overly taxonomic only the more interesting cases will be taken up.

(a) Only one producer in either country

Suppose that the demand patterns are such that in the home country $n_1 > 0$ and $n_2 = 0$ while in the foreign country $n_1^* = 0$ and $n_2^* > 0$, and furthermore that the only producer is located in the home country.

Clearly the existing firm produces model θ_1. (There is no point in selecting a model slightly to the right of θ_1 and preventing entry for $n_2 = 0$.) When a a possibility of trade arises the producer may try to sell to the market in the foreign country. The domestic firm will begin to export to the foreign market if:

$$[\bar{p} - (\theta_2 - \theta_1) - c] (n_1 + n_2^*) > (\bar{p} - c) n_1. \qquad (5.13)$$

The larger is the foreign country and the more similar are the demand patterns, the more likely it is that trade will occur between the two countries.

In our example trade benefits only the country exporting the differentiated commodity. The producer's profit will be larger and home consumers will gain through price reduction. Foreign consumer's welfare will not improve for the sole producer of the differentiated product will be able to exact a price which will leave foreign consumers practically indifferent between consuming only the homogeneous good or consuming both the differentiated and homogeneous product. (Introducing elastic demand would modify this result, allowing them in part to benefit as well.)

Since only the home country has a producer under autarky, unless it has a cost advantage, it must be the larger country (i.e. $n_1 > n_2^*$). Hence in this case it is the larger country that gains from the opening of trade while the smaller one is indifferent, in contrast with the Ricardian result.

(b) Two producers

This case may consist of a number of sub-cases. Suppose first that initially there is one producer in each country. The opening of trade is likely to benefit consumers both in terms of lower prices and (possibly) in terms of providing them access to a model that is closer to their ideal. With only one firm operating in each country each producer charges the monopoly price under autarky. Trade creates price competition. The biggest reduction in prices occurs if the two firms produce the same model, as is the case if the two countries are identical in all respect. A mere possibility of trade would force each producer to charge marginal cost.

The welfare effects of the case of identical location are rather straightforward. The opening of trade would result in the producers' welfare being reduced and in the consumers being made better off. The improvement in the consumers' welfare would stem entirely from a price reduction for there would be no change in product variety. If the initial location of the firms were different, however, then *some* consumers would gain from the availability of a product closer to their ideal, and consumers would gain from price changes. It is possible that under autarky some consumers did not consume the differentiated product; with the opening of trade this could not happen. The price reduction in this case would be necessarily smaller than in the previous case. The producers' welfare could go either way. Increased price competition reduces profits; however, the possibility of selling to a larger market can benefit the producers.

Consider now the case where under autarky there were two producers in the home country and none abroad. From equations (5.10) and (5.11) the effects of trade on prices would depend upon the relative number of consumers of each type in the two economies. If the relative number of type-2 consumers in the importing country is larger than in the exporting country, then the price of commodity 2 will fall (since trade has lowered λ), and similarly, the reverse will also be true. Thus consumers in the exporting country benefit from trading with an economy where there are relatively more consumers of their type.

(c) More than two firms

If initially there are two firms in one country and one or two in the other, at least one and possibly all firms lose from trade since there must be negative profits in the new equilibrium. There will be, however, some consumers who will benefit from lower prices.

Although the opening of trade may involve a number of different outcomes, one characteristic runs through all possible cases: in no instance does trade, *given* the initial number of firms and distribution of models, lead to a *Pareto-inferior* outcome in either country: at least one group benefits or else no group loses. In some cases (e.g. when there is initially only one firm anywhere) trade can lead to a Pareto-superior outcome.

3.2. The Effects of Trade in the Long Run

We now consider the effect of trade on welfare in the long run taking into account its effect on both the number of firms and the type of models produced. As developed so far, our theory yields no predictions about the *location* of production. For concreteness we will assume, in this section, that producers locate in the country in which their market is largest. We will also assume in this section that all potential entrants in either country have access to the same technology to produce the differentiated commodity.

The opening of trade can have myriad effects on the nature of the resulting long-run equilibrium. We do not attempt a complete taxonomy. Rather we discuss some examples that we find of particular interest. We categorize them according to whether trade has increased, left constant, or reduced the number of firms.

(a) Trade that increases the number of producers

Trade can increase the number of firms (i) from zero to one, (ii) from zero to two, or (iii) from one to two. In all cases the welfare of at least one producer, the one who entered, rises (unless in the new equilibrium his profits are exactly zero). Consumers cannot be made worse off by an increase in the number of firms. Thus in cases (i) and (ii) trade yields a *Pareto-equivalent* or *Pareto-superior* outcome. In case (iii) the welfare of the existing firm may rise or fall, so that trade may not lead to a Pareto-superior outcome. In no case does it yield a Pareto-inferior one.

(b) Trade that leaves the number of producers unaffected

Trade can leave the number of firms in both countries unchanged at one or two. In the case where there is only one firm, trade can affect the location of the firm either because the opening of trade makes a model adjustment profitable or else because the opening of trade requires a new position to deter further entry. We develop an example of the second in which trade can yield a *Pareto-inferior* outcome.

Assume that the home country has n_1 type-1 and n_2 type-2 consumers, where

$$(\bar{p} - c)\,n_1 > [\bar{p} - (\theta_2 - \theta_1)/2 - c]\,(n_1 + n_2) \tag{5.14}$$

$$(\bar{p} - c)\,n_1 > 0 \tag{5.15}$$

and

$$\frac{(1 + \lambda)\,(\theta_2 - \theta_1)}{(1 - \lambda + \lambda^2)}\,n_2 - K < 0. \tag{5.16}$$

Expressions (5.14) and (5.15) imply that a single producer selling only to the home market will establish $Z = \theta_1$ and sell only to type-1 consumers. Expression (5.16) guarantees that once a firm has taken this action that there is no room for further entry. In autarky, then, the home country will have a single producer selling only to type-1 consumers.

Consider the case in which the home country opens trade with a foreign country with n_2^* type-2 consumers and zero type-1 consumers. In the foreign country

$$(\bar{p} - c) n_2^* - K < 0 \tag{5.17}$$

so that it sustains no production at all. In the integrated market, however, (5.19) may no longer be obtained. For example, if $n_1 = 9$, $n_2 = 1$, $n_2^* = 1$, $\theta_2 - \theta_1 = 2$, $K = 8\,16/103$, $c_a = c_b$ and $\bar{p} - c = 5$, then under autarky a single entrant will establish $Z_a = \theta_1$ in the home country without providing an inducement for further entry. The foreign country will not be able to sustain any production at all. The opening of trade will, on impact, result in no trade actually taking place. However, given that $Z_a = \theta_1$, a second entrant establishing $Z_b = \theta_2$ will, in the resulting equilibrium, earn positive profits. By establishing a model $Z_a = \theta_1 + 1/11$, however, the first entrant can make further entry unprofitable. At the same time this entrant will continue to find that his profits are higher if he continues to sell only to type-1 consumers. Establishing $Z_a = \theta_1 + 1/11$ and selling to type-1 consumers also dominates establishing $Z_a = (\theta_2 + \theta_1)/2$ and selling to both types of consumers. The first entrant's profits have fallen, however, from $(\bar{p} - c) n_1 - K$ to $(\bar{p} - 1/11 - c) n_1 - K$.[7] Type-1 consumers' utility levels are unchanged (they pay a lower price for a product that is inferior by an exactly compensating amount) while type-2 consumers continue not to buy the differentiated commodity at all. Since all consumers' utility levels are unchanged while the single producer's profit has fallen, the opening of trade has yielded a Pareto-inferior outcome, even though no trade actually occurs. Note that the home country would improve welfare by prohibiting trade.

Trade can also leave the number of firms at two. It may be that initially each country had one firm, or one country two firms and the other zero. In the second case trade yields a Pareto improvement if the share of type-1 consumers is the same in each country. The two producers and the consumers are indifferent. If the share of type-1 consumers is *larger* in the foreign country type-1 consumers at home gain while type-2 consumers lose and conversely. Again, consumers benefit from trading with a country where tastes are predominantly *most like* their own.

If, initially, each country has one firm, consumers cannot lose and may gain from trade while producers may gain or lose.

(c) Trade that reduces the number of producers

The opening of trade can reduce the number of producers from three or four to two or from two to one.[8] When two firms remain, the remaining producers may benefit or lose. Consumers in a country which initially had one producer cannot lose while consumers in the country in which there were initially two firms gain or lose according to whether the trading partner has relatively more or fewer consumers of their own type.

Trade can reduce the number of producers from two to one only if the two producers were in different countries under autarky. It is possible, in this case, that trade again can lead to a Pareto-inferior outcome. Consider an example much like the one given earlier:

$\theta_2 - \theta_1 = 2$, $K = 8\ 16/103$, $c_a = c_b$, $\bar{p} - c = 5$. As before, let $n_1 = 9$, but assume that $n_2 = 0$ while $n_2^* = 2$; i.e. all the type-2 consumers are in the foreign country. In this case, under autarky, both countries can sustain a single producer who produces a model exactly congruent with tastes in that country. If trade opens up, no transactions take place but prices fall. Producers lose while consumers gain.

The first producer, by modifying his model to $Z_a = \theta_1 + 1/11$, can insure that he is the only producer in the consolidated market. In the new equilibrium there will be no production or consumption of commodity B in the foreign country. Consumers are indifferent between the trade and autarky situations while producers in each country lose; the foreign producer stops producing, forgoing his profit while the home producer must now sell at a price $\bar{p} - 1/11$.

This example indicates how trade can *reduce* the variety of products in the world economy. It does so by eliminating producers serving a small market with idiosyncratic tastes. In the new equilibrium the consumers in this market do not necessarily buy a less desirable product but may cease consuming altogether. Trade does not necessarily lower the price of the commodities that *are* produced, either, but the threat of price competition can deter entry.[9]

4. COMMERCIAL POLICY AND DIFFERENTIATED PRODUCTS

Our model can readily incorporate elements of commercial policy, such as tariffs and quotas. To give the reader a smattering of the results we consider the case in which there is only one producer (in the home country) and the demand patterns are such that $n_1 > 0_1$, $n_2 = 0$, $n_1^* = 0$ and $n_2^* > 0$. It has previously been shown that if equation (5.13) holds, trade flows will be generated. The gains from trade entirely accrue to the larger country with no gains at all to the smaller country.

In the case considered, the small country can improve its welfare by imposing a tariff on imports of the differentiated product. The optimal (specific) tariff, $\tilde{t}$, is given by:

$$\tilde{t} = [\bar{p} - (\theta_2 - \theta_1) - c]\frac{(n_1 + n_2^*)}{n_2^*} - (\bar{p} - c)\frac{n_1}{n_2^*}. \tag{5.18}$$

Effectively the small country can, through a tariff, tax away from the foreign producer all profits in excess of profits he makes by selling only to consumers in his own country. It is easy to see that, in general, free trade will not be the first-best policy for a small country in the type of setting considered here.

Tariffs and quotas are not equivalent in the case at hand.[10] Suppose that the government of the smaller country introduces a quota in place of a tariff. The effect will be to shrink the size of the foreign market exactly by the amount of the quota. Quota holders cannot derive any profits from auctioning off the rights to import. Any increase in the price paid by the foreign consumers for the imported product would result in their restoring the pre-trade consumption pattern. The producer, in other words, reaps all the revenue from the quota.

5. CONCLUSION

The ability to trade, even if no exchange actually occurs, can affect the allocation of resources within an economy. Furthermore, the effect may be harmful. The opportunity to trade can eliminate the domestic production of a commodity even if there is then no subsequent importation of that commodity. Diaz-Alejandro (1982) reports that the disruption in international trade that occurred during the Great Depression and Second World War led to a burgeoning of industrial activity in several Latin American countries. The model developed in this paper suggests how the loss of trade could have fostered domestic industries' activity far beyond the substitution of previous imports.

NOTES

1. The last two papers, Brander (1981) and Brander and Krugman (1983), do not impose a zero-profit constraint but consider the number of firms as predetermined. There is consequently scope for positive profits but there is no attempt to explain the number of entrants and the choice of product.
2. This utility function has been used by Salop (1979).
3. Since our model has only one factor of production, labour, K should be thought of as 'overhead' workers independent of the level of output.
4. As before, price discrimination is precluded by assumption. The two firms, 1 and 2, produce models embodying characteristics Z_1 and Z_2, respectively, with respective marginal costs c_1 and c_2 which can, in principle, differ.
5. For a discussion of the problem of consistent conjectures in models of oligopolistic competition the reader is referred to Bresnahan (1981). See Eaton and Kierzkowski (1982) for a formal proof of the result that the semi-reactive Bertrand equilibrium is based on consistent conjectures.
6. We follow Prescott and Visscher (1977) in this specification.
7. The details of this example are tedious but straightforward to work out.
8. It cannot reduce the number from three or four to one or from any number to zero.
9. Dixit and Norman (1980) also provide an example in which trade leads to the elimination of a model. In their case, however, consumers of the commodity continue to consume a differentiated model of the product rather than stop consuming the product altogether. Their example arises in a framework in which there is a single monopolistic producer *ex ante* as well as *ex post*, and thus is rather different from ours.

10.   This is a larger topic which calls for a in-depth treatment, especially in the context of alternative models of product differentiation and international trade.

REFERENCES

Baumol, W. J. (1982), 'Contestable Markets: An Uprising in the Theory of Industry Structure', *American Economic Review*, 72, 1–15.

Brander, J. A. (1981), 'Intra-Industry Trade in Identical Commodities', *Journal of International Economics*, 11, 1–14.

Brander, J. A. and Krugman (1983), 'A Reciprocal Dumping Model of International Trade', *Journal of International Economics* (in press).

Bresnahan, T. F. (1981), 'Duopoly Models with Consistent Conjectures', *American Economic Review*, 71, 934–45.

Diaz-Alejandro, C. F. (1982), 'The 1940s in Latin America', Discussion Paper No. 394, Economic Growth Center, Yale University.

Dixit, A. K. and Norman, V. (1980), *Theory of International Trade* (Cambridge: Cambridge University Press).

Eaton, J. and Kierzkowski, H. (1982), 'Oligopolistic Competition, Product Variety and Entry Deterrence', *Rand Journal* (forthcoming).

Feenstra, R. and Judd, K. (1982), 'Tariffs, Technology Transfer and Welfare', *Journal of Political Economy*, 90, 1142–65.

Grossman, S. J. (1981), 'Nash Equilibrium and the Industrial Organization of Markets with Large Fixed Costs', *Econometrica*, 49, 1149–72.

Grubel, H. G. and Lloyd, P. J. (1975), *Intra-Industry Trade* (London: Macmillan).

Helpman, E. (1981), 'International Trade in the Presence of Product Differentiation, Economies of Scale and Monopolistic Competition: A Chamberlin–Heckscher–Ohlin Approach', *Journal of International Economics*, 11, 305–40.

Krugman, P. (1979), 'Increasing Returns, Monopolistic Competition, and International Trade', *Journal of International Economics*, 9, 369–79.

Krugman, P. (1980), 'Scale Economies, Product Differentiation, and the Pattern of Trade', *American Economic Review*, 70, 950–9.

Krugman, P. (1981), 'Intra-industry Specialization and the Gains from Trade', *Journal of Political Economy*, 89, 959–73.

Lancaster, K. J. (1971). *Consumer Demand: A New Approach* (New York: Columbia University Press).

Lancaster, K. J. (1980), 'Intra-Industry Trade Under Perfect Monopolistic Competition', *Journal of International Economics*, 10, 151–76.

Linder, S. B. (1961), *An Essay on Trade and Transformation* (New York: Wiley).

Prescott, E. C. and Visscher, H. (1977), 'Sequential Location among Firms with Foresight', *Bell Journal of Economics*, 8, 378–93.

Salop, S. C. (1979), 'Monopolistic Competition with Outside Goods', *Bell Journal of Economics*, 10, 141–56.

Spence, A. M. (1977), 'Entry, Capacity, Investment, and Oligopolistic Pricing', *Bell Journal of Economics*, 8, 534–44.

Vernon, R. (1966), 'International Investment and International Trade in the Product Cycle', *Quaterly Journal of Economics*, 80, 190–207.

6

Recent Theories of International Trade: Some Implications for the South

Frances Stewart*

1. INTRODUCTION

Over the last twenty years, a set of new theories has been put forward to complement (and/or substitute for) the simple Heckscher–Ohlin (H–O) model. The new theories were a response to two deficiencies in the H–O paradigm. First, the oversimplified and often patently unrealistic, assumptions behind H–O, especially in the simplest textbook versions: these include 'perfect competition, international identity of production functions and factors, non-reversibility of factor intensities and international similarity of preferences',[1] together with constant returns to scale, if the usual free trade, and specialization in accordance with factor endowment, conclusions are to be derived. Second, the theory, at least superficially, seemed incapable of explaining certain significant empirical findings about the world economy. These included the Leontief paradox; the growth in trade between *similar* economies with near-identical factor endowment; the fact that a considerable portion of trade in manufacturers (and its growth) is intra-industry; and the fact that there appears to be a strong tendency for growth in trade to exceed growth in income.

The focus of the new theories, which aim to adopt a more realistic set of assumptions and to incorporate some or all of these awkward facts, has been on trade between advanced countries (i.e. N–N trade),[2] because it is between these economies that growth in trade has been greatest, while factor endowment theories are least applicable. Grubel and Lloyd (1975) have shown that intra-industry trade is greatest for N–N trade, much less significant for N–S and S–S trade; in addition, while trade growth has greatly exceeded income growth among advanced countries, this has not been the case for poor countries.[3] Moreover, the Leontief paradox (with capital-abundant US exporting labour-intensive commodities and importing capital-intensive), which can be 'explained' by incorporating skill into factor endowment,[4] does not apply to poor countries. In general N–S trade is in accordance with H–O theory, with the North exporting capital and skill-intensive products and the South exporting (unskilled) labour-intensive goods.[5]

None the less, in one vitally important respect — that of eventual factor price equalization — the Samuelson–Stolper development of H–O has not shown much sign of coming to fruition; and this respect, that of substantial and in absolute terms growing, income differences between N and S is the one that the third world cares about most. In addition, the assumptions of H–O are in some respects even less realistic with respect to N–S than N–N (or S–S) trade – in particular with respect to the assumed identical production functions between countries (which involves equal knowledge about and access to technology) and similar preferences. Moreover, since the prime concern of developing countries is development, i.e. to *change* their factor endowment, their incomes, and their consumption patterns, they tend to find a theory, such as H–O, which assumes all these as given and unchanging, particularly unattractive.

None the less despite some problems for the S about the H–O theories, the new theories have been directed in the main to N–N trade. The aim of this paper is to explore what relevance (if any) these theories have for the South, given this predominantly Northern focus, and the satisfaction of many observers with an H–O model for predicting trade patterns for the South.[6] Perhaps because of the Northern focus, the new theories in the main remain surprisingly undynamic, particularly with respect to the direction of technical change in products and processes. For the North this may not be of great significance since technical change being endogenous to them can be assumed to be broadly in line with factor availability and income levels, while for the South, where technical change is largely exogenous coming from the North, it can incorporate significant biases.

This paper therefore will try to add a dynamic dimension to the theories under discussion, especially with respect to technical change.

2. THE 'NEW' THEORIES

A very brief description of the main features of the various theories, 'old' and 'new', to be considered is helpful before exploring implications for the South:

1. Simple factor proportions theory, described as H–O, with two factors of production, capital and labour, in which, given the assumptions already described, trade flows in accordance with relative factor endowment of capital and labour (Heckscher–Ohlin).

2. Factor proportions theory encompassing 'human capital' as a third factor of production. Again trade flows occurs according to endowment, including human capital (Leontief, 1953; Kenen, 1965; Keesing, 1966).

3. Scale economies with homogeneous products, where a large home market gives a cost advantage in products with significant economies of scale. Small countries with small markets would specialize in constant returns/diminishing returns products (Drèze, 1960).

4. Technological gap theory: countries which innovate gain an advantage and export to countries which are technologically lagging in particular lines.

This trade is eliminated when the laggards catch up, but new innovations create new possibilities for trade (Posner, 1961; Hufbauer, 1966).

5. Product cycle theory: advanced countries develop and then export new products. Once the technology has been standardized (matured) it is transferred to low-wage-cost countries and the product re-exported to the technological leaders (Vernon, 1966).

6. Preference similarity: differentiated products are developed for the home market in accordance with domestic preferences. These preferences depend in large part on income levels. The products are exported to markets with similar tastes (Linder, 1961).

7. Economies of scale through intra-industry specialization, where specialization is limited by the extent of the *international* market. International trade takes the form of intra-industry trade in intermediate products to exploit economies of specialization (Ethier, 1979; Krugman, 1979a.)

8. The significance of *intra-firm* trade. This has been shown to be of substantial and growing importance. Its existence suggests certain advantages (which could consist of organization, or market access or technology access, which accrues within firms as compared to trade between firms). The convenience of intra-firm trade may help overcome some of the disadvantage of geographic dispersion in trade in intermediate products and thus help explain its existence, i.e. theory 7 (Lall, 1973; Helleiner, 1981).

In the absence of international firms, it seems likely that much trade in intermediate products would take place at the national level, since national sales are easier to organize than international. This possibility is illustrated by the large amount of national subcontracting and national trade in intermediate products in Japan, in the absence of multinational firms, while in Europe many of the major multinationals deploy their production to exploit economies of scale in different countries (e.g. Ford producing bodies in one country and engines in another). However, marketing agencies can substitute for the organizational advantage of the multinationals, as in S. Korea. According to this view, the growing predominance of multinational intra-firm trade both explains and is explained by specialization and consequent trade in intermediate products.

9. Economies of scale in differentiated products, with diversity of preference. Each economy produces a limited number of differentiated products and international trade widens potential choice (Lancaster, 1980; Krugman, 1980).

10. Economies of scale in differentiated products, in the presence of transport costs. In this case, the larger the home market, the greater the possibility of exploiting economies of scale so that there is a terms-of-trade advantage to the larger market (Krugman, 1980).

11. Product variety plus transport costs. Each country produces a limited variety of products. Because of transport costs, foreign products generally cost more than home products. As incomes rise, the propensity to import rises

as consumers can satisfy their inherent desire for variety, while exports also rise in response to similar tendencies in other countries. The net result is that international trade rises faster than incomes (Barker, 1977).

12. The implications of *learning* economies for international trade. Here increasing returns are related to the accumulation of experience, rather than scale alone. These learning economies may be internal to the firm, external to the firm but internal to an industry, or may accrue as a result of the accumulation of manufacturing experience as a whole. Learning economies generate cumulative tendencies between countries, so that countries that acquire an initial advantage in any area where learning economies are significant enjoy an increasing advantage over time (Westphal, 1982; Stewart, 1982; Krugman, in this volume).

It should be noted that none of these theories needs to be treated as an exclusive explanation of trading patterns. Indeed it is unlikely that any one of the theories would explain all trading patterns. This is a major deficiency of many empirical tests of different theories which tend to apply to all manufactured commodities (e.g. Hufbauer, 1970). In some cases, commodities may fit into just one of the categories – e.g. homogeneous goods produced under constant returns to scale, with capital and labour as the major elements in production costs, would fit the H–O model. For other types of trade, more than one of the theories may be applicable. For example, some intra-industry trade takes advantage of different factor costs in locating production of different elements of the productive process, and thus both exploits economies of specialization and is located along H–O lines.

3. SPECIAL FEATURES OF SOUTHERN ECONOMIES

Certain features of Southern economies are of particular relevance to the applicability and implications of the various theories. These features all stem from lower levels of development. The first concerns patterns of demand: the remainder affect conditions of supply.

(i) The substantial difference in per capita incomes between North and South have implications for consumer preferences, not only as between broad categories of goods (food and manufactures, for example) but also as between particular characteristics of goods. If, as a short cut, we assume that goods embody varying combinations of 'high-income' and 'low-income' characteristics (following Lancaster's approach to consumer demand), then one would expect low-income countries to have preferences more weighted towards low-income characteristics, as shown in Fig. 6.1. Actual preferences, as expressed through the market, depend on the distribution of money income. Countries with highly skewed income distribution will exhibit demand for goods similar to those demanded in the North, from their high income groups. But they will then have large numbers of consumers with very low incomes, and consequently

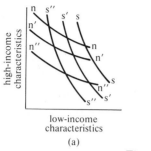
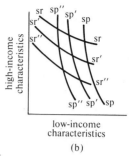

Fig. 6.1

with a greater preference for low-income characteristics than in countries where incomes are more evenly distributed. This is also shown in Fig. 6.1.

(ii) In general, most Southern economies are capital-scarce and skilled-labour scarce, and unskilled-labour abundant, as compared with Northern countries. (There are, however, exceptions: for example, the oil-rich countries tend to be capital-rich, but skilled- and unskilled-labour scarce; some Asian countries have quite abundant supplies of particular types of educated/skilled labour.)

(iii) Southern economies have small domestic markets, relative to most Northern economies.

(iv) Industrial experience in general, and in particular types of production, is more limited (in terms of time and quantity) than in Northern countries.

(v) For the most part, the South does not initiate technical change. Recently a few countries have shown some technical innovations but these are very small in magnitude compared with the innovations coming from the North. The fact that — in the main — the South are recipients of technical change from the North means that the characteristics of the technical change reflect Northern environment. It therefore exhibits biases in terms of the Southern environment. These biases relate both to techniques of production and to product characteristics. More formally, Lancaster (1984) shows how, in equilibrium, in the presence of economies of scale and therefore with a finite number of firms, products actually produced will tend, relatively, to be in accordance with the tastes of the larger market. Since developed countries constitute the largest market, this theory, applied to N–S, would mean that the product space filled would be proportionately biased towards markets of the North. Similarly, Sutton's analysis suggests that with vertical product differentiation, firms will tend to fill up the space at the higher-income end of the spectrum — which means that new products emanating from the North would tend to have increasingly high-income characteristics.

New technologies from the North tend to be increasingly capital-intensive (higher K/L) and (often) skill-intensive, while the products tend to embody increasingly high-income characteristics, as illustrated by Fig. 6.2.

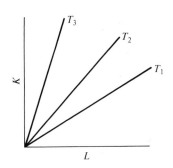
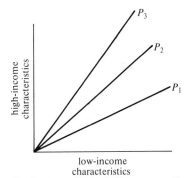

T_1-T_3 shows technical change over time, in relation to K/L.

P_1-P_3 shows technical change over time in relation to product characteristics.

Fig. 6.2

(vi) Southern economies are characterized by very substantial elements of x-inefficiency — in terms of under-employment of some resources and poor productivity of resources in use.

(vii) For the most part the organization (and headquarters) of multinational corporations is in the North, not the South. This is being gradually modified, but remains true for the vast bulk of MNCs — see Lall (1982) and Lecraw (1977).

(viii) Owing to colonial and neo-colonial experience the infra-structure (of trade, finance, administration, experience and contacts, transport) has a heavy N–N and N–S bias and is relatively highly deficient with respect to S–S trade.

As already noted, these generalizations do not apply uniformly to all countries, but they are of sufficient generality to permit some conclusions with respect to the implications of the various theories for the South. Among the three major directions of trade, N–N, N–S, S–S, it is helpful to distinguish two sub-groups, regional N–N and regional S–S. These regional groups are distinct in that organizational problems and transport costs are generally less than for non-regional trade.

4. SOME IMPLICATIONS OF THE THEORIES

As far as the South is concerned the criteria for assessing international trade are generally broader than in much 'gains-from-trade' literature. As well as the obvious gains from allocational efficiency, general development effects need to be considered. These include effects on the accumulation of capital, skills, learning (and hence on future 'endowment'), the terms of trade effects (including the terms of trade for technology acquisition), effects on x-inefficiency and on the employment of resources, since the 'full employment' assumption of much trade theory is singularly inappropriate, and effects on the distribution of income and of consumption. In addition, some would include 'independence' or 'self-reliance' as a significant consideration. 'Self-reliance' forms one of the major objectives of the Group of 77, but it is not included in the discussion of the theories below.

Most of the theories apply to trade in manufactures, not primary products where climatic conditions play a significant role. The advantages and disadvantages for the South of trade in primary goods is normally mainly discussed in terms of trends and fluctuations in the terms of trade. Aspects of production and trade in primary products do fit into some of the theories, but in this paper we confine attention to manufactures.

Table 6.1 briefly summarizes some implications of the theories outlined in Section 2 in the light of the special features of the South suggested in Section 3. Here I will briefly discuss the main findings.

A. Theory 1: simple H–O. Given the substantial difference in factor availability between N and S, with the North capital-abundant and labour-scarce and the South labour-abundant and capital scarce, the H–O theory explains N–S trade in terms of this difference, with the North exporting capital-intensive goods and importing labour-intensive goods from the South. The theory concludes that both parties gain from the exchange. With some minor qualifications, the theory leads to free trade policy conclusions. This is a strong conclusion with, for the most part, strong empirical backing in the form of evidence on the actual characteristics of trade in manufactures between North and South. The remaining eleven theories all suggest the need for some qualification to this theory both as descriptions of actual trade flows and in terms of policy prescriptions.

B. Theory 2: H–O plus human capital. The introduction of a third factor of production – human skills – as an explanation of trade flows involves a major change as far as the South is concerned. The theory suggests that the North will export both capital-intensive and skill-intensive products and import unskilled-labour-intensive products. The South specializes in unskilled-labour-intensive manufactures, as it is relatively short of human skills. But from a South point of view this is likely to involve adverse terms of trade, since human skills (and their products) command a higher price than unskilled labour. This indeed is one of the causes of Emmanual's 'unequal exchange'. Because human skills can be created, the South may wish to subsidize the creation of human skills, and interfere with the workings of free trade in order to do so.

C. The technology gap–product cycle theories (5 and 6). The relevant special feature of the South in relation to these theories is that, for the most part, the South is a recipient and not an innovator of technical change. While Northern countries may both initiate and receive technological change, the South is in an asymmetrical position, receiving but not initiating new technologies. This has implications both for the terms of trade and for the direction of technological change.

The South first imports the products of technological innovation from the North, then imports the technology and may re-export the product back

TABLE 6.1. *Summary of implications of theories for the south*

	Theory	Special feature of south	Direction of trade	Nature of trade	Terms of trade	Technical change	Other factors	Policy implications
1.	Simple 2-factor H–O	Capital-scarce, labour-abundant	N ↔ S	Mainly inter-industry	'Unequal' exchange as S specializes in low-wage activities.	May undermine comparative advantage, e.g. garments t.c.: 'inappropriate'	S wishes to change endowment	'Free' trade; S may need to innovate to maintain comparative advantage
2.	H–O plus 'human capital'	S generally human-capital scarce but varies between countries	N → S; some N ↔ N; some S ↔ S	Mainly inter-industry	'Unequal' exchange as skilled labour receives higher rewards	Changes skill requirements and comp. advantage	—	—
3.	Scale economies in homogeneous commodities	S small domestic markets	N → S; N ↔ N for scale econ. goods: S → N; S ↔ S, non-scale econ. goods	Mainly inter-industry	Tends to favour countries with scale econ. where imperfect competition may prevail	Tends to accentuate scale economies	—	—
4.	Technological gap	S generally technological laggards	N ↔ N; N → S	Inter- and intra-industry	N receives Schumpeterian profits as innovators.	Direction of t.c. in products and techniques inappropriate for S	Tendency for t.c. to create dualistic development	S. needs to create own innovatory capacity to enter this trade as technological leader
5.	Product cycle	S does not innovate in products	Initially N → S; subsequently S → N	Inter-industry	N receives quasi-rents as 4	Direction of t.c. inappropriate as 4; reverse trade may be undermined by innovations, as 1	As 4	S needs to promote own product innovations
6.	Preference similarity	S lower incomes per capita than N; does not innovate in products	N ↔ N; S → S for élite markets; S ↔ S, but limited by lack of S innovations	Inter- and intra-industry (final products)	—	Products likely to be for increasingly high-income markets	Potential for S–S trade if S innovates	S promote own product innovations
7.	Econ. of scale, intra-industry specialization in intermed. products	S earlier stage of development; weaker trading intra-structure	Mainly N ↔ N; some S → N with H–O element Limited S ↔ S	Intra-industry	—	H–O element in such trade in S changed by t.c.	Potential for productivity gains for S from S–S trade	Improve S–S infra-structure, organization; reduce S–S trade barriers
8.	Intra-firm trade	N dominate MNCs	N ↔ N; and N → S	Intra-industry	Major gains to countries which control MNCs	t.c. leads to relocation of industry via MNC	—	S may bargain; also promote own MNCs
9.	Intra-industry specialization in differentiated final prods.	S markets and scale of production smaller	Primarily N ↔ N; potentially S ↔ S	Intra-industry	Equivalent for producers of differentiated prods. May be against producers of homogeneous products	Element of product differentiation may increase	Being late-starter may be disadvantage where ec. of scale significant	Promotion policies to enter market. Potential for S–S
10.	As 8 with transport costs	S smaller markets	As 8	As 8	Larger market secures better terms of trade	—	—	—
11.	Product variety-dynamic	S lower per capita incomes	Primarily N ↔ N; tendency for N → S	Intra-industry	—	Product differentiation increases	As S incomes rise greater variety of products demanded	Need for policies to deal with demand for greater variety
12.	Learning economies	S at earlier stage of 'learning'	N → S where learning significant factor	Inter- and intra-industry	S produces less 'learning-intensive' products: probably lower returns	t.c. requires ability to adapt to new processes	Learning economies present disadvantage (and potential) for S	Justifies S protection against N

to the North. But because of continuous innovation, countries in the South are permanently in a position of importing the products of later and later innovations and of having their own competitiveness in existing lines undermined unless they import recent technologies, or are able to introduce sufficient innovations in the technologies they are using to maintain competitiveness. The terms of trade tend to be adverse to the South because they pay a form of Schumpeterian profits to the innovators, in the form of high product prices, when a new innovation first occurs. In the initial phases of a new product, prices are high enough for the entrepreneur to reap 'abnormal' profits *and* to pay the high wages necessary in developed countries. But as more producers enter the market, the price tends to fall so that eventually production is transferred to low wage countries. Thus when the South is *importing* the product, they pay the high prices which cover Schumpeterian profits and high DC wages; by the time they become producers and start to export the product the price has fallen, so that it is sufficient to cover the low LDC wages, but not the high DC wages. So long as firms in developed countries maintain property rights over the technology, even when they are producers of a particular product, they will still pay the North for the use of the technology. Meanwhile, while the South begins to export the product whose price has fallen, new products will have been developed in the North, which they will sell to the South for prices high enough to cover their wages and to earn some Schumpeterian profits. Hence an intrinsic aspect of the product cycle process is that the technology-initiating high-wage economy enjoys high prices for its products relative to the technology-receiving low-wage economy. Krugman (1979b) has presented a formal model of aspects of this process.

The second implication of the asymmetry is that the South has to accept the direction of technological change emanating from the North. As described earlier this tends to be inappropriate in both process and product dimensions, with the techniques being yearly more capital-intensive and the products embodying more high-income characteristics (see Fig. 6.2).

The technological gap explanation of trade as initially put forward was supposedly a two-way phenomenon between equally developed countries, so that the net terms of trade effect would be insignificant and the direction of technology change could be assumed equally appropriate for each country. But this is not the case between North and South. To benefit from such a process and avoid the adverse consequences the South would need to become innovators themselves.

D. The preference similarity theory (6) is primarily applicable to N–N trade, since it explains trade between innovating and similar economies. It is assumed, with some empirical justification, that products are first designed for the home market; they are then exported to countries with similar tastes, where tastes are assumed to be mainly determined by income level. Strictly then the South — which generally does not innovate, especially in products, and which has

substantially lower-income levels, on average, and consequently according to
the theory, different tastes from the North – would not participate in this
form of trade. In practice, as is well known, the South does import consumer
products from the North, despite the difference in incomes. This may be
explained by two factors: first, marked inequality of incomes among some
South economies means that the incomes of the rich in these economies are
similar to those in the North – hence among these groups there is a market
for Northern products (as depicted earlier in Fig. 6.1b). Second, in the absence
of alternative products, the South may consume products from the North, as
shown in Fig. 6.3. While the South has different tastes (represented by indifference curves ss), if product OP_n is the only available product there is a market
for it. The main lesson for the South from this theory is that potentially the
South could enjoy preference-similarity trade with other South economies
but only if the South innovates and produces its own products. For example,
if a South product OP_s, which cost the same as OP_n, were available it would
be preferred to OP_n (Fig. 6.3).

E. Theories of monopolistic competition and product differentiation (9
and 10) are fairly closely related to the preference similarity theory. The existence of economies of scale in the production of differentiated products means
that each nation produces only a limited variety of the infinite possible combination of characteristics. International trade permits consumers to enjoy a
wider range of choice.

Models of this type of trade have shown that the actual combination of
characteristics of the products produced and traded will tend to be nearer to the
tastes of the larger market (Lancaster, in this volume), while, with transport
costs, the terms of trade will tend to favour producers in the larger market
(Krugman, 1980). With this type of trade, then, those in smaller markets will
tend to get worse terms both as consumers (in terms of the availability and/or
price of the combination of characteristics they prefer) and as producers. The
South can be thought of as a smaller market, relative to the North, in this context.
Given economies of scale and transport costs in the production of differentiated

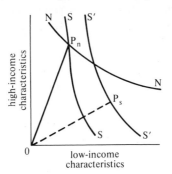

Fig. 6.3

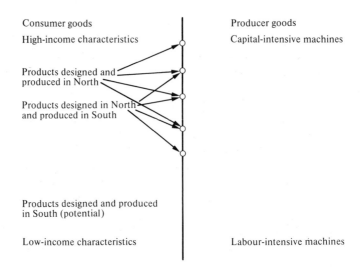

Fig. 6.4. Potential combinations of characteristics

products, the South generally has a comparative disadvantage in the production of these goods which, for the most part, it produces only with heavy protection. International trade in these products permits Southern consumers a wide choice of products produced in the North, but these tend all to have high-income characteristics since it is among high-income consumers that the main market lies.

One major difference then, for this type of trade in differentiated products, for N–S trade, as compared with N–N for which the models have been primarily developed, lies in the different preferences of South consumers arising from different (lower) levels of income so that the combination of characteristics preferred in the North and embodied in most Northern products may differ from the preferred combination of the majority of South consumers, as depicted in Fig. 6.3 in relation to the preference similarity theory. This difference in preferences is not confined to consumer goods, but also applies to producer goods, where differences in conditions of production, notably in factor availability and scale of market, make for demand for different producer goods. However, as shown in Fig. 6.3, in the absence of any alternative the South may and does consume Northern products (both consumer and producer) but the combination of characteristics offered gives less welfare than a specifically designed South-product would. Though the South may produce differentiated products, in general it does so on the basis of Northern designs. Hence Southern production does little to modify the range of characteristics available.

In Fig. 6.4 we depict one dimension of possible combinations of characteristics that might potentially be embodied in actual products as being represented by a vertical line running from high-income characteristics to low-income characteristics (for consumer goods), and capital-intensive to labour-intensive (with respect to producer goods), while the circles depict actual products. The upper portion of the line shows the type of products the North would be likely to design and produce, while over time new products would tend to move upwards along the line. So long as the South does not design its products but uses Northern designs it will be confined to a similar range, although it may select the most appropriate (lowest) out of the range, and may, by minor modifications, shift the range further downwards. New products designed in and for the South would tend to be in the lower portion of the line.

Where the South produces differentiated consumer goods, it tends to do so on a small scale and hence fails to realize potential economies of scale. Lacking a natural comparative advantage in the production of these goods, especially in the initial stages of production when there are diseconomies of small scale and x-inefficiency is high due to lack of experience, most countries start production under heavy protective barriers, where the market is confined to the relatively small domestic market. In the pre-import substitution stage, consumers are able to import a variety of products made by different manufacturers. When it is decided to establish domestic production, governments often permit this variety to be reproduced locally, establishing, e.g. a Fiat plant, a VW, a Ford etc., thus ensuring that each plant will have a very limited market. For example, in Mexico in 1977, thirty-seven different automobile models were being produced, with costs that were over 50 percent higher than country-of-origin costs. In contrast, in Brazil, a much smaller number of car producers had been allowed and Volkswagen had captured nearly 90 percent of the domestic market with the 'beetle', producing on a scale that reduced costs to internationally competitive levels, so that a substantial export market was built up.[7] The two cases illustrate a dilemma for LDC governments in relation to the production of differentiated consumer goods, subject to economies of scale. If local production is to be established on a sufficient scale to realize economies of scale, then normally very few varieties can be justified, given the small scale of the domestic market. Hence there appears to be a trade-off between efficiency and variety, unless international trade can perform the role of permitting specialization, economies of scale and variety to be exploited, as occurs within the North. But in the South, in the initial stages at least, free trade would normally eliminate local production. Here trade within the South, with one country specializing on one type of car, and others on others, could provide a means of combining infant industry protection (against the North), exploitation of economies of scale and economies of specialization and variety. This conclusion may be especially relevant to the pressures that arise over time, as the demand for variety increases with incomes.

F. The Barker theory of product variety plus economic growth (11) is a dynamic development of theories which explain trade by preferences for product characteristics. In this theory, as incomes rise the variety of products consumed tends to rise, as people are able to afford to buy goods more nearly representing their preferred combination of characteristics. Because of economies of scale, each nation produces only a limited variety of goods and additional variety is achieved by spending an increasing proportion of income on imported goods. For the North, the increase in proportion of income imported can be expected to be paralleled by an increase in the proportion of differentiated products exported, since rising incomes abroad also cause a rise in the variety of goods consumed and imported. But the position is rather different for the South. In general it seems correct to argue that for the South too a rise in incomes will be accompanied by a demand for increasing variety of products consumed. It is helpful to interpret this 'demand for increasing variety' rather more broadly than simply a question of more variants of a rather narrowly defined product (e.g. demand for Fiats as well as Minis), as in the original article. The demand for additional variety also encompasses demands for goods which were not consumed when incomes were lower, e.g. at very low levels of income a move away from spending most income on food and housing towards also spending on textiles and shoes; at higher incomes a move towards a variety of consumer durables.

A consumer survey in Brazil in 1972 illustrates how consumer demand alters with income level (Table 6.2). As incomes rise, each income group will tend to demand different products and a greater variety within any product group. If there were no restrictions on trade, this change in preferences associated with rising incomes could be expected to lead to increasing (proportionate) expenditure on imports. But for the South this leads to a major difficulty because the South produces only a limited number of differentiated products of the type for which demand is increasing. While most countries will produce some of the goods demanded at the lower- and middle-income ranges, the new demands that arise among the upper-income groups, as incomes rise, will generally not be satisfiable by local production, or by imports from other South economies except at very high cost. With unrestricted trade then there will be a strong tendency for imports of differentiated products to rise, but no parallel tendency (in contrast to North economies) for exports to rise. There will therefore be a tendency for the N–S trade balance to deteriorate, as a result of changes in preferences with rising incomes.

The tendency for preferences for imports of differentiated products to rise as incomes rise is liable to occur irrespective of the initial income distribution. Even with egalitarian income distribution, the incomes of those at the top of the scale will rise as incomes rise, unless income distribution becomes more egalitarian over time to such an extent that the incomes of the rich are stabilized over time. For income distribution to become steadily more equal over time is very unusual. In the typical case, as Kuznets first noted, incomes tend to become more unequal with development.

The tendency for demand for increasing variety of differentiated consumer

Table 6.2. *Brazil: the percentage of households in each decile of the household income distribution owning a series of consumer durable goods (1972)*

	0–10	10–20	20–30	30–40	40–50	50–60	60–70	70–80	80–90	90–100	Average for all households
Gas and electric stoves	10	14	24	33	56	56	77	82	88	92	53
Electric iron	7	10	18	26	45	45	69	75	84	95	47
Table radio	19	24	32	36	43	43	48	49	49	43	39
Portable radio	10	13	18	21	29	29	37	42	49	67	31
Refrigerator	3	3	6	10	16	24	41	53	68	87	31
Television	3	3	6	10	17	27	45	57	70	85	32
Liquefier	2	3	5	8	16	16	36	46	60	81	27
Floor-polisher	1	1	2	3	7	7	19	28	41	65	17
Bicycle	5	7	11	13	18	18	21	23	24	26	17
Gramophone	1	1	2	3	5	7	13	19	27	50	13
Motor car	0.4	0.6	0.9	1.6	2.4	4.2	8.2	14.8	24.9	59.7	11.7
Fan	1	1	1	1	5	5	11	15	22	38	10
Washing-machine	0	0	0	1	1	2	3	6	12	33	6
Cake-mixer	0	0	0	1	1	1	4	7	13	36	6
Vacuum-cleaner	0	0	0	0	0	1	1	3	6	25	4
Air-conditioner	0	0	0	0	0	0	0	0	1	7	1
Motor-cycle	0	0	0	0	0	0	1	1	1	1	0
Average annual household income (US $)	128	254	400	506	686	934	1305	1819	2636	8663	1726

Souce: J. Wells (1978), p. 260.

goods as incomes rise has long been apparent to governments of LDCs, and they have dealt with it in a number of different ways. On the one hand, governments in some rather inegalitarian states have tried to keep domestic production in line with domestic demands, leading to the production domestically of a wide proliferation of consumer goods. This has tended to mean rather inefficient production because of the small scale of the domestic market, and involved capital-intensive production with a heavy reliance on imports of machinery and technology and parts. Some of the Latin American patterns of development, for example in Brazil and Mexico, have been on these lines. At the other extreme, radical governments have tried to repress these demands by prohibiting imports and local production of certain luxury items. But this leads to pent-up demand, black markets, and political protests. In India colour television provides an example. Until recently, colour television was not available in India. But after considerable pressure, it has been decided to permit local production of a limited number of colour sets: 'So starved are the comparatively few rich Indians of entertainment that there is a ready market for these sets even at the price (£2,470).'[8] The production of these sets will involve a heavy foreign exchange cost initially. Only countries with no balance-of-payments constraints are able to 'solve' the problem by permitting unlimited imports. The problem is compounded by the increasing number of goods available, at a world level, as technical change in the developed countries generates new consumer goods.

This problem is the dynamic version of the general problem noted above of production of differentiated products, subject to economies of scale, in small and highly protected markets. South–South trade could, as suggested above, contribute to a solution by permitting specialization on particular differentiated products within LDCs and exchange between them. In this way some of the demand for variety may be met without leading to a deteriorating trade balance.

S–S trade is unlikely to present a total solution to the problem, especially in relation to the élite demand for the latest products, but it would make a major contribution compared with the existing country-by-country solution.

If one set of countries specializes in differentiated products (the North) while another (the South) specializes in homogeneous products, this is liable to mean poor terms of trade for the non-differentiated producers, since some rent is normally associated with brand-name differentiated product production, as shown by the high price that companies can charge for permission to use the brand name.

G. Intra-industry trade in intermediate products and intra-firm trade (theories 7 and 8). According to Ethier, the size of the international market is the limiting factor in determining specialization and economies of scale, and geographic location becomes almost irrelevant. Yet clearly geographic proximity is an advantage in providing intermediate products. However, the MNC may use its organizational facilities to substitute for geographic proximity. There is therefore a close association between intra-industry trade of this type and intra-firm trade. Even so geographic proximity remains an advantage and there have to be strong cost advantages for it to be worth locating production of different parts in a very dispersed way. Much of the N–N trade of this type is concentrated geographically if not nationally – e.g. within Europe. As far as production in the South is concerned, where some parts of the productive process are very labour-intensive, such trade may be justified despite the transport and communication costs involved. Hence for S–N trade, this tends to be a special variant of H–O trade, normally organized by an MNC (see Helleiner, 1973).

N–S trade of this type is very vulnerable to technical progress, which can eliminate the labour-intensive parts of the productive process, as seems to be happening in electronics, for example. Moreover, because the trade is mostly organized by Northern MNCs, the gains for the South tend to be confined to the employment generated and wage-payments, while the profits are located in the North. While then this type of traders offers some advantages to those economies who participate, it is unlikely to form the basis for sustained development.

As far as S–S trade is concerned, the (limited) available evidence suggests that such intra-industry specialization and trade within the South is rather small. Yet this type of trade within the South is potentially of enormous development value. As Adam Smith pointed out with his famous pin example, division of labour and specialization in the production of a single product enables huge growth in productivity; not only does it enable productivity to rise through repetition of simple processes and through learning and new methods which evolve as a result of that repetition, but it also gives rise to mechanization of processes that would not be justified with lesser specialization because of indivisibilities in machinery. A large proportion of the growth in producitivity that has occurred with and since the industrial revolution has been associated with increasing specialization and division of labour within industries. But as Adam Smith noted, such specialization is limited by the extent of the market; the size of the market determines how much division of labour and mechanization is justified. International trade extends the market and hence the scope for specialization. This could be of great significance for LDC economies, whose markets are small. This type of trade within and across regions could increase the size of the market and hence give rise to increased specialization and productivity.

S–S trade of this type is limited by two factors – institutional deficiencies and trade barriers. In the North the rapid growth of this trade occurred when trade barriers were being dismantled, especially with the European Economic Community, while the institutional vehicle for much of the trade was the multinational company. As well as a dismantling of trade barriers, the South needs institutions to facilitate this type of trade. Specialization and trade within an industry across national frontiers is difficult to organize without institutions which operate easily across nations. South-based multinationals offer one possibility: there is evidence that these are developing quite fast in certain areas (see Lecraw, 1977; Lall, 1982, L. Wells, 1983). Other institutional possibilities are trading agencies such as those in Japan and S. Korea.

A number of common markets and regional trading agreements have tried to provide the required trading infrastructure and to reduce trade restrictions within the South. But for this purpose many of the arrangements have been somewhat misconceived, in that they have been designed for *inter*-industry, rather than *intra*-industry trade. For example, industries are sometimes 'allocated' to countries. Both for the Adam Smith trade being considered here, and for trade in differentiated consumer products discussed above, what is required is rather different since the major trade expansion is likely to be within industries. An industry allocation exercise becomes irrelevant; it is likely that the specialization will most readily evolve within a liberal trading environment, with the actual 'allocation' occurring as a result of market forces. Where generalized relaxation of trade restrictions has occurred within the South, there is evidence that intra-industry trade has expanded rapidly (see Willmore (1972) on the Central American experience).

While then in fact, in the past, expansion of trade in intermediate products has been greatest between Northern economies, its greatest potential today for promoting growth and development may well be within the South.

H. Learning and international trade (theory 12): a major deficiency of the H–O theory for the South is the assumption that each country faces identical production functions. In fact, as is well known, the South normally operates the 'same' technology at much less efficiency than the North. Moreover, the degree of lesser productivity varies across technologies. The exact explanation of these differences (in general and as between different technologies) is not known, but learning seems to play some role. The efficiency with which a technology is operated varies with the time over which it has been operated. In most countries, productivity with any given technology tends to rise over time. In those industries where learning economies are known to be substantial, the South may appear at a disadvantage in the short run despite a potential advantage in the long run. This forms the classic infant industry case for protection. It may be confined to a single industry or extend to the whole of manufacturing sector depending on the nature of the learning process.

The learning justification for protection may have different implications according to the direction of trade: while the South may justify general protection of their manufacturing inudstry against the North because of the earlier stage of development and lesser accumulation of learning, the justification is much smaller (or non-existent) in relation to trade with other countries at a similar level of development and of accumulated learning.

5. SUMMARY OF IMPLICATIONS

As stated at the outset, most of these new theories have been specifically designed to explain N–N trade, while there tends to be a certain widespread complacency that H–O can deal with N–S trade, since the country groups exhibit the required difference in factor endowments. This brief sketch of a great number of theories has, however, suggested that they do contain a large number of insights for trading patterns and policies for the South. The most general conclusion is that while the theories explain N–N trade, S–S trade would offer a potential way for the South to gain from the types of trade being considered — in products for countries with similar preferences, in differentiated products and in intermediate products. This S–S trade is mainly *potential* rather than actual, and is likely to remain so without significant changes. Yet, the gains for the South from making the trade actual are likely to be great. These gains stem from:

(i) extending the choice of product for South consumers, through South countries specializing in differentiated products and exchanging them without running into a chronic tendency for balance-of-payments problems, which tends to arise if product variety comes from importing differentiated products from the North;

(ii) extending the gains from specialization, increasing division of labour and economies of scale through trade in intermediate goods and trade in differentiated consumer goods within the South.

Both (i) and (ii) represent classic gains from specialization through trade, but on a S–S basis.

(iii) permitting a more appropriate direction of technology change in products and processes;

(iv) making the terms of trade more 'equal', than for N–S trade.

The first two points have been elaborated sufficiently above, but it is worth saying more here about the last two.

Trends in technology: As indicated earlier (Fig. 6.2) there is a tendency for technology in products and processes, emanating from developed countries to be increasingly inappropriate for South countries although, of course, in some respects new technologies offer substantial productivity gains and product improvements, which represent gains for the South as well as the North. Let me illustrate this point with respect to printing inks.[9]

Initially printing inks used simple (inexpensive) machinery and raw materials that were widely available (mainly vegetable material). But over time, the industry has moved towards the (near-exclusive) use of petrochemical products, which most South countries have to import. Even where vegetable matter is retained, modern processes require such standards that most countries have to import the processed materials from developed countries. The machinery has become much more expensive, more automated, and less labour-using. The quality of the end product has also improved substantially – with printing of highly defined quality, robust (e.g. won't wash off, withstands low temperatures for freezing, and is capable of adhering to a wide variety of surfaces). Technical change in this industry follows neatly the diagrammatic presentation earlier, in terms of changes in both product and technique characteristics – in both cases the tendency has been for a move away from characteristics which would best suit the South. Moreover, there has also been a close link between choice of technique and choice of product. If a recent product is chosen then the corresponding technique also has to be selected, and conversely.

It is illuminating to consider how an actual case of technical change relates to the various theories considered above. If LDCs aim to trade with the North, in labour-intensive commodities along H–O lines, they would have very little choice in printing ink technology but to follow many of the latest technological developments because consumers in the North require advanced standards in the print they receive, in terms, e.g., of colour fastness in textiles, packaging with printing of high definition and durability etc. A focus on trade with the North tends to lock countries into the trends in technological change in the North. Trade with other South countries might potentially permit the use of more appropriate technology producing more appropriate products.[10] But here, too, countries face competition from the high-quality North products, which they find it difficult to withstand for two reasons: first, in countries with unequal income distribution, actual monetary preferences may be on Northern lines, as illustrated in Fig. 6.1. Second, lack of R & D into products for the South may mean that they are of poor quality and the technology is of low productivity so that, although more appropriate, they remain inferior to Northern products. This is illustrated in Fig. 6.5. Some improvement in the quality of the

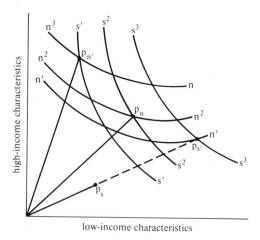

Fig. 6.5

South products P_s, to $P_{s'}$ is necessary before it will be freely chosen in the South.

P_n shows the combination of characteristics obtainable initially with a North-product; after technical change a new combination, $P_{n'}$ (assumed to use the same amount of resources) is obtainable; P_s shows the combination possible for the same resource expenditure with South technology. Assume the South preferences are given by the ss set of indifference curves, and the North by nn. With North preferences the new product, $P_{n'}$ is unambiguously preferred. With South preferences, the old North product is preferred. The South project is inferior offering less of both characteristics than the North. If a South country trades with the North, it may need to move to the North preferred product, $P_{n'}$. If it trades with the South, it would be able to succeed producing the old North product, P_n. If South products were to become competitive they would need to be improved so that they are on a preferred indifference curve, e.g. as at $P_{s'}$. Even with this technical change the new South product would not be chosen by Northern consumers. The range of product choice itself affects welfare, as indicated. But in addition, each technology corresponds to a different production technology, with the more recent products from the North being generally more capital-intensive[11] than earlier techniques.

Kaplinsky's study of sugar technology developments[12] provides an example of the developments illustrated in Fig. 6.5. The open-pan sulphitation techniques (OPS) have long been advocated as more appropriate for developing countries. But their productivity was so low that they were not competitive, without subsidies, with conventional large-scale techniques (see Forsyth, 1977; Tribe, 1979). But recent developments in the technology have greatly improved it, pushing it out from P_s, to $P_{s'}$, so that now the technology offers potential for S–S trade.

In terms of the technology gap–product cycle theories, taking into account the direction as well as the existence of technical change means that if the South participates in this trade, as technological followers, they will be tied into the technology trends of the North, while their advantage in 'mature' products may be temporary, to be displaced by new technological developments.

Fig. 6.5 illustrates how preference-similarity works in international trade. Among similar countries where each country innovates, each can be expected to develop products similar to $P_{n'}$ and to exchange them — hence trade in differentiated final products. But the South, with different preferences, and little innovation, cannot participate in this type of trade. While it can potentially participate in such trade among South countries, this will only occur if it innovates sufficiently to make these products competitive with advanced products from the North.

While S–N trade much restricts the possibilities for generation and use of more appropriate technologies, S–S trade provides an environment in which such technical change is likely to be encouraged.[13]

Terms of trade. Much of the literature of N–S terms of trade has concentrated on the tems of trade between primary products and manufactures, while industrialization was advocated as a means by which the South might avoid the supposed worsening in the terms of trade for primary products as against manufactured goods. But as the South moves into manufactured exports, it is relevant to look also at the likely terms of trade within manufactures. In general, as illustrated in the Table 6.1, there is a tendency for the terms of trade to favour the North because the North tends to export technology-intensive and product-differentiated products while the South exports 'mature', standardized, and homogeneous products. In various ways, the North is able to levy a rent (which may take a number of actual forms, e.g. over-invoicing technology payments, payments for use of brand names and so on) for its products, while the products the South exports face a much more competitive environment. S–S trade offers a way in which these rents may be more equally distributed among South countries.

6. CONCLUSIONS

The discussion has suggested that the South could benefit from the types of trade described in the new theories by developing trade ties on a regional and S–S basis. To do so effectively would require three types of policy change: (i) improved South-trading infrastructure, including transport, payments systems,[14] financial services; (ii) liberalization of trade restrictions within the South; (iii) organizational ties which would make it easier to exploit the economies of specialization in intra-industry trade; and (iv) the creation of an effective innovatory capacity for the development of more efficient products and techniques suitable to South conditions and preferences.

One important question is whether S–S trade can add to and complement N–S trade in manufactures or whether it is a substitute for it. If it is a question of substitution, then more consideration of the various costs and benefits is required. While there are undoubted advantages for the South of trading within the South, these may not outweigh the gains from trade with the North, including the large markets and access to goods and technology not available within the South.

As fare as intra-industry specialization and exchange is concerned, it is solely a matter of more efficient deployment of resources within the South, and should raise productivity and not divert resources. In other words, this is a form of trade creation, not diversion. Other types of trade under consideration will also fit the 'trade creation' categorization. For example, if countries in the South specialized on particular differentiated final products and then exchanged them (as in the exchange of Minis for Fiats, for example) each country should be able to use its resources more efficiently, raising output without diverting resources.

In other cases — e.g. where the South specializes in the production of appro-priate consumer and producer goods which it exchanges within the South — there may be some re-orientation away from trade with the North. Whether this makes much difference to trade with the North will depend on the major constraint on manufacturing output. For many products, it appears that the size of the *market* provides the major constraint. Where this is so, S–S trade may be additional to N–S trade. Market constraints appear particularly critical in the current world depression, where depressed markets everywhere, but especially in the North, and growing protectionism, are threatening Southern exports. Lewis (1980) has recently argued that in the current conjuncture, Northern markets can no longer act as the 'engine of growth' and that this is a sufficient reason for the promotion of S–S trade.

The new theories considered in this paper provide powerful support for the conclusion: specialization and the division of labour within the South can raise productivity in the production of producer goods, intermediate goods and consumer goods; similarity of environment means that technology development and trade within the South could create the conditions for the development of efficient, dynamic, and appropriate technologies.

NOTES

* I am grateful for comments from Subrata Ghatak, Gustav Ranis, and partici-pants at the Conference on Monopolistic Competition in International Trade.
1. H. G. Johnson, in R. Vernon (ed.) (1970), p. 11.
2. In the rest of this paper N–N trade refers to trade between advanced nations; N–S to trade between rich and poor nations. We recognize the obvious non-homogeneity within both N and S but maintain the fiction, for the most part, that they represent two distinct and relatively homogeneous groups.
3. Barker (1977) shows the following growth rates:

	1950–1970 % growth p.a.	Imports
Developed	4.5	7.9
Developing	4.9	5.0

4. See Kenen (1965), Roskamp and McMeekin (1968), and Keesing (1966).
5. See Rahman (1973), also Hubauer (1970). The fact that trade in manu-factures between N and S is in accordance with H–O predictions does not mean that it is explained by H–O since the facts are also in accordance with other theories (see Hufbauer). But it does mean that there is no awkward inconsis-tency between theory and facts for N–S trade, as there is for N–N.
6. E.g. Little, Scitovsky, and Scott (1970), Bhagwati (1978), Krueger (1978).
7. Example from SRI International (1980), Appendix B.
8. *Financial Times*, 18 July 1982.
9. Example based on an interview with Mr S. Tingley of Coates Brothers.
10. The definition of 'appropriate' products/techniques has been subject to

much discussion. Very broadly, appropriate techniques are techniques in line with resource availability and productive environment, while appropriate products are products whose characteristics correspond to the needs and incomes of the majority of consumers. But see also, e.g., Morawetz (1974), Stewart (1983), and Singh (1981). In this paper the many difficulties involved in the definition are ignored.

11.   Technique's characteristics vary in many dimensions of which capital-intensity is one, other relevant ones include scale of product nature of inputs and skills.

12.   See Kaplinsky (1982, 1984).

13.   See also Kaplinsky (1982), who develops this argument for S–S trade and illustrates the argument with reference to the implications of the electronics revolution for N–S trade and technology choice.

14.   For one possible financial mechanism for promoting S–S trade see Stewart and Stewart (1980).

REFERENCES

Barker, T. S. (1977), 'International Trade and Economic Growth: an Alternative to the Neoclassical Approach', *Cambridge Journal of Economics*, 1, 153–72.

Bhagwati, J. (1978), *Anatomy and Consequences of Exchange Control Regimes, NBER*.

Drèze, J. (1960), 'Quelques reflexions sereines sur l'adaptation de l'industrie belge au Marché Commun', *Comptes Rendus des Travaux de la Société Royale d'Economie Politique de Belgique*, 275.

Emmanual, A. (1972), *Unequal Exchange, A Study of the Imperialism of Trade*, (London: Monthly Review Press).

Ethier, W. (1979), 'Internationally Decreasing Costs and World Trade', *Journal of International Economics*, 9, 1–24.

Forsyth, D. (1977), 'Appropriate Technology in Sugar Manufacturing', *World Development*, 5, 189–202.

Grubel, H. G. and Lloyd, P. J. (1975), *Intra-Industry Trade* (London: Macmillan).

Helleiner, G. K. (1973). 'Manufactured Exports from Less-developed Countries and Multinational Firms', *Economic Journal*, 83, 21–47.

Helleiner, G. K. (1981), *Intra-firm Trade and the Developing Countries* (London: Macmillan).

Hufbauer, G. C. (1966), *Synthetic Materials and the Theory of International Trade* (London: Duckworth).

Hufbauer, G. C. (1970). 'The Impact of National Characteristics and Technology on the Commodity Composition of Trade in Manufactured Goods', in R. Vernon (ed.).

Johnson, H. G. (1970), 'The State of Theory in Relation to the Empirical Analysis', in Vernon (ed.).

Kaplinsky, R. (1982), 'Trade in Technology — Who, What, Where and When?',

Paper for International Workshop on Facilitating Indigenous Technological Capability, Edinburgh, May 1982.

Kaplinsky, R. (1984), *Sugar Processing: the Development of a Third World Technology* (London: Intermediate Technology Development Group).

Keesing, D. B. (1966), 'Labor Skills and Comparative Advantage', *American Economic Review*, 56, 249–58.

Kenen, P. B. (1965), 'Nature, Capital and Trade', *Journal of Political Economy*, 73, 437–60.

Krueger, A. O. (1978), *Foreign Trade Regimes and Economic Development. Liberalisation Attempts and Consequences* (Cambridge, USA: Ballinger).

Krugman, P. (1979a), 'Increasing Returns, Monopolistic Competition and International Trade', *Journal of International Economics*, 9, 469–79.

Krugman, P. (1979b), 'A Model of Innovation, Technology Transfer, and the World Distribution of Income', *Journal of Political Economy*, 87, 253–63.

Krugman, P. (1980), 'Scale Economies, Product Differentiation and the Pattern of Trade', *American Economic Review*, 70, 950–9.

Lall, S. (1973), 'Transfer Pricing by Multinational Firms', *Oxford Bulletin of Economics and Statistics*, 35, 173–95.

Lall, S. (1982), 'The Emergence of Third World Multinationals', *World Development*, 10, 127–46.

Lancaster, K. J. (1971), *Consumer Demand: a New Approach* (New York: Columbia University Press).

Lancaster, K. J. (1980), 'Intra-industry Trade under Perfect Monopolistic Competition', *Journal of International Economics*, 10, 151–76.

Lecraw, D. J. (1977), 'Direct Investment by Firms from Less Developed Countries', *Oxford Economic Papers*, 29, 442–57.

Leontief, W. W. (1953), 'Domestic Production and Foreign Trade: the American Capital Position Re-examined', *Proceedings of the American Philosophical Society*, 97, 332–49.

Lewis, W. A. (1980), 'The Slowing Down of the Engine of Growth', *American Economic Review*, 70, 555–64.

Linder, S. B. (1961), *An Essay on Trade and Transformation* (Stockholm: Almqvist and Wiksell International).

Little, I. M. D., Scitovsky, T., and Scott, M. (1970), *Industry and Trade in Some Developing Countries* (London: Oxford University Press).

Morawetz, D. (1974), 'Employment Implications of Industrialisation in Developing Countries', *Economic Journal*, 84, 491–542.

Posner, M. V. (1961), 'International Trade and Technical Change', *Oxford Economic Papers*, 13, 323–41.

Rahman, A. (1973), 'Exports of Manufactures from Developing Countries', *Erasmus*, 1–11.

Roskamp, K. W. and McMeekin, G. C. (1968), 'Factor Proportions, Human Capital, and Foreign Trade: the Case of West Germany Reconsidered', *Quarterly Journal of Economics*, 82, 152–60.

Singh, H. V. (1981), 'Appropriate Technology', M. Phil. thesis, Oxford.

SRI International (1980), 'Technology Choices in Developing Countries', Final Report, SRI Project, 7295.

Stewart, F. (1977), *Technology and Underdevelopment* (London: Macmillan).

Stewart, F. (1982), 'Industrialization, Technical Change and the International Division of Labour', in G. K. Helleiner, (ed.) *For Good or Evil: Economic Theory and North-South Negotiations* (London: Croom Helm).

Stewart, F. (1983), 'Macro-policies for Appropriate Technology: an Introductory Classification', *International Labour Review*, 122, 279–93.

Stewart, F. and Stewart, M. J. (1980), 'A New Currency for Trade among Developing Countries', *Trade and Development*, 2, 69–82.

Tribe, M. A. (1979), 'The choice of Technique in the Sugar Industry in Some Developing Countries', mimeo, David Livingstone Institute, Strathclyde.

Vernon, R. (1966), 'International Investment and International Trade in the Product Cycle', *Quarterly Journal of Economics*, LXXX, 190–207.

Vernon, R. (1970), *The Technology Factor in International Trade* (New York: Columbia University Press).

Wells, J. (1977), 'The Diffusion of Durables in Brazil and its Implications for Recent Controversies concerning Brazilian Development', *Cambridge Journal of Economics*, 1, 259–79.

Wells, L. T. (1983), *Third World Multinationals*, (Cambridge: MIT Press).

Westphal, L. (1982), in M. Syrquin and S. Teitel (eds.), *Trade, Stability, and Equity in Latin America* (London: Academic Press).

Willmore, L. N. (1972), 'Free Trade in Manufactures among Developing Countries: The Central American Experience', *Economic Development and Cultural Change*, 20, 659–70.

7

Growth and Terms of Trade
under Imperfect Competition

Avinash Dixit*

1. INTRODUCTION

The argument that the less-developed countries (LDCs) have failed to gain from their trade with the developed countries (DCs) is of long standing and contains many strands.[1] Some of the important economic issues can be enumerated as follows: (i) LDC exports cover a narrow range of primary products, the demand for which fails to keep up with growth, due to low income-elasticities in the case of consumer goods, and technical progress in the case of raw materials; (ii) with isolated exceptions, there are good substitutes for these raw materials produced within the DCs, thus limiting LDC monopoly power in exports; (iii) LDCs depend on imports of manufactured goods, and their demand for such goods is high because of demonstration effects or advertising; (iv) monopoly power is exercised against LDCs importing manufactures, by DC-based multinationals or by DC governments; and (v) as a result of these forces, LDCs face adverse and worsening terms of trade. They fail to share in the benefits of trade and growth, and may even lose in an absolute sense.

Textbook analyses of trade under perfectly competitive setting yield clear and robust results that ensure mutual gains from trade.[2] Therefore imperfect competition must be an essential ingredient of the conditions under which LDCs are supposed to lose from trade. This has different conceptual aspects: (i) Each firm may face a demand curve that is less than perfectly elastic; (ii) firms may collude with one another, and (iii) existing firms may prevent new entry.

In this paper I focus on the first of these, i.e. the setting is one of mono-polistic competition. Using techniques developed in recent studies of intra-industry trade,[3] I construct a similar stylized model to examine the effects of growth and technical progress on terms of trade and welfare for an LDC which exports a raw material and imports manufactured consumer goods under conditions of monopolistic competition.

The model has two countries, a representative LDC and a representative DC. Each has labour as its only primary factor of production. Each also has a non-traded good, produced under constant returns. The traded good for the LDC is an intermediate product, also produced by its labour under constant returns. This may be an agricultural product like cotton, or an industrial product like

electrical components, or an extractive material like metal ore; however, the
aspect of scarcity rent on exhaustible raw materials is not considered here.
This is exported to the DC, where it combines with labour in producing a
range of traded differentiated final products under conditions of increasing
returns and monopolistic competition. Each country's consumers have broadly
similar tastes for its non-traded good and the range of traded goods produced
only in the DC. An equilibrium with balanced trade is established, and its comparative statics with respect to growth and technology parameters constitute
the analysis of the dependence hypotheses stated at the outset.

Three features of the model should be remarked upon at this stage. First,
the set-up is static, but can be thought of as the steady state of a more complex
model where each country's labour also produces other non-traded intermediate
and capital goods, by interpreting the unit labour requirements as the direct-
cum-indirect ones. Second, the structure of the DC-traded-goods industry is
modelled as Chamberlinian monopolistic competition. This captures the first
aspect of monopoly power stated above, but not collusion or entry-deterrence.
Since the DC really stands for the totality of such countries, this model seems
fairly realistic. However, I recognize that some would argue for a collusive
monopoly model.

Finally, the LDC is modelled as a Ricardian economy with labour mobile
between the sectors. This could be easily reinterpreted as a Harris–Todaro
dual economy governed by expected wage equalization; this acts just like an
increase in the labour input coefficient in the tradeables sector.[4] However,
important differences remain between this model and two recent models of
LDC–DC trade. In Kemp and Ohyama (1978), the final output of the DC is
the only consumption good. By raising the export tax on it without limit, the
DC is able to drive the LDC's real income to zero and thus exploit it completely.
In my model, LDC labour (and consumers) have a fall-back opportunity. Findlay
(1980) models the LDC as the modern sector of a Lewis-type dual economy.
There is a traditional sector in the background, but its output is not formally
recognized in consumption and welfare. In my model, the non-traded sector
plays an explicit part. Again, I believe this to be an improvement.

The question of LDC gains or losses from trade is often examined by looking
at changes in terms of trade. The net barter or commodity terms of trade are
the usual measure. Recently, interest has been revived in the double-factoral
terms of trade.[5] In the context of imperfect competition, neither of these
measures is adequate for calculation of the effect on LDC welfare. By modelling
demand explicitly from utility-maximization, I shall be able to find the welfare
effect directly, and show how the alternative terms of trade measures can give
misleading information.

There are two themes in the results. On the positive side, several of the
qualitative results are independent of the new featurs of scale economies and
monopolistic competition. On the normative side, what these features generally

introduce is the possibility of further gain from trade because of the availability of greater product variety. Thus the setting of monopolistic competition does not appear to be conducive to any unequal development. The model thereby serves the purpose of narrowing down the forces we must investigate in order to find any basis for the claims of LDC loss from trade, namely collusion and entry-deterrence.

2. THE MODEL

The LDC will be labelled country 1 and the DC country 2. Their labour endowments will be respectively L_1 and L_2; the wage rates w_1 and w_2. The quantities of their respective non-traded goods will be y_1 and y_2; the corresponding prices q_1 and q_2. The unit labour requirements in the production of these non-traded goods will be α_1 and α_2. Then in equilibrium,

$$q_i = \alpha_i w_i \quad (i = 1, 2). \tag{7.1}$$

The LDC produces a raw material with a unit labour requirement β. Let r be its price, so

$$r = \beta w_1. \tag{7.2}$$

The output of this good will be denoted by z.

The DC has a manufacturing sector with differentiated products. Each has a fixed cost $F(w, r)$ and a constant marginal cost $c(w, r)$. A cost-minimizing producer will, by Shepherd's Lemma, employ F_w of labour and F_r of raw materials in the overhead part, and c_w and c_r per unit of output, where subscripts w and r denote partial derivatives. One would expect the variable part to be more raw-material intensive than the fixed part. To highlight this case and reduce algebraic detail, I shall later consider a special case where the fixed part does not use imported raw materials, i.e. where $F(w, r) = fw$ for fixed f.

I shall consider only symmetric equilibria, denoting by n the number of varieties produced, p the price of each, and x the quantity of each.

Each consumer has a utility function which is parametrized as

$$u = \left(\sum_j x_j^\delta \right)^{\gamma/\delta} y^{1-\gamma} \tag{7.3}$$

as in Krugman (1979), where γ and δ are parameters in the range $(0, 1)$, y the consumption of the non-traded good and x_j the amounts consumed of the differentiated products. Then it is easy to show that a constant fraction γ of income is spent on the differentiated products. Also, when n is large (as will be assumed to be the case), the own price elasticity of demand for each product of this sector is $1/(1 - \delta)$. I shall allow the γs to differ between the two countries, thus capturing somewhat imperfectly the possibility that the LDC consumers' tastes for foreign goods are not quite on par with those in the DC. In the symmetric equilibrium, a representative consumer in country i with wage w_i will then consume $(1 - \gamma_i)w_i/q_i$ units of the non-traded good and $\gamma_i w_i/(np)$ units of each differentiated good, and achieve a utility level

$$u_i = k_i\, w_i\, p^{-\gamma_i}\, n^{\gamma_i(1-\delta)/\delta}\, q_i^{-(1-\gamma_i)}, \tag{7.4}$$

where k_i is a constant.

The parameter δ captures the desirability of product diversity. When $\delta < 1$, the products x_j are imperfect substitutes in (7.3), and each has a less than infinitely elastic demand. Further, in (7.4), utility increases if the number of products available increases even when each sells for the same price.

I have used this specification of demand for its algebraic simplicity in comparative statics. In other models, e.g. Helpman (1981), the expression replacing (7.4) would be more complex, but the qualitative dependence of utility on numbers would be similar, and quantitatively stronger. This is because in such models greater product variety increases the elasticity of demand for each firm and therefore lowers the equilibrium mark-up, an influence that is neglected here. Thus my formation gives an understatement of gains from greater product variety, a point that should be remembered when interpreting the results.

Next consider production decisions. Non-collusive price-setting by each firm will produce the usual condition for profit-maximization:

or

$$p[1 - (1 - \delta)] = c(w_2, r)$$

$$\delta p = c(w_2, r). \tag{7.5}$$

Also, free entry will eliminate profit, i.e.

$$px = F(w_2, r) + c(w_2, r)x. \tag{7.6}$$

Now turn to the LDC labour market. Its production of the non-traded good to meet demand must be

$$y_1 = (1 - \gamma_1)w_1 L_1/q_1 = (1 - \gamma_1)L_1/\alpha_1$$

using (7.1). Therefore

or

$$L_1 = \alpha_1 y_1 + \beta z = (1 - \gamma_1)L_1 + \beta z$$

$$z = \gamma_1 L_1/\beta. \tag{7.7}$$

This is easy to interpret: with constant returns to scale and constant budget share, a fraction $(1 - \gamma_1)$ of labour L_1 must be employed in producing non-traded goods to meet the demand. This has an unfortunate consequence: changes in α_1 have no effect on the equilibrium allocation of labour. With more general demands, γ_1 would depend on relative prices and so on α_1.

Similarly in the DC

$$y_2 = (1 - \gamma_2)w_2 L_2/q_2 = (1 - \gamma_2)L_2/\alpha_2$$

and

$$L_2 = \alpha_2 y_2 + n\{F_w(w_2, r) + x\, c_w(w_2, r)\}$$
$$= (1 - \gamma_2)L_2 + n\{F_w(w_2, r) + x\, c_w(w_2, r)\},$$

where the labour input in the manufacturing sector is calculated by applying Shepherd's Lemma as indicated earlier. Then

$$\gamma_2 L_2 = n\{F_w(w_2, r) + x\, c_w(w_2, r)\}. \tag{7.8}$$

Finally, we have the derived demand for the raw material input:

$$z = n\{F_r(w_2, r) + x\, c_r(w_2, r)\}. \tag{7.9}$$

This completes the determination of equilibrium. I have omitted a redundant aggregate income–expenditure equation (or equivalently, the trade balance condition). Only relative prices are determinate. I shall usually choose the LCD wage as the numeraire, and then abbreviate w_2 as w. This corresponds to the double-factoral terms of trade. The LDC gains less, or loses more, than the DC if w rises, thus an increase in w is a worsening of the LDC's double-factoral terms of trade. The corresponding measure of the commodity terms of trade is $t = p/r$, the ratio of import to export prices. A rise in t is a worsening of the LDC's commodity terms of trade. This being a model of monopolistic competition, it will be found that welfare is only partially governed by the terms of trade.

The new features of the model are scale economies and product differentiation. In the limiting case of $F = 0$ and $\delta = 1$, the model will reduce to a neo-classical one with perfect competition.

3. GROWTH

The first comparative static exercise I consider is a change in L_1 and L_2. This can be thought of as aggregate growth, or an economy-wide technical shift. Sector-specific technical progress will be considered in the next section.

Setting $w_1 = 1$, writing w for w_2, and substituting from (7.7) into (7.9), the relevant equations of equilibrium can be restated as

$$r = \beta \tag{7.10}$$

$$\delta p = c(w, r) \tag{7.11}$$

$$(1 - \delta)p\, x = F(w, r) \tag{7.12}$$

$$\gamma_1 L_1 = \beta\, n[F_r(w, r) + x\, c_r(w, r)] \tag{7.13}$$

$$\gamma_2 L_2 = n[F_w(w, r) + x\, c_w(w, r)] \tag{7.14}$$

Now let L_1 and L_2 change. Denoting infinitesimal proportional changes by a circumflex, we have $\hat{r} = 0$ from (7.10). Then (7.11) gives

$$\hat{p} = (1-\theta)\hat{w},$$

where $\theta = r\,c_r/c$ is the distributive share of the raw materials in the variable costs. Similarly, from (7.12),

$$\hat{p} + \hat{x} = (1-\theta')\hat{w},$$

where $\theta' \equiv r\,F_r/F$ for the fixed cost. Hence

$$\hat{x} = (\theta - \theta')\hat{w}.$$

Our presumption that fixed costs are more labour-intensive entails $\theta > \theta'$. Then a higher w raises x. This is because fixed costs become relatively more important in production, making the optimum scale of each plant bigger.

Turning to (7.13) and (7.14), we have

and

$$\hat{L}_1 = \hat{n} + \lambda'(1-\theta')\sigma'\hat{w} + (1-\lambda')[\hat{x} + (1-\theta)\sigma\,\hat{w}]$$

$$\hat{L}_2 = \hat{n} - \lambda\theta'\sigma'\hat{w} + (1-\lambda)[\hat{x} - \theta\,\sigma\,\hat{w}],$$

where σ, σ' are the elasticities of substitution in variable and fixed costs, and $\lambda \equiv F_w/(F_w + x\,c_w)$, $\lambda' \equiv F_r/(F_r + x\,c_r)$ are the proportions of labour and raw materials employed in the fixed part of the manufacturing sector production process.[6] Our factor intensity assumption entails $\lambda > \lambda'$. While λ and λ' are useful abbreviations in several formulas, they are not independent parameters. Using (7.11) and (7.12), it is easy to verify that

$$\frac{1-\delta}{\delta} = \frac{\lambda}{1-\lambda}(1-\theta) + \frac{\lambda'}{1-\lambda'}\theta.$$

The neoclassical case of no fixed costs and no product differentiation corresponds to $\lambda = \lambda' = 0, \delta = 1$.

Let us continue with the solution. Substituting for $\hat{x}$ on the right hand sides of the $\hat{L}_1$ and $\hat{L}_2$ equations, we have

$$\hat{L}_1 = \hat{n} + A_1\hat{w}$$

$$\hat{L}_2 = \hat{n} - A_2\hat{w},$$

where

$$A_1 \equiv \lambda'(1-\theta')\sigma' + (1-\lambda')(1-\theta)\sigma + (1-\lambda')(\theta - \theta')$$

$$A_2 \equiv \lambda\theta'\sigma' + (1-\lambda)\theta\,\sigma - (1-\lambda)(\theta - \theta'). \tag{7.15}$$

Given our factor intensity presumption, A_1 is sure to be positive. So will A_2 if, as is commonly believed, σ and σ' are reasonably large. In fact $\sigma \geqslant 1$ is enough to ensure positive A_1 and A_2 irrespective of any factor-intensity comparisons. I shall therefore take this to be the normal case. Also note that

$$\Delta \equiv A_1 + A_2 = [\lambda'(1-\theta') + \lambda\theta']\sigma' + [(1-\lambda')(1-\theta) + (1-\lambda)\theta]\sigma$$

$$+ (\lambda - \lambda')(\theta - \theta') \tag{7.16}$$

is a positive weighted average of σ, σ', and 1, again irrespective of factor intensities. In the neoclassical case, $\Delta = \sigma$.

The solution is readily completed. We have

$$\hat{w} = (\hat{L}_1 - \hat{L}_2)/\Delta \tag{7.17}$$

$$\hat{t} = \hat{p} = (1 - \theta)(\hat{L}_1 - \hat{L}_2)/\Delta \tag{7.18}$$

and

$$\hat{n} = (A_2\hat{L}_1 + A_1\hat{L}_2)/\Delta. \tag{7.19}$$

Thus we find that DC growth ($\hat{L}_2 > 0$) improves the LDC's terms of trade
both in the commodity sense ($\hat{t} < 0$) and the double-factoral sense ($\hat{w} < 0$).
The LDC's own growth has the opposite effects.

However, the effect on the utility of a representative LDC consumer has
to be found using (7.4), or in differential form,

$$\hat{u}_1 = \gamma_1 \left(\frac{1 - \delta}{\delta} \hat{n} - \hat{p} \right).$$

In view of the argument concerning the likely signs of A_1 and A_2, we expect any
growth to yield greater product variety. For DC growth, this effect reinforces
the commodity terms of trade effect and guarantees an increase in LDC welfare.
For LCD growth, it counteracts the adverse effect of the commodity terms of
trade. The larger are σ and σ', the more likely is the variety effect to prevail
and produce an increase in LDC welfare.

This result is paradoxical in two ways. First, the variety effect is absent in
the neoclassical case, and the LDC is bound to lose from its own growth. Thus
the incorporation of monopolistic competition has increased the possibility of
gain to the LDC. At least to this extent, the assertion of harm from monopolistic
trade is not valid.

The second paradox is that the possibility of LDC gain is greater when σ or σ'
is larger. According to conventional beliefs, it is precisely in this case that an
LDC would be very vulnerable to damage from trade: the DCs could easily
substitute away from the good the LDC exports. However, we find that the
supposed vulnerability works to the LDC's advantage. Such results will recur
in the following sections.

It might be argued that LDC consumers are not homogeneous, that only a
subset exposed to modern goods consume them and stand to benefit from
variety in such goods. This is what might be roughly captured by allowing the
γs to differ across the countries. However, this does not upset the welfare conclusions. Those LDC consumers who spend all their income on the non-traded
good have a constant real income $1/\alpha_1$, and are neither helped nor hurt by trade.
The others stand to gain as shown above. Thus, in the Pareto sense, the analysis
remains valid.

4. TECHNICAL PROGRESS

When we consider production of the raw material, and fixed and variable costs in the manufacturing sector, there is a large variety of rates and biases of technical progress. To keep the algebra more manageable, I shall consider a special case that captures in an extreme form the earlier relative factor-intensity assumption. I shall henceforth assumed that fixed costs are entirely labour costs, i.e. $F(w,r) = f w$ for fixed f. Then, in the notation of the earlier section, $\lambda' = \theta' = \sigma' = 0$, and $\Delta = \lambda\theta + \sigma(1 - \lambda\theta)$. The more general case yields qualitatively similar results.

Now two types of technical progress can be considered: a reduction in the labour coefficient β in production of raw materials, referred to as LDC technical progress. and reduction of a parameter μ in the cost function c, referred to as DC technical progress. The equilibrium conditions are

$$r = \beta \tag{7.20}$$

$$\delta p = c(w,r,\mu) \tag{7.21}$$

$$(1 - \delta)p = f w/x \tag{7.22}$$

$$\gamma_1 L_1 = \beta n x c_r(w,r,\mu) \tag{7.23}$$

$$\gamma_2 L_2 = n\{f + x c_w(w,r,\mu)\}. \tag{7.24}$$

There are two aspects of DC technical progress that are of interest. One is its contribution to overall cost reduction. This is measured by the partial elasticity $\partial \log c/\partial \log \mu$, and will be denoted by π. The other is its Hicksian raw-material-saving bias, as measured by the partial elasticity of the factor proportions ratio, $\partial \log (c_r/c_w)/\partial \log \mu$. This will be denoted by ξ. By homogeneity, we have

$$\partial \log c/\partial \log \mu = (1 - \theta)\partial \log c_w/\partial \log \phi + \theta\partial \log c_r/\partial \log \mu.$$

Hence

$$\partial \log c_w/\partial \log \mu = \pi - \theta\xi \tag{7.26}$$

and

$$\partial \log c_r/\partial \log \mu = \pi + (1 - \theta)\xi. \tag{7.27}$$

We can now proceed with the comparative statics. From (7.20) we have $\hat{r} = \hat{\beta}$, and from (7.21)

$$\hat{p} = (1 - \theta)\hat{w} + \theta\hat{\beta} + \pi\hat{\mu}.$$

Next, (7.22) gives $\hat{p} = \hat{w} - \hat{x}$, so

$$\hat{x} = \theta\hat{w} - \theta\hat{\beta} - \pi\hat{\mu}.$$

Using (7.26) and (7.27), the differentials of (7.23) and (7.24) are

$$0 = \hat{\beta} + \hat{n} + \hat{x} + (1 - \theta)(\hat{w} - \hat{\beta}) + [\pi + (1 - \theta)\xi]\hat{\mu}$$

and

$$0 = \hat{n} + (1 - \lambda)\{\hat{x} - \theta\sigma(\hat{w} - \hat{\beta}) + [\pi - \theta\xi]\hat{\mu}\}.$$

On subtracting,

$$0 = \hat{\beta} + \lambda\hat{x} + [(1-\theta) + \theta(1-\lambda)]\sigma(\hat{w} - \hat{\beta})$$
$$+ [\pi + (1-\theta)\xi - (1-\lambda)\pi + (1-\lambda)\theta\xi]\hat{\mu}$$
$$= \hat{\beta} + \Delta(\hat{w} - \hat{\beta}) + (1 - \lambda\theta)\xi\hat{\mu}.$$

The change in the relative wage is

$$\hat{w} = \left(1 - \frac{1}{\Delta}\right)\hat{\beta} - \frac{(1-\lambda\theta)\xi}{\Delta}\hat{\mu}$$

or

$$\hat{w} = \{(\sigma - 1)\hat{\beta} - \xi\hat{\mu}\}(1 - \lambda\theta)/\Delta, \tag{7.28}$$

while

$$\hat{t} = \hat{p} - \hat{r}$$
$$= (1 - \theta)(\hat{w} - \hat{\beta}) + \pi\hat{\mu}$$

or

$$\hat{t} = -\frac{1-\theta}{\Delta}\hat{\beta} + \left\{\pi - \frac{(1-\lambda\theta)\xi}{\Delta}\right\}\hat{\mu}. \tag{7.29}$$

Thus LDC technical progress ($\hat{\beta} < 0$) worsens its commodity terms of trade ($\hat{t} > 0$), but improves its double factoral terms of trade ($\hat{w} < 0$) iff $\sigma > 1$. Once again we have the paradox that the LDC especially vulnerable to substitution stands to gain. The point is that increased productivity in the raw-material sector lowers the price of this input in DC production, so the high degree of substitution works in favour of the LDC.

The effect of DC technical progress ($\hat{\mu} < 0$) on the double-factoral terms of trade depends solely on its bias: raw material saving technical progress ($\xi > 0$) is to the relative advantage of the DC. This is somewhat in keeping with the usual assertions. However, there are further subleties. A special case of interest is one where the DC technical progress is Harrod-neutral or purely raw-material augmenting, i.e. the cost function has the form

$$c(w, r, \mu) = g(w, r\mu).$$

Then $c_\mu = rg_2$ and $c_r/c_w = \mu g_2/g_1$ in obvious notation, so $\pi = \theta$ and $\xi = 1 - \sigma$. Thus $\sigma > 1$ ensures that such technical progress has a raw-material-using bias, and this works to the relative advantage of the LDC. The effect of raw-material augmenting technical progress is to lower its input price in efficiency units. If large substitution possibilities exist, they operate in favour of this input. Thus the vulnerability of an LDC when σ is large really comes from technical progress which augments other inputs.

Once again, it should be noted that the signs of all these comparative static effects would be the same in the neoclassical case, i.e. the qualitative results are unaffected by the existence of scale economics and monopolistic competition.

To complete the welfare analysis we need the effect on price

$$\hat{p} = \left\{ \frac{(1-\lambda\theta)(\sigma-1)+\theta}{\Delta} \right\} \hat{\beta} + \left\{ \frac{(1-\lambda\theta)\xi}{\Delta} - \pi \right\} \hat{\mu} \qquad (7.30)$$

and on product variety

$$\hat{n} = \frac{(1-\lambda)\theta}{\Delta} \{ -(\sigma-1)\hat{\beta} + \xi\hat{\mu} \}. \qquad (7.31)$$

The change in utility of a representative LDC consumer is given by

$$\hat{u}_1/\gamma_1 = \frac{1-\delta}{\delta} \hat{n} - \hat{p}.$$

LDC technical progress increases variety for $\sigma > 1$, and the same condition is sufficient to ensure a price fall. The precise condition for LDC technical progress to raise welfare is

$$\sigma > 1 - \frac{\theta}{(1-\theta)+\theta(1-\lambda)/\delta} = 1 - \frac{\theta}{(1-\theta)+\theta(1-\theta)/(1-\theta\delta)}. \qquad (7.32)$$

In the neoclassical case this reduces to $\sigma > 1 - \theta$. Resource-saving DC technical progress reduces product variety; if its overall rate is sufficiently rapid, it can still raise welfare by lowering the price. In the neoclassical case the criterion reduces to the terms-of-trade effect.

5. TARIFFS

Finally, consider an LDC seeking to improve its terms of trade by levying an export tariff on the raw material. When interpreting the model, this must be understood to be done collusively by all the countries concerned. Such proposals have been an important part of the attempt to establish the New International Economic Order.

Let τ be the tariff rate in specific terms, the LDC wage being numeraire. Then the price of the raw material to the DC users is

$$r = \beta + \tau \qquad (7.33)$$

so $dr = d\tau$ and $\hat{r} = d\tau/r$. The initial equilibrium has $\tau = 0$.

LDC income inclusive of tariff revenue is $L_1 + \tau z$ where z is the quantity of the raw material produced and exported. For its labour market equilibrium, we have

$$L_1 = \alpha_1 y_1 + \beta z$$

$$= \alpha_1 (1-\gamma_1)(L_1 + \tau z)/\alpha_1 + \beta z$$

or

$$\gamma_1 L_1 = z[\beta + (1-\gamma_1)\tau], \qquad (7.34)$$

replacing (7.7). Less labour is available in the traded-good sector since some income from tariff revenues is spent on the non-traded good.

Production decisions in the DC are as before, and the equilibrium is determined by

$$\delta p = c(w, r) \tag{7.35}$$

$$(1 - \delta)p = f w / x \tag{7.36}$$

$$\gamma_1 L_1 = [\beta + (1 - \gamma_1)\tau] \, n \, x \, c_r(w, r) \tag{7.37}$$

$$\gamma_2 L_2 = n\{f + x \, c_w(w, r)\}. \tag{7.38}$$

As τ, or equivalent r, increases, we can differentiate this system and solve in the now-familiar manner. We find

$$\hat{w} = \hat{r}\{1 - (1 - \gamma_1)/\Delta\}. \tag{7.39}$$

Thus w is raised, i.e. the LDC's double-factoral terms of trade worsen, if $\Delta > 1 - \gamma_1$, or

$$(1 - \lambda\theta)(\sigma - 1) + \gamma_1 > 0. \tag{7.40}$$

If γ_1 is large, there is a serious risk that the tariff will rebound to the relative benefit of the DC, even when $\sigma < 1$.

Turning to the (tariff-inclusive) commodity terms of trade, we find

$$\hat{t} = \hat{p} - \hat{r} = (1 - \theta)(\hat{w} - \hat{r}) = -(1 - \theta)(1 - \gamma_1)\hat{r}/\Delta, \tag{7.41}$$

i.e. the tariff is bound to improve the commodity terms of trade.

Welfare analysis again requires consideration of product variety. We find

$$\hat{n} = -\theta(1 - \lambda)(1 - \gamma_1)(\sigma - 1)\hat{r}/\Delta. \tag{7.42}$$

When $\sigma > 1$, therefore, a tariff reduces product variety. A rise in the input price raises the variable cost of production of each good. This makes scale economies relatively less important, and so acts in the direction of greater variety. But the rise in cost and hence this effect, is smaller when σ is larger. Then the effect of the rise in w can outweigh it.

We also find

$$\hat{x} = -\theta(1 - \gamma_1)\hat{r}/\Delta, \tag{7.43}$$

i.e. the scale of manufacturing production is lowered, and

$$\hat{p} = \{1 - (1 - \theta)(1 - \gamma_1)/\Delta\}\hat{r}, \tag{7.44}$$

so the conditions under which a tariff raises w suffice to ensure that it also raises p.

To find the effect on LDC utility, we note that per capita income is

$$1 + \tau z / L_1 = 1 + \gamma_1 \tau / [\beta + (1 - \gamma_1)\tau]$$

$$= (\beta + \tau) / [\beta + (1 - \gamma_1)\tau].$$

The proportional change in this is

$$d\tau/(\beta + \tau) - (1 - \gamma_1)d\tau/[\beta + (1 - \gamma_1)\tau]$$

$$= \hat{r}\{1 - (1 - \gamma_1)\} \qquad \text{at} \qquad \tau = 0$$

$$= \gamma_1 \hat{r}.$$

Then

$$u_1 = k(1 + \tau z/L_1)p^{-\gamma_1} n^{(1-\delta)\gamma_1/\delta} \alpha_1^{-(1-\gamma_1)}$$

and

$$\hat{u}_1 = \gamma_1 \hat{r} - \gamma_1 \hat{p} + (1 - \delta)\gamma_1 \hat{n}/\delta.$$

Substituting and simplifying, this becomes

$$\hat{u}_1/\gamma_1 = \hat{r}\left\{(1-\theta)(1-\gamma_1) + \frac{1-\delta}{\delta}\theta(1-\lambda)(1-\sigma)\right\}\Big/\Delta. \qquad (7.45)$$

This is bound to generate a benefit if $\sigma < 1$. Also, if σ exceeds 1 by a small amount, the adverse effect on diversity is weak and there is positive net benefit. Recall that in this case the double-factoral terms of trade worsen. Here is an instance where attention to a fashionable measure might cause the LDC to miss a beneficial policy.

We can also find the effect on the utility of the typical DC consumer. We have

$$u_2 = k \, w \, p^{-\gamma_2} n^{\gamma_2(1-\delta)/\delta} (\alpha_2 w)^{-(1-\gamma_2)},$$

which gives

$$\hat{u}_2 = \gamma_2\left(\hat{w} - \hat{p} + \frac{1-\delta}{\delta}\hat{n}\right).$$

Substituting from earlier expressions,

$$\hat{u}_2/\gamma_2 = \hat{r}\left\{-\theta(1-\gamma_1) + \frac{1-\delta}{\delta}\theta(1-\lambda)(1-\sigma)\right\}\Big/\Delta. \qquad (7.46)$$

Thus, if $\sigma > 1$, a tariff is bound to harm the DC.

However, a monopolistically competitive equilibrium is not Pareto-efficient, and there is scope for mutually beneficial policies. An inspection of (7.45) and (7.46) shows that if σ is sufficiently above 1, a subsidy on raw material exports by the LDC can bring benefit to both countries, while for σ is sufficiently less than 1 a tariff can do this. In each each, it is the variety effect that helps both, overcoming the conflicting effects of the terms of trade change.

6. CONCLUDING REMARKS

The model has not produced any strong arguments to support the thesis of harmful effect of trade on LDCs. The implications for producers of raw materials that permit easy substitution are particularly surprising. Such countries benefit from most technical progress, and can be harmed by attempts to turn the terms of trade in their favour. Nor is the often-emphasized aspect of monopoly power found to cause notable harm. On the contrary, the associated increase in product diversity yields welfare gains to the LDC in some cases where the neoclassical terms of trade effect works against it. If there is truth in the claims of dependent or unequal development, it must be substantiated using aspects of market power that go beyond monopolistic competition in trade, i.e. collusion and entry-deterrence at the international level.

APPENDIX

Here I show how the model can be reinterpreted to allow unemployment in the LDC along the Harris–Todaro expected wage equalization lines. The country subscript 1 is omitted for simplicity.

The non-traded goods sector is identified with the traditional sector, and denoted by subscript t; the traded good sector is taken to be the modern or urban sector, indicated by subscript m. Total labour force allocates itself among the sectors:

$$L = L_t + L_m. \tag{7.A1}$$

In the modern sector, there is a distinction between the employed E_m and the unemployed U_m

$$L_m = E_m + U_m. \tag{7.A2}$$

The technology of production gives

$$L_t = \alpha y, \qquad E_m = \beta z, \tag{7.A3}$$

where α, β are the input coefficients and y, z the output levels.

If ϵ is the probability of employment for each member of the modern sector labour force, expected wage equalization implies

$$w_t = \epsilon w_m. \tag{7.A4}$$

For rationality of expectations of employment,

$$\epsilon = U_m/L_m \tag{7.A5}$$

or

$$1 - \epsilon = E_m/L_m.$$

Substituting in (7.A1) and using (7.A3)

$$L = \alpha y + \frac{\beta}{1 - \epsilon} z. \tag{7.A6}$$

Now w_t is determined by the average productivity $1/\alpha$ in the traditional sector, and w_m is exogenous. This fixes ϵ. Then this model is formally identical to the one in the text, with β replaced by the higher number $\beta/(1 - \epsilon)$. The point is that each unit of modern sector output 'requires' not only the actual workers who produce it but also the induced migrants. This is just like having a worse technology.

The welfare calculations are also valid in terms of the expected utility, which is governed by the wage w_t.

NOTES

*   I am grateful for valuable comments received in seminars ar Princeton, Harvard and IIES, Stockholm, as well as the conference session.
1.   A fairly comprehensive statement can be found in Diaz-Alejandro (1978, pp. 94–104).
2.   See Smith (1979) and Dixit and Norman (1980, ch. 3).
3.   See Krugman (1979), Lancaster (1980), Dixit and Norman (1980, ch. 9), and Helpman (1981).
4.   This formally shown in the Appendix.
5.   See Lewis (1978).
6.   The procedure is very similar to the usual two-by-two Rybczynski theory, and mathematically identical if we regard L_1 and L_2 as producing two 'outputs' n and $(n\,x)$. See Jones (1965).

REFERENCES

Diaz-Alejandro, C. F. (1978), 'Delinking North and South: Unschackled or Unhinged?' in A. Fishlow *et al.*, *Rich and Poor Nations in the World Economy* (New York: McGraw-Hill).

Dixit, A. and Norman, V. (1980), *Theory of International Trade* (Welwyn, England: James Nisbet & Co.; and Cambridge, England: Cambridge University Press).

Findlay, R. (1980), 'The Terms of Trade and Equilibrium Growth in the World Economy', *American Economic Review*, 70(3), 291–9.

Helpman, E. (1981), 'International Trade in the Presence of Product Differentiation, Economies of Scale and Monopolistic Competition: A Chamberlin–Heckscher–Ohlin Approach', *Journal of International Economics*, 11(3), 305–40.

Jones, R. W. (1965), 'The Structure of Simple General Equilibrium Models', *Journal of Political Economy*, 73(4), 557–72.

Kemp, M. C. and Ohyama, M. (1978), 'On the Sharing of Trade Gains by Resource-poor and Resource-rich Countries', *Journal of International Economics*, 8(1), 93–115.

Krugman, P. (1979), 'Increasing Returns, Monopolistic Competition and International Trade', *Journal of International Economics*, 9(4), 469–79.

Lancaster, K. (1980), 'Intra-Industry Trade under Perfect Monopolistic Competition', *Journal of International Economics*, 10(2), 151–75.

Lewis, W. A. (1978), *The Evolution of the New International Economic Order* (Princeton, N.J.: Princeton University Press).

Smith, A. (1979), 'Intertemporal Gains from Trade', *Journal of International Economics*, 9(2), 239–48.

8

Increasing Returns, Monopolistic Competition, and Factor Movements: a Welfare Analysis*

Elhanan Helpman and Assaf Razin

1. INTRODUCTION

The welfare economics of international factor movements have been widely discussed in the literature. In private ownership economies factor owners choose the location of employment of their factors of production according to the highest reward and when permitted this includes locations in different countries. In competitive economies with convex technologies these private considerations coincide with social welfare (except for monopolistic considerations of large countries). As one might suspect, this coincidence of goals does not necessarily hold in economies which are characterized by industries which operate with increasing returns to scale and in which firms engage in monopolistic competition. The aim of this study is to identify the channels of influence of factor movements on social welfare which are special to such market structures, and in view of their existence to evaluate in welfare terms the performance of the private sector's decisions about the international allocation of productive resources. In the main analysis we will use foreign investment as a case study, but it should be clear that our findings apply to all factor movements except for labour migration. An analysis of labour migration requires as an input the results reported below, but since migration is guided by utility differentials rather than wage differentials it requires a separate treatment (see, for example, the discussion in Helpman and Razin, 1980).

Our main concern is with welfare aspects. For this reason we will assume that reward differentials exist (thereby inducing factor movements) without specifying the factors that generate these reward differentials. In the case discussed in this paper primary inputs can be differently priced in different countries for the same reasons that are advanced in the standard trade models (see, for example, Jones, 1967). It should only be pointed out that in the present framework they can also be differentially priced due to pure size differences among countries (see Helpman and Razin, 1980).

In order to have a benchmark for our main findings, we present in Section 2 a standard analysis of the welfare effects of capital mobility. In Section 3 we provide a detailed analysis of the effects of changes in the capital stock on a country's gross domestic product for economies with an increasing-returns-to-scale sector in which firms engage in average-cost pricing. The results of this analysis are then used in Section 4 to perform a cost–benefit analysis of international capital movements for an economy which produces differentiated products under increasing returns to scale. Concluding comments are provided in Section 5.

2. THE STANDARD WELFARE ANALYSIS OF FACTOR MOVEMENTS

As a prelude to our main discussion, we present in this section an analysis of welfare gains from factor movements for a competitive economy with a convex technology. For simplicity, we aggregate all traded goods into a single commodity Y and choose $p_Y = 1$ as its price. The aggregation is based on the assumption that relative prices of traded goods do not change as a result of factor movements (the small country assumption in commodity markets) in order to avoid welfare changes that result from adjustments in the terms of trade, because our main analysis sheds no new light on this issue. We also assume that there is a single non-traded good X whose price in terms of Y is p (an extension to many non-traded goods is straightforward).

Assuming the existence of a representative consumer, or a social welfare function which is maximized with costless income redistribution, our country's welfare level can be represented by an indirect utility function $v(p, GNP)$, where GNP stands for gross national product measured in units of Y, which equals net national product due to the lack of depreciation of the capital stock. Assuming that all foreign source income stems from international mobility of capital, GNP equals GDP minus rental payments on domestically employed foreign capital. Hence,

$$GNP = GDP(p, L, K + \Delta) - \rho\Delta \tag{1}$$

where $GDP(\cdot)$ is the gross domestic product function (which has the standard properties of a restricted profit function as discussed, for example, in Varian (1978)), L and K stand for domestically owned labour and capital (assumed to be inelastically supplied), Δ stands for foreign capital employed in the home country when $\Delta > 0$ and domestic capital employed abroad when $\Delta < 0$. Finally, ρ represents the rental rate on Δ.

When foreign capital is employed in the home country $\rho = r$, where r is the domestic rental rate on capital and it equals the domestic marginal product value of capital $\partial GDP(\cdot)/\partial K$. Here the assumption is that foreignly owned capital commands the same rental rate as domestically owned capital. On the other hand, when domestic capital is employed abroad its rental rate in the foreign country is ρ, which may be a function of the size of foreign investment.

Choosing a transformation of the utility function such that in equilibrium the marginal utility of income (i.e. $\partial v/\partial GNP$) equals one, differentiation of $v(\cdot)$, using (8.1) and the properties of the indirect utility and *GDP* functions yield:

$$dU = (r-\rho)d\Delta - \Delta d\rho + (X - D_X)dp,$$

where X is the output level of sector X and D_X is consumption of X. Since X is not traded, in equilibrium $X = D_X$, and we obtain:

$$dU = (r-\rho)d\Delta - \Delta d\rho. \tag{8.2}$$

Suppose that r is smaller than the rental rate that domestic capital can obtain abroad. Then owners of domestic capital will shift part of it into foreign operations thereby increasing domestic welfare due to the first term on the right-hand side of (8.2) (since $r < \rho$ and $d\Delta < 0$). If the foreign rental rate is unaffected by the home country's investment abroad, the second term on the right-hand side of (8.2) equals zero. If, on the other hand, the foreign rental rate on domestic capital invested abroad declines with the size of the investment and we start with a positive investment level ($\Delta < 0$), the second term generates a negative welfare effect, but this negative welfare effect is negligible for small investment levels. In the case under discussion dU evaluated at $\Delta = 0$ is positive, so that it pays to invest abroad at least a little. The negative welfare effect (which doesn't exist at $\Delta = 0$) stems from monopoly power in foreign investment and we will disregard it in what follows because our main analysis sheds no new light on this particular aspect of international capital mobility.

Now suppose that r exceeds the rental rate that foreign capital receives abroad. Then foreigners will invest in the home country. In this case $r \equiv \rho$ and (8.2) reduces to $dU = -\Delta dr$. However, due to the concavity of the GDP function in the employed levels of factors of production the rental rate on capital declines with capital inflows so that for positive investment levels ($\Delta > 0$) welfare increases. This shows that private considerations about the location of capital coincide with social benefits in the sense that social welfare increases as a result of private decisions to shift capital to the high-return location.

3. INCREASING RETURNS AND INCOME EFFECTS OF CAPITAL MOVEMENTS

We have seen in the previous section that in a competitive economy with convex technologies private decisions about the location of capital coincide with the goal of social welfare maximization. An important ingredient in that analysis was the effect of capital movements on GDP. In particular, an inflow of one unit of capital increases GDP by exactly the market rental rate on capital ($r = \partial GDP/\partial K$), thus making the private and social returns on capital coincide. This is achieved in a competitive economy due to marginal-cost pricing.

In sectors with increasing returns to scale marginal-cost pricing is incompatible with profitable production. In such cases free entry drives firms to engage in average-cost pricing and indeed this assumption is common in much of the recent literature on international trade in the presence of economies of scale (see the literature surveyed in Helpman, 1984). If this is the case, an inflow of one unit of capital (or an increase in the employed capital stock due to, say, invest-ment) will not increase GDP by the market rental rate on capital. A similar argument also applies to other factors of production. However, for every welfare analysis of factor movements their effect on GDP will be of major importance. For this reason we provide in this section the relevant analysis (which we believe to be of interest in its own right) which will be used in the next section for welfare evaluations.

The following analysis applies to models in which sectors with economies of scale are populated by firms which have identical technologies. They charge the same price and, due to free entry, engage in average-cost pricing. For example, recent models of monopolistic competition in differentiated products which confine attention to symmetric equilibria satisfy these requirements (see Helpman, 1984). Assuming again that there are two goods, X and Y, which are produced with labour and capital, where this time Y is produced with constant returns to scale and X is produced with increasing returns to scale, the equilibrium conditions in production can be represented as follows:

$$1 = c_Y(w, r), \qquad (8.3)$$

$$p = C_X(w, r, x)/x, \qquad (8.4)$$

$$a_{LY}(w, r)Y + l_X(w, r, x)N = L, \qquad (8.5)$$

$$a_{KY}(w, r)Y + k_X(w, r, x)N = K + \Delta, \qquad (8.6)$$

where $c_Y(\cdot)$ is the marginal cost function of Y, w and r are the wage rate and the rental rate on capital, $C_X(\cdot)$ is a single firm's cost function in industry X, x is the output level of a single firm in industry X, $a_{LY}(\cdot) (= \partial c_Y/\partial w)$ is the employed labour/output ratio in the production of Y, $a_{KY}(\cdot) (= \partial c_Y/\partial r)$ is the employed capital/output ratio in the production of Y, $l_X(\cdot) (= \partial C_X/\partial w)$ is the employment of labour by a single firm in industry X, $k_X(\cdot) (= \partial C_X/\partial r)$ is the employment of capital by a single firm in industry X, Y is the output of product Y and N is the number of firms in industry X.

Equation (8.3) represents the condition of marginal-cost pricing in the production of Y (the price of Y equals one) while equation (8.4) represents the condition of average-cost pricing in the production of X. Equations (8.5) and (8.6) represent equilibrium conditions in factor markets. The demand for labour and capital by a firm in sector X and its cost function are not proportional to its output level x due to economies of scale. In fact, the elasticity of $C_X(\cdot)$ with respect to x is smaller than one, because due to scale economies the standard measure of economies of scale:

$$\theta(w, r, x) \equiv \frac{C_X(w, r, x)/x}{\partial C_X(w, r, x)/\partial x} \qquad (8.7)$$

is larger than one.

Given a single firm's output level x, the price of output in the X sector p, and the employment of factors of production L and $K + \Delta$, equations (8.3)–(8.6) provide a solution to factor prices w and r, the output level Y and the number of firms N in the industry producing with increasing returns to scale. We can use equations (8.3)–(8.6) to derive a GDP function for the economy under analysis, which is an analogue of the GDP function used in the previous section. For this purpose we transform these equations as follows. Let:

$$c_X(w, r; x) \equiv C_X(w, r, x)/x \ = \ \text{average-cost function of a firm in sector X}$$

$$a_{LX}(w, r; x) \equiv l_X(w, r, x)/x \ = \ \text{labour/output ratio in sector X}$$

$$a_{KX}(w, r; x) \equiv k_X(w, r, x)/x \ = \ \text{capital/output ratio in sector X}$$

$$X \equiv Nx \ = \ \text{output level in sector X.}$$

Using the new variables, equations (8.3)–(8.6) can be rewritten as:

$$1 \ = \ c_Y(w, r), \qquad (8.3')$$

$$p \ = \ c_X(w, r; x), \qquad (8.4')$$

$$a_{LY}(w, r)Y + a_{LX}(w, r; x)X \ = \ L, \qquad (8.5')$$

$$a_{KY}(w, r)Y + a_{KX}(w, r; x)X \ = \ K + \Delta. \qquad (8.6')$$

Equations (8.3')–(8.6') have the standard form of the production equilibrium conditions in a competitive constant returns to scale economy as long as x is given. In particular, $c_X(\cdot)$ has the usual properties of a unit cost function as far as its dependence on factor prices is concerned. Moreover, $a_{LX}(\cdot) = \partial c_X(\cdot)/\partial w$ and $a_{KX}(\cdot) = \partial c_X(\cdot)/\partial r$, so that by duality there exists a sectoral constant returns-to-scale production function of X from which $c_X(\cdot)$, $a_{LX}(\cdot)$, and $a_{KX}(\cdot)$ are derivable.[1] Hence, system (8.3')–(8.6') implies the existence of a GDP function, $GDP(p, L, K + \Delta; x)$, such that it has the usual properties with respect to $(p, L, K + \Delta)$. In particular, $\partial GDP/\partial p = X = Nx$, $\partial GDP/\partial L = w$, $\partial GDP/\partial K = r$ and GDP is convex in p and concave in $(L, K + \Delta)$. The difference between this GDP function and that used in the previous section is the dependence of the present one on x, the individual firm's output level. It is obvious from (8.5')–(8.6') that x operates like technical progress; an increase in x reduces unit output costs $c_X(\cdot)$, because due to (8.7) the elasticity of $c_X(\cdot)$ with respect to x is $-1 + 1/\theta(\cdot) < 0$. Let $b = 1 - 1/\theta$ be the absolute value of the elasticity of $c_X(\cdot)$ with respect to x, then following the analysis of technical progress in Jones (1965) $b = \theta_{LX} b_L + \theta_{KX} b_K$ where b_L is minus the elasticity of $a_{LX}(\cdot)$ with respect to x, b_K is minus the elasticity of $a_{KX}(\cdot)$ with respect to x, and θ_{jX} is the share of factor j in costs of production; $j = L, K$.

As Jones (1965) has shown, a one percentage point increase in x has the same effect on *output* levels as a b per cent increase in the price p plus a $\lambda_{LX} b_L$ per cent increase in the labour force plus a $\lambda_{KX} b_K$ per cent increase in the capital stock, where λ_{LX} is the share of labour employed in the production of X and λ_{KX} is the share of the capital stock employed in the production of X.[2] This can be explained as follows. Suppose x is increased by a one percentage point and the number of firms N is reduced by a one percentage point so that aggregate output in sector X does not change. As a result of the increase in x each firm will increase its employment of labour by ϵ_{LX} per cent, where ϵ_{LX} is its elasticity of labour demand with respect to output, so that the sector's demand for labour will increase by ϵ_{LX} per cent. On the other hand, due to the decline in the number of firms in the industry, the industry's labour demand will fall by one per cent, so that $b_L \equiv 1 - \epsilon_{LX}$ is the proportion of the industry's labour force that is being released as a result of these changes. Since the industry employs the proportion λ_{LX} of the total labour force, $\lambda_{LX} b_L$ is the industry's saving of labour as a proportion of the total labour force. Similarly, $\lambda_{KX} b_K$ is the proportion of total capital saved by industry X as a result of a one per cent increase in x, holding aggregate output X constant (with the adjustment being made by means of an increase in the number of firms in the industry). In addition to these factor supply effects, a one percentage point increase in x reduces unit production costs by b per cent.

Using the above-described relationship between the effects on output levels of a one percentage point increase in x and a b per cent increase in the price p plus $\lambda_{jX} b_j$, $j = L, K$, per cent increases in the supply of factors of production, one can calculate the change in GDP as a result of a one percentage point increase in x as follows:

$$\frac{\partial GDP}{\partial x} x = \left(p \frac{\partial X}{\partial p} + \frac{\partial Y}{\partial p}\right) pb + \left(p \frac{\partial X}{\partial L} + \frac{\partial Y}{\partial L}\right) L \lambda_{LX} b_L + \left(p \frac{\partial X}{\partial K} + \frac{\partial Y}{\partial K}\right) K \lambda_{KX} b_K.$$

The term in the first bracket on the right-hand side equals zero (due to the standard tangency condition between the GDP line and the transformation curve), the term in the second bracket is the wage rate w and the term in the third bracket is the rental rate on capital r. Hence, using the definition of λ_{jX}, $j = L, K$, we obtain:

$$\frac{\partial GDP}{\partial x} x = w a_{LX} X b_L + r a_{KX} X b_K = pX(\theta_{LX} b_L + \theta_{KX} b_K) = pX$$

and

$$\frac{\partial}{\partial x} GDP(p, L, K + \Delta; x) = pN(1 - \theta^{-1}),$$

where use has been made of the relationships $X = Nx$ and $b = (1 - \theta^{-1})$.

Now define r^* to be the increase in GDP that results from an increase in Δ *holding p constant*. In the competitive case with convex technologies this was shown to equal r – the market rental rate on capital. In the case considered here it is:

$$r^* = \frac{\partial}{\partial \Delta} GDP(\cdot) + \frac{\partial}{\partial x} GDP(\cdot) \frac{dx}{d\Delta},$$

where $dx/d\Delta$ is a *total* derivative. Using the previous result this can be written as:

$$r^* = r + pN(1 - \theta^{-1}) \frac{dx}{d\Delta}. \tag{8.8}$$

Since $\theta > 1$ (economies of scale), (8.8) tells us that an inflow of one unit of capital will increase GDP by more than the market rental rate on capital if it brings about an expansion of every firm's output level in sector X and it will increase GDP by less than the market rental rate on capital or even reduce GDP (as we will show) if it brings about a contraction of every firm's output level in sector X. This means that the private sector may undervalue or overvalue the marginal productivity of capital (and labour) as far as GDP is concerned, depending on its marginal effect on the size of operation of firms in the sector with economies of scale (with constant returns to scale $\theta = 1$ and $r^* = r$). However, this is but one consideration in the cost–benefit analysis of international capital movements, although it is an important one. A complete welfare analysis for an economy that produces differentiated products is presented in the next section.

4. DIFFERENTIATED PRODUCTS AND THE WELFARE ECONOMICS OF CAPITAL MOVEMENTS

A complete analysis of the welfare effects of international movements of factors of production in the presence of economies of scale and monopolistic competition requires a complete specification of the economy's structure. We chose to analyse an economy in which sector X produces differentiated products and we model it along the lines suggested in Lancaster (1980) and Helpman (1981). However, here we assume that Y is a composite traded good while the differentiated products are non-traded goods. The assumption of non-tradedness of the differentiated products simplifies the analysis by enabling us to employ the small country assumption without having to deal explicitly with the effects of factor movements on the number of varieties supplied on world markets. Moreover, it is an assumption of interest in its own right because many services (such as restaurant meals) are non-traded differentiated products.

Following Lancaster (1979) we assume that every consumer has a utility function $u(\cdot)$ defined on the consumption level of good Y, α_Y, and the consumption level of his most preferred differentiated product X, α_X. We assume that these preferences can be represented by a Cobb–Douglas utility function:

$$u = s^{-s}(1 - s)^{s-1} A \alpha_X^s \alpha_Y^{1-s}, \quad 0 < s < 1, A > 0. \tag{8.9}$$

If an individual has to consume a variety which is at distance δ from his ideal product then $\alpha_X(\delta)$ units of this variety provide him with the same level of utility as $\alpha_X(\delta)/h(\delta)$ units of the ideal product, where $h(\cdot)$ is Lancaster's compensation function. This means that the effective price a consumer pays for a unit of his ideal product is $p(\delta)h(\delta)$ if he buys for the price $p(\delta)$ a variety which is at distance δ from his ideal product. Given his income level I in terms of Y and measuring $p(\delta)$ in units of Y his demand functions are:

$$\alpha_X = \frac{sI}{p(\delta)h(\delta)},$$

$$\alpha_Y = (1-s)I$$

and his indirect utility function is:

$$v = AI[p(\delta)h(\delta)]^{-s}. \tag{8.10}$$

All consumers are assumed to be identical except for their most preferred variety. They are, however, uniformly distributed over the set of varieties in terms of their preferences, where this set is assumed to consist of a circumference of a circle whose length is one (see Helpman, 1981).

Assuming that Y is produced with constant returns to scale while every variety in sector X is produced with the same increasing-returns-to-scale technology, and assuming that firms in industry X engage in monopolistic competition with free entry which enforces average-cost pricing, we can describe a symmetric equilibrium of this economy (in a symmetric equilibrium all varieties are equally priced and produced in equal quantities) which translates in the present case into equations (8.3)–(8.6) plus the following two conditions (see Helpman, 1981):

$$R(N) = \theta(w, r, x), \tag{8.11}$$

$$s(pxN + Y - \rho\Delta) = pxN. \tag{8.12}$$

The production conditions (8.3)–(8.6) were discussed already. It should only be pointed out that due to the economies of scale every firm in sector X produces a different variety so that N stands for both the number of firms and the number of varieties supplied by local firms. Since X-goods are not traded, N is also the number of varieties that are consumed. Condition (8.11) stems from monopolistic competition which leads every firm in sector X to equate marginal costs to marginal revenue, and from average-cost pricing. These two imply the equality of the degree of monopoly power represented by $R(\cdot)$ to the degree of economies of scale $\theta(\cdot)$. The degree of monopoly power is measured by the ratio of average revenue to marginal revenue which equals in the case of a Cobb–Douglas utility function (and a unit length of the circumference of the circle) to one plus twice the elasticity of $h(\cdot)$ evaluated at $\delta = 1/N$ (see equation (49) in Helpman, 1981). Finally, equation (8.12) describes the equilibrium condition in the market for non-traded goods – proportion s of GNP is spent on X-products. From the system of equations (8.3)–(8.6) and (8.11)–(8.12) we can calculate the effect of capital movements on all endogenous variables, and in particular on x which is required in order to find out whether the market rental rate on capital r under-values or overvalues the GDP effect of capital movements.

Producers in sector X supply in equilibrium N varieties. Since every product is sold for the same price, consumers whose ideal product is one of the N that are being produced are better off than other consumers. Using the indirect utility function (8.10), the fact that all varieties are equally priced and the fact that a proportion $1/N$ of consumers is served by a single firm in sector X, the average utility level is calculated to be:

$$AIp^{-s}N \int_0^{1/N} [h(\delta)]^{-s} d\delta$$

If the produced varieties are drawn from a uniform distribution this represents the *ex-ante* expected utility level of *every* consumer. Multiplying the average welfare level by L and taking advantage of the accounting equation $LI = GDP - \rho\Delta$, we obtain the following measure of the economy's aggregate welfare level:

$$U = Ap^{-s}[GDP(p, L, K + \Delta; x) - \rho\Delta]\phi(N), \qquad (8.13)$$

where $GDP(\cdot)$ is a function with the properties discussed in the previous section and $\phi(N) \equiv N\int_0^{1/N} [h(\delta)]^{-s} d\delta$ is an increasing function of N.

It is seen from (8.13) that the welfare effects of capital movements (a change in Δ) can be decomposed into four parts. Two traditional effects and two new ones. The traditional effects are the direct effect of Δ on GNP both through its effect on GDP and on repatriation payments and the indirect effect through an induced change in the price p of X-goods. These were discussed in Section 2 in which we presented the traditional analysis and we showed that the price effect is nil due to the non-tradedness of X-goods. This will be shown to be true also in the present case. The new channels of influence that appear in (8.13) are an induced change in the scale of operation of firms in the differentiated-product industry, that was discussed in detail in Section 3, and an induced change in the number of varieties that are available to consumers, whose welfare implications are similar to those of public goods.

Total differentiation of (8.13), using properties of the $GDP(p, L, K + \Delta; x)$ function that were derived in the previous section and the definition of r^* in (8.8), we obtain:

$$dU = \frac{U}{\phi}\phi' dN + \frac{U}{GNP}[(r^* - \rho)d\Delta - d\rho\Delta] + \frac{U}{p}\left(\frac{pxN}{GNP} - s\right) dp,$$

where $\phi' > 0$ is the derivative of ϕ with respect to N. Due to the equilibrium condition in the market for non-traded goods the last term – which captures the induced price effect – equals zero, just as in the standard analysis. Choosing the constant A so that $U = GNP$ at the initial equilibrium point (which means that the marginal utility of income equals one), the change in welfare is:

$$dU = \frac{U}{\phi}\phi'dN + (r^* - \rho)d\Delta - d\rho\Delta, \qquad (8.14)$$

where (from (8))

$$r^* = r + pN(1 - \theta^{-1})\frac{dx}{d\Delta}.$$

Comparing this equation to (8.2) we see immediately the two novel elements in the present welfare analysis of capital flows, the effect on the number of varieties and the difference between the social value of capital as a contributor to GDP, r^*, and the private value r, which do not coincide unless the scale of operation of firms in sector X does not change.

The above-described considerations suggest that private decisions to locate capital in the highest private return location may have negative social welfare effects. This is demonstrated by the following two cases.

Case 1.

Suppose that a capital outflow reduces the number of varieties supplied in the investing country and it reduces the scale of operation of a representative firm in sector X (i.e. $dN/d\Delta > 0$ and $dx/d\Delta > 0$). In this case $r^* > r$. Suppose also that foreigners offer a rental rate on domestic capital ρ which exceeds r but falls short of the social productivity of domestically employed capital r^*. Disregarding the effect of foreign investment on ρ, it is seen that in this case private owners of capital will invest abroad ($d\Delta < 0$) bringing about a reduction of domestic welfare ($dU < 0$). The reduction of welfare stems from the fact that the rental rate on capital offered by foreigners falls short of the domestic social productivity of capital in terms of GDP and that a capital outflow makes less varieties available to consumers. Nevertheless, atomistic individuals will invest abroad because they maximize their own income.

Case 2.

Suppose that a capital inflow reduces the number of varieties produced in the home country and the scale of operation of a representative firm in industry X. In this case $r^* < r$, which means that the domestic market rental rate on capital overstates its marginal product value. Suppose also that $r^* < \rho < r$. Then foreigners will find it profitable to invest in the home country (because $\rho < r$), but domestic welfare will decline because the capital inflow will reduce GNP and the number of varieties available to domestic consumers.

The two cases discussed above show that an investing country as well as a recipient country may lose from foreign investment, provided the number of varieties and the scale of operation of firms producing these varieties can respond to capital flows as indicated in the suppositions of these cases. Generally, the response of x and N to changes in Δ can be calculated from the general equilibrium system described by equations (8.3)–(8.6) and (8.11)–(8.12). For present purposes it is sufficient to bring examples to the effects discussed in Cases 1 and 2, which we do below.

1. Let Y be produced only by means of labour and let X be produced only by means of capital. Let the production function of X be:

$$x = \begin{cases} 0 & \text{for } k_X < \bar{\beta}_X \\ (K_X - \bar{\beta}_X)/\beta_X & \text{for } k_X \geqslant \bar{\beta}_X \end{cases} \qquad \bar{\beta}_X, \beta_X > 0.$$

This is a production function with increasing returns to scale which has associated with it the linear cost function:

$$C_X = r(\bar{\beta}_X + \beta_X x) \quad \text{for } x > 0$$

and the measure of economies of scale:

$$\theta = 1 + \bar{\beta}_X/(\beta_X x) \quad \text{for } x > 0.$$

In this case equilibrium conditions (8.6) and (8.11) become:

$$(\bar{\beta}_X + \beta_X x)N = K + \Delta \tag{8.6a}$$

$$R(N) = 1 + \bar{\beta}_X/(\beta_X x). \tag{8.11a}$$

Choosing a compensation function $h(\delta)$ whose elasticity is increasing in δ at $\delta = 1/N$ assures that $R(N)$ declines in N. In this case (8.6a) and (8.11a) imply $dN/d\Delta > 0$ and $dx/d\Delta > 0$; i.e. a capital outflow reduces the number of varieties and the scale of operation of a representative firm, and $r^* > r$.

2. Suppose that Y is produced with a Lenotief technology in which the input–output coefficients a_{LY} and a_{KY} are fixed and X is produced only with labour according to the following production function:

$$x = \begin{cases} 0 & \text{for } l_X < \bar{\gamma}_X \\ (l_X - \bar{\gamma}_X)/\gamma_X & \text{for } l_X \geqslant \bar{\gamma}_X \end{cases} \qquad \bar{\gamma}_X, \gamma_X > 0.$$

In this case the equilibrium conditions (8.5), (8.6), and (8.11) can be written as follows:

$$a_{LY} Y + (\bar{\gamma}_X + \gamma_X x)N = L \tag{8.5b}$$

$$a_{KY} Y = K + \Delta \tag{8.6b}$$

$$R(N) = 1 + \bar{\gamma}_X/(\gamma_X x). \tag{8.11b}$$

It is straightforward to see that in this case $dN/d\Delta < 0$ and $dx/d\Delta < 0$, provided $R(\cdot)$ is declining in N, which happens when the elasticity of $h(\delta)$ is increasing in δ at $\delta = 1/N$.

Our examples show that indeed the social productivity of a factor of production can be understated or overstated by its market reward and that an expansion in the quantity of a factor of production may increase or reduce the number of varieties available to consumers. With a suitable reinterpretation of the equilibrium conditions, taking $d\rho \equiv 0$, the last example can be used to produce $r^* < 0$ which shows that in a closed economy with differentiated products capital accumulation may be welfare-reducing — an immiserizing growth result. Finally, the reader should not be left with the impression that changes in the capital stock always affect N and x in the same direction; this is a special feature of our examples in which X-goods are produced with a homothetic production function. In Helpman and Razin (1980) there is an example with a non-homothetic production function in which they can be affected in opposite directions.

5. CONCLUDING REMARKS

We have shown in this paper that in economies with sectors which produce differentiated products under increasing returns to scale, foreign investment may flow in the wrong directions thereby harming the recipient as well as the investing country. This was demonstrated by identifying two channels of influence which are special to such economies and which are not taken into account by private capital owners; the contribution of capital flows to GDP through its inducement of changes in the scale of operation of individual firms and its contribution to welfare through an inducement of changes in the number of varieties supplied to consumers. This finding has a clear policy implication — it calls for an intervention to prevent harmful capital flows by bringing the private return on foreign investment in line with the social return, with the social return being the one derived in our cost–benefit analysis.

Although this paper deals with capital movements, the issue that is raised in it is much broader; the issue is really that in economies with increasing returns and a monopolistic market structure — even if it is perfect competition according to Lancaster's (1979) terminology — private valuations of productive resources do not coincide with social valuations. We have, for example, already indicated in the main text that in such economies the contribution of a factor of production to GDP may be negative and that capital accumulation may bring about a decline in welfare. However, given the market structure, one can use our techniques to compute appropriate shadow prices for policy evaluation purposes.

NOTES

*This paper is based on Seminar Paper No. 155, Institute for International Economic Studies, University of Stockholm. It was first published in *Journal of International Economics*, 1983, and is reprinted here by kind permission of North-Holland Publishing Company.
1.   This function is implicitly defined by $F(xL_X/X, xK_X/X) = x$, where $F(\cdot)$

is the single firm's production function and (L_X, K_X) are employment levels in industry X.
2.   This can be easily verified by logarithmic differentiation of $(8.3')$–$(8.6')$.

REFERENCES

Helpman, E. (1981), 'International Trade in the Presence of Product Differentiation, Economies of Scale and Monopolistic Competition: a Chamberlin-Heckscher-Ohlin approach', *Journal of International Economies* 11, 305–40.

Helpman, E. (1984), 'Increasing Returns, Imperfect Markets and Trade Theory', Ch. 7 in R. W. Jones and P. B. Kenen (eds.), *Handbook of International Economics* (Amsterdam: North-Holland Publishing Company).

Helpman, E. and Razin, A. (1980), 'Monopolistic Competition and Factor Movements', Seminar Paper No. 155, Institute for International Economic Studies, University of Stockholm.

Jones, R. W. (1965), 'The Structure of Simple General Equilibrium Models', *Journal of Political Economy* 73, 557–72.

Jones, R. W. (1967), 'International Capital Movements and the Theory of Tariffs and Trade', *Quarterly Journal of Economics* 81, 1–38.

Lancaster, K. (1979), *Variety, Equity and Efficiency* (New York: Columbia University Press).

Lancaster, K. (1980), 'Intra-industry Trade under Perfect Monopolistic Competition', *Journal of International Economics* 10, 151–75.

Varian, H. R. (1978), *Microeconomic Analysis* (New York: Norton).

9

Protection and Product Differentiation*

Kelvin Lancaster

This paper is devoted to some initial exploration of the relationship between protection, product differentiation, and product variety — in particular, the way in which the degree of product differentiation or variety is changed by tariffs or other protective measures.

Note that a distinction is being made here between product differentiation and product variety, a distinction that is not usually drawn. The reason is that, in a trade context, we need to keep track of two measures involving numbers of products: the number of products produced by the industry in a particular country, and the number of products available to the consumers in that country. The two numbers are the same in an isolated economy, but obviously need not be the same when there is trade. Since the term 'product differentiation' is an active term, it will be used to denote the number of distinct products produced by the relevant industry, a number that is the result of active decision-making by its existing and potential member firms. The passive term 'product variety' will be used to describe the number of different products available to the consumers in a given country.

A study of the effect of protection on product differentiation and/or product variety presumes, of course, that the degree of product differentiation is endogenously determined and in such a way as to be potentially capable of being affected by trade restrictions. Some models of monopolistic competition and product differentiation used in the growing recent work on trade in differentiated products have been simplified to answer questions of a different kind, and are not suitable for use here. Differentiated-product trade models by Dixit and Norman (1980), Helpman (1981), and Krugman (1979, 1980), for example are so structured that the number of different products produced in each country is predetermined by the parameters of the system. Trade increases the degree of product variety because the number of products available in the world is the sum of the number produced in each country (no two firms will produce the same product, so there is no duplication after trade), and costless free trade makes all of these available in every country. Indeed, since outputs are constant and there are no increased scale economies, the gains from trade in the Krugman and Dixit–Norman models are due to the increased product variety, the utility functions being structured so that $1/n$ units of each of n goods gives more utility than $1/(n-1)$ units of each $(n-1)$ goods. Neither the degree of product differentiation nor the degree of product variety is affected by the level of protection —

the number of products produced by the local industry is always the same, whether there is trade or not, and the number of products available to the consumer is always the same (the world total) so long as there is *any* trade, although the products will not all be available on equal terms.

THE MODEL

The context in which the effect of protection on variety will be examined here is a version of the model of monopolistic competition which was developed earlier by the author.[1] This model resembles other analyses of monopolistic competition modified for the investigation of problems in international trade in that it is based on a two-sector economy, the output of one sector being a single homogeneous numeraire good produced under constant returns to scale and that of the other being a heterogeneous mix of product differentiates each of which is produced under some kind of economies of scale. The product-differentiated sector is modelled in the neo-Hotelling tradition, that is, the degree of substitutability between any two products is related to some measure of the distance between them in a space of product characteristics. Such an approach might be contrasted with the neo-Chamberlinian approach of such a model as that of Dixit and Stiglitz (1977), in which all goods are equal substitutes for one another and the degree of substitutability is a parameter of the system, not one of the endogenous variables.

Consumers are assumed to have separable utility functions, with one subutility a function of the amount of the homogeneous good, and the other a function of the amount and characteristics of the differentiated product. There are assumed to be only two relevant characteristics for the differentiated product, so that its characteristics specification can be defined along a one-dimensional spectrum. Each consumer has some point on the spectrum which is his 'most preferred specification', the particular way in which he would choose to have the characteristics combined if he were ordering the product custom-made. The consumer has also a 'compensating function', $h(v)$, where v is the distance along the spectrum between his most preferred specification and the specification of some good actually available, such that he would be indifferent between the available good at price P and his most preferred good at price $h(v)P$. Obviously, $h(v)$ is an increasing function of v and $h(0) = 1$.

The utility function is formulated in constant elasticity of substitution form as

$$U(q, v, y) = [\alpha q^\rho h(v)^{-\rho} + (1 - \alpha)y^\rho]^{1/\rho}, \qquad (9.1)$$

where q is the quantity of the differentiated good available, v the distance between its specification and the most preferred specification of the consumer, and y is the quantity of the homogeneous numeraire good. The individual's demand function for the given product differentiate can easily be shown to be

$$q(P, v, I) = \frac{I}{[1 + Ah(v)^{\sigma-1}P^{\sigma-1}]P},\qquad(9.2)$$

where σ $(= 1/(1 - \rho))$ is the elasticity of substitution.[2] P the price of the differentiated product in terms of the homogeneous product, and I the income in units of homogeneous good.

The economy is taken to be populated with individuals whose preferences are identical except as to their most preferred specifications, and these preferences to possess a uniformity such that individual demand is, as it is written above, a function of price, income and the *relative* specifications of the consumer's most preferred good and the available good, and independent of the *absolute* position on the spectrum. The population distribution is taken to be such that most preferred specifications are distributed continuously over the spectrum with constant density, and income is assumed to be distributed uniformly.

Since we shall be confining our attention to cases in which there are some economies of scale in the differentiated industry, the number of goods actually produced will be finite. These goods will each be defined by the position of their product specification on the spectrum. In general, a consumer will not find his most preferred specification among those of the goods actually available, and he must choose one of the latter. There will be two goods which are closest to his most preferred, one in each direction along the spectrum. If the goods sell at prices P, P' and are situated at distances v, v', the consumer will choose the unprimed good if $h(v)P < h(v')P'$ and the primed good if the inequality is reversed.

Aggregate market demand for a good selling at price P, with the next good on the spectrum at distance D and selling at price P' in one direction, and at distance D' and price P'' in the other, is determined in the following way:

(i) The total market for the good is made up of two half-markets, one in each direction. The half-markets are determined independently, so we can confine our attention to one only.

(ii) The half-market is made up of all the individuals who choose the target good rather than the neighbouring one, that is, all individuals with most preferred specifications out to a distance u, where u satisfies the *dividing condition*:

$$h(u)P = h(D - u)P'.\qquad(9.3)$$

(iii) Each of the individuals in the market has a demand for the product given by the expression (9.2) set out previously, which is a function of v, the individual's spectral position relative to that of the good. Thus the aggregate demand in the half-market is a function of P, P', and D and given by

$$Q(P, P', D) = \int_0^u q(P, v)\, dv,\qquad(9.4)$$

where $u = u(P, P', D)$ is given by the dividing condition (9.3) above.

The demand function has the following properties which are relevant to the later analysis:

(i) Using subscripts to represent partial derivatives:

$$Q_D < 0, \quad Q_{P'} > 0, \quad Q_D > 0,$$

as expected.

(ii) The elasticity of demand $E(P, P', D)$ is not a constant as in some other models of monopolistic competition,[3] but is a variable. Changes in the elasticity (and thus in the ratio of price to marginal revenue) form an important mechanism in attaining equilibrium. The properties of the elasticity function are given by:

$$E_P > 0, \quad E_{P'} < 0, \quad E_D < 0.$$

In particular, $E \to \infty$ as $D \to 0$ — goods become perfect substitutes as their specifications converge.

On the production side, firms are assumed to have the same cost functions for all specifications within the product-differentiated industry. For simplicity this cost function is taken to be determined by a constant marginal cost plus a fixed cost.

In order to provide numerical results with which to back up the various stories which will be given to describe the effects of protection on product differentiation and variety, a special model is used which satisfies all the assumptions of the more general analysis. To obtain this specific model, details of which are given in the Appendix, (a) the compensating function was assumed to have the quadratic form[4] $h(v) = 1 + v^2$, and (b) the elasticity of substitution in (9.2) was taken to have the value $\sigma = 2$. In addition, numerical values were chosen for the marginal and fixed costs in production and for the constant A in expression (9.2). The particular form chosen for the compensating function not only satisfies all the criteria, but permits integration of the demand function (9.4), to give:

$$Q(P, P', D) = \frac{k}{4P^2} \arctan \frac{2P^{1/2}[P'(PP'D^2 - (P-P')^2)^{1/2} - P'D]}{(P-P')(1+4P)^{1/2}} \quad (9.5)$$

with an explicit, but complicated expression, for the elasticity $E(P, P', D)$, details of which are given in the Appendix. Unfortunately, although explicit expressions for Q, E can be found, solutions of the various equilibrium equations can only be found by numerical methods.

THE REFERENCE SITUATION

Consider first an isolated economy with an industry group conforming to the model as detailed. Within the product-differentiated industry, each firm has two variables at its disposal, the specification of its product (the mix of characteristics) and the price of the product. Assuming perfect information, costless adjustments, free and willing entry, and no collusion, the equilibrium of the product-differentiated industry will be taken to be the zero-profit Nàsh equilibrium in which each firm takes the specification and price of the other firms as given. The equilibrium will, of course, be such that marginal cost and marginal revenue are equal for each firm and that price and average cost are also equal. A zero-profit Nash equilibrium will not necessarily exist,[5] but it does exist under the conditions of the model being used here – in particular, because of the uniform distribution of consumers over the spectrum and the assumed absence of boundary effects. With this uniformity of distribution and the assumed uniformity of preferences, the demand conditions for any product depend only prices and the *relative* positions of goods on the spectrum, but not on *absolute* spectral locations. Thus the Nash equilibrium is such that the equilibrium values for the individual firms (price, quantity, profit) will be identical except for specification, and furthermore, that the specifications of the various goods produced will be evenly spaced along the spectrum.

The above equilibrium is fully characterized by the price, output, and profit for any one firm, since these will be the same for all firms, and by the spacing between adjacent goods along the spectrum. In fact, only two values – price and spacing – are sufficient for a specific model, the remaining values being derivative. We shall normally use the inverse of the spacing, defined as the degree of product differentiation or degree of product variety (according as whether the spacing is that between products produced in the country, or all products available), rather than the inter-good spacing itself. For the specific model used for illustration in this paper, the equilibrium solution values can be obtained by numerical methods. Since the absolute numbers have meaning only relative to the arbitrarily chosen units of the model, they will be utilized only for reference in discussing what happens to the same economy under different trade regimes. Thus we shall give equilibrium values for all the variables (prices, quantities, degree of product differentiation) as indexes to base 100 relative to the solution values for the reference situation, which we shall take initially to be the economy in isolation.

Now consider costless free trade between two identical economies, each exactly like the economy described above. Since there are no comparative advantage effects, there will be no trade in the homogeneous outside good even if it is tradeable (and not leisure, for example). Trade will consist solely of differentiated products, each country producing half the total number of different goods and supplying consumers in both countries. Under free trade with zero transport costs and identical cost and demand conditions at home and abroad, the equilibrium values for the representative firm will be the same as those for a firm in a single isolated country having twice the population density of the country used as reference.

What should our expectations be as to the relationship between the equilibrium in isolation and the configuration resulting from free trade? The initial effect of opening trade between absolutely identical countries will be that there are now two firms producing each product, so we can expect one of the two firms to be forced out.[6] The main difference from the pre-trade situation will then be in the quantity produced by each firm, since it is the expanded market open to the single surviving firm that provides the driving force toward the new equilibrium as well as much of the gains from trade. But we would not generally expect that the trade solution would simply be one in which the number of products remained the same as before, with the number of firms in each country halved but their outputs doubled. Consider an initial post-trade situation in which half the original firms in each country have left the industry and each surviving firm has a market of double the size but with other parameters (in particular, elasticity of demand) unchanged.[7] At the original price the firm can sell twice the quantity at the same marginal revenue as before, which will still equal the marginal cost (this having been assumed constant). But average cost is declining with output, so that these firms will be making positive profits and thus new firms will enter and the number of products will increase.

TABLE 9.1. *The effects of trade*

	Autarchy	Free trade (intermediate)	Free trade (final)
Price (local good)	100	100	93.3
Price (import)	–	100	99.4
Product variety	100	100	159.7
Number of local firms	100	50	79.9
Output per firm	100	200	138.4
Excess profit	0	101	0

Thus the free trade equilibrium, when fully established, can be expected to be such that each country has more than half the number of firms that existed in isolation, but necessarily less than the original number. Price will be lower after trade, since it is equal to average cost which will certainly have fallen. Table 9.1 shows the actual solution values for the model, relative to the autarchy values, and the expectations are seen to be fulfilled. The centre column labelled 'inter-mediate' refers to the situation after the first impact (when one of the two firms producing each product is assumed to be forced out), but before the new round of entries and changes in products. Note that this intermediate situation is put in for reference only – a real scenario might never include such a stage, since firms may commence by varying their products immediately after the opening of trade rather than competing head-on by price wars, exits, then some re-entries. The figure 'excess profit' is the percentage by which the excess of revenue over variable cost exceeds the fixed cost.

Note that free trade *increases* the degree of product variety available to consumers, although it *reduces* the degree of product differentiation in each country. The gains from trade come partly from the greater degree of product variety and partly from the lower-price per product. When there is variable product specification, trade improves the distribution of welfare as well as its average level, since greater variety means more consumers can find a good closer to their most preferred specification.

SYMMETRIC TRADE RESTRICTIONS

To consider the effect of tariffs and protection on product differentiation, let us commence with the simplest case to analyse, that of the completely symmetric case in which two identical countries impose identical non-prohibitive tariffs on each others' imports.

Before proceeding further, however, we need to consider the effect of different simplifying assumptions concerning the relative arrangement of goods on the spectrum in the two countries. As in the free trade case, the final equilibrium will be such that each country will produce half the total number of different goods. In the free trade case, however, it did not matter which goods were produced in which country since the equilibrium configurations were the same in all markets. In this case, it is obvious that the equilibrium configuration for a home good will be different from that for an import because of the effects of trade restrictions. Since the equilibrium for a single market depends on the equilibria in the adjacent markets, the world equilibrium will depend on the arrangement of goods. For example, consider two different arrangements which are both symmetrical:[8]

(i) in which the products of the two countries alternate in specification as we move along the spectrum, so that every home good has an imported good as its immediate neighbour on each side. (There is a Japanese car closely similar to every American car.)

(ii) in which one country makes all the goods on the right half of the spectrum and the other makes all those on the left. (Japan makes all the small cars and the United States all the large cars, for example.)

We shall refer to (i) as the 'Interleaved Case', (ii) as the 'Split Case'. The two cases will lead to quite different world equilibria, since each market is surrounded by dissimilar markets in the interleaved case (home goods surrounded by imports, and imports by home goods) and by similar goods (home goods surrounded by other home goods, imports by other imports) in the split case. If we ignore the boundary effects in the split case, both cases can give simple symmetric solutions defined by two equilibria, one for the home market which will apply to all home markets in both countries, and one for the export market which will also apply universally. In both cases, the solution will be such that:

(i) the number of firms is the same in each country, each firm selling in both the local and export markets;

(ii) the price, quantity, and elasticity of demand are the same for foreign sales at home as for home sales abroad;

(iii) the price, quantity, and elasticity of demand are the same in the local markets of both the home and foreign producers; and

(iv) total sales and total profits (from combined local sales and exports) are the same for all firms in both countries.

Consider first the interleaved case. Denote the constant marginal cost assumed in the model by m and the revenue, marginal revenue, and price in the market for the home good by R, MR, and P respectively. Primes will denote equivalent values for the market for imports. Denote the distance between adjacent goods by D, which will be constant along the spectrum because of the assumption that home and foreign goods alternate.

In any of the home markets, the demand conditions and thus the marginal revenue will be determined by the product price (P), the price of adjacent goods (P', the same in both directions), and the inter-good distance (D in both direction). The same will be true of the market for imports, with the roles of P, P' interchanged. Thus we can write the net revenues (revenue less variable cost – linear in quantity and thus assignable between markets) from home sales and from exports as $NR(P, P', D)$, respectively, with the same relationships between functions and arguments for MR, MR'. The profit $\Pi(P, P', D)$ is given by

$$\Pi(P, P', D) = NR(P, P', D) + NR'(P', P, D) - FC \qquad (9.6)$$

where FC is the fixed cost.

If we take the tariff to be a specific one of value t, then the Nash equilibrium for the system, given the number of firms (and thus the value of D), will be the solution to the pair of equations:

$$MR(P, P', D) = m$$
$$MR'(P', P, D) = m + t \qquad (9.7)$$

provided the non-arbitrage condition

$$P' \leq P + t$$

is satisfied. The profit Π then becomes a function of D only, with the equilibrium value of D found by the condition $\Pi = 0$.

For the split case, the home market has other home markets adjacent to it, so that the net and marginal revenues are functions of P and D alone. Similarly the net and marginal revenues in the import markets are functions of P', D alone. Thus the Nash equilibria for the home and import markets are determined independently, given D (which must be the same for both types of markets since every good is solid in a home market in one country and an import market in the other), the system being as follows:

$$MR(P, D) = m$$

$$MR'(P', D) = m + t$$

$$\Pi(P, P', D) = 0. \tag{9.8}$$

Although it will be argued later that the interleaved case represents the final equilibrium situation in a world of full information and costless adjustment, the split case has a more clear-cut solution, and will be analysed first. Suppose, in particular, that the free trade equilibrium happened to result in this configuration and then consider the effect of adding the specific tariff t, a move reciprocated by the other country. Take the short-term temporary equilibrium to be that in which no firms have yet entered or exited following the trade restrictions, but each firm sells in the home and export markets at prices which equate marginal revenue and marginal cost (including tariff, where relevant). The Nash equilibrium for the home markets will be unchanged, since marginal revenue is independent of the import market price, the spacing between adjacent goods has not yet changed, and marginal cost is unchanged. Thus the home market price will be the same as under free trade and the profit on the home market will be unchanged. But the profit on export sales will necessarily fall because of the tariff, so that total profit will fall (to less than zero) and firms will exit. Thus the final equilibrium will be with fewer firms (and products) than under free trade. The price of the home product will be slightly higher (since reducing the number of home goods will lower the elasticity of demand for each and increase the mark-up of price over marginal cost), and the price of the import considerably higher because of the same effect plus the tariff effect. The story is illustrated, for the model being used, in Table 9.2. Note that the reference situation is now the free trade equilibrium.

TABLE 9.2. *The split case*

	Free trade	Restricted trade	
		(intermediate)	(final)
Price (local good)	100	100	100.7
Price (import)	100	119.4	119.9
Product variety	100	100	98.0
Number of firms	100	100	98.0
Excess profit	0	− 4.4	0

In this case, as in all the symmetric cases, the degree of product differentiation (number of local firms) will always be half the number of different goods, as with free trade. Thus the degree of product variety and the number of firms will always stand in the same relationship to their free trade levels, and only the degree of product variety need be traced.

There are no ambiguities in the solution of the split case, since profit per firm will necessarily fall when a tariff is imposed and the number of firms (and thus of products) will be reduced. Formal comparative static analysis can be used to show that the sign of dD/dt is unambiguously positive.

The interleaved case is more complex, since the home and import markets are adjacent and intimately related instead of being separable. Assume that the initial free trade structure is one of alternating home and imported goods, then consider the effect of equal specific tariffs introduced by the two countries. The very first effect will be that the firms will be out of equilibrium in their export markets, the marginal cost of selling in which has risen by the amount of the tariff, so the export price will be raised. From the point of view of the other country, the (consumer) price of imports will rise — but import and home markets are adjacent on the spectrum so that there will be substitution in favour of home goods. Since this is happening in all markets in both countries, the price of home goods will rise. In the initial stage (with the same firms as under free trade) the price of both home and imported goods will rise. It is clear that the firms will each make less profit on their exports, but more profit on their home sales, than in the free trade position. Does this mean that firms gain or lose from the tariff? In the specific model being used here, the firms gain — increased home market profits outweigh decreased export market profits, as shown by the figures in the centre column of Table 9.3.

TABLE 9.3. *The interleaved case*

	Free trade	Restricted trade	
		(intermediate)	(final)
Price (local good)	100	105.2	103
Price (import)	100	112.6	110.3
Product variety	100	100	112.6
Excess profit	0	23.3	0
Home firms' share of market	50%	74.9%	81.2%

As the table shows, the pre-entry pre-exit effect of the tariff is to give positive profits to the existing firms. These profits will then induce entry so that the number of firms (and the number of products) is larger with protection than with tariffs. This is the opposite result from that found in the split case. There is a perfectly reasonable explanation for the existence of positive profits at the intermediate stage of the interleaved case (as compared with the negative profits in the split case): since the immediate competitors for every home good are imports in the interleaved case, protection reduces that competition and increases the monopoly power and thus the profits in the home market. Although the effect of the tariff is necessarily to reduce profits in the export market, this loss can be outweighed by the home market gains. In the split case, on the other hand, the immediate competitors of home goods are other home goods, so that protection brings no home market gains from increased monopoly power to outweigh reduced export profits.

The increased degree of product variety may seem paradoxical when restricted trade is compared with autarchy and with free trade. Since the equilibrium number of products is less under autarchy than under free trade, it might seem that restricted trade should give an intermediate result — fewer products than with free trade but more than in isolation — rather than a result in the opposite direction from autarchy. The outcome is less paradoxical, however, when it is noted that the number of *firms* (degree of product differentiation) does have this intermediate property, being 13 per cent more than under free trade but 10 per cent fewer than in isolation.

While the number of firms converges to the autarchy level as the tariff converges to the prohibitive level, the degree of variety shows a discontinuity. What happens is as follows: the higher the tariff, the smaller the import sales (home sales are 81 per cent for the model) so that, although the number of products available to consumers is twice the number produced at home, the half that are imported have very small markets because of the high price due to the tariff. As the tariff approaches the prohibitive level, the number of firms approaches the autarchy level while the product variety approaches twice the autarchy level, but with half the products having minute sales. At the prohibitive tariff, these minute sales become zero and the number of goods available in either country collapses to the autarchy value.[9]

The effect of protection on product differentiation and product variety depends, as shown above, on the relationship between arrangements of products on the spectrum in the two countries. In the split case, the degree of product differentiation falls as a result of tariffs; in the interleaved case, it rises. But the arrangement of the goods on the spectrum could itself be endogenously determined, and if so, there should be a clear choice between the two cases. There has been some considerable recent study of the problems of predicting patterns from entry in spatial and quasi-spatial models of competition, and the subject is a difficult one.[10] One criterion that has considerable merit is to assume that a final equilibrium will be that configuration which contains the largest number of firms possible that can all be sustained without loss, a kind of 'minimum entropy' property. For any other zero-profit configuration, there is some reorganization of the firms and product specifications such that at least one firm can make a positive profit. The author has referred elsewhere to the possibility of 'innovative entry' which can arise in such a case,[11] so that the long-run full-information, full-flexibility equilibrium should be such that no innovative entry is possible. As between the split and interleaved case, only the interleaved case possesses this property, since there are clearly profits to be made by rearrangement from the split configuration.

Thus the conclusion for the case of symmetric tariff protection is that the interleaved case is the appropriate one, and thus that protection leads to *increased* product differentiation and product variety, at least in this specific model. The generality of this result will be considered later.

It should be noted that protection has distributional effects (meaning distribution with respect to a consumer's location on the spectrum) resulting from the change in the product mix which will tend to pull in two different directions:

(i) In so far as there is an increase in the degree of product variety, distribution is more even — the average distance between consumers' most-preferred goods and the goods actually provided by the market is reduced.

(ii) Because of the direct effect of the tariff, however, consumers whose most-preferred goods are close in specification to the imported good will be worse off (higher prices) relative to consumers close to the home products, making the distribution less even.

In the split case, or in any circumstances in which the degree of product variety is reduced by the tariff, the distributional effects will all be in the direction of increasing the unevenness of the welfare distribution.

ASYMMETRIC PROTECTION

In order to study the effects of unilateral tariff protection, we shall change the context somewhat from the above symmetrical case to that of a small country in a large world. We will assume that the home country does not export the product-differentiated industry's output, but that there is an industry abroad which does sell products of this group in the home market. The industry abroad has the same marginal cost as the home industry[12] (but not necessarily the same fixed costs), and it reacts passively to home country tariffs.

Take the initial situation to be that in which there is no tariff, the home market being shared equally between home goods and imports,[13] where this is taken to mean that home and foreign products alternate on the spectrum and sell at the same prices. For the model under consideration, this implies an equilibrium at the same values as autarchy except that only half the goods are produced by the home firms. Measurements of the properties of other situations will be taken with reference to this situation as base.

Now consider the effect of a tariff which, for convenience, we will take to be a specific tariff of level t, as in the analysis of the symmetric cases. Since the foreign supplier has the same marginal cost (m) as the domestic industry, the effect of the tariff on the foreign firms is to make their effective marginal cost equal to $m + t$ for sales in the home market. The effect of the tariff will be a consequence of the foreign firms' adjustment to equate marginal revenue in the home market with the new marginal cost in that market. Since the pre-tariff marginal revenue is less than the new marginal cost, the initial post-tariff change will a rise in the price of the foreign good on the home market. The market widths for imports will fall as some consumers with most-preferred specifications lying in between the domestic and foreign goods shift from the latter to the relatively cheaper domestic products. But the expanded size of the market for the home goods will reduce their elasticity of demand and the price of domestic goods will rise to re-equate marginal revenue with marginal cost. Both prices will rise, but the foreign price more (since the foreign material cost has risen relative to the domestic), and the sales of the foreign models will drop while those of the domestic models will expand. Since both price and quantity of the domestic model increase, zero profits change into positive profits. With the specifications of goods unchanged, the post-tariff, pre-entry equilibrium will be related to the pre-tariff situation as shown in the centre column of Table 9.4. As before, the values given are those for the numerical solution of the specific model being used to illustrate the events.

Table 9.4. *The asymmetric case*

	Free trade	Post-tariff	
		Pre-entry	Post-entry
Price (local good)	100	104.2	97.6
Price (import)	100	112.5	104.6
Product differentiation	100	100	129.2
Excess profit	0	44	0
Home firms' share of market	50	67.1	73.4

The existence of positive profits will attract new domestic firms. We will assume that the rest of the world is large, so that foreign firms will continue to sell in the home market so long as revenue more than covers variable cost plus tariffs. Somewhat more heroically, we shall also assume that the imports remain interleaved with the home goods. Since the spacing between the home firms will change as a result of new entry, this implies that the specifications of imports also change – even though it is being assumed that the country is too small to cause restructuring of foreign industry. Such a situation might arise when (a) the rest of the world is very large and produces a wide range of products and (b) the only kinds of these products that will be imported are those having specifications midway between those of home goods, since these will always be the most profitable.

As a result of entry, there is an increase in the degree of product differentiation and product variety. Since the goods are now closer to each other on the spectrum, the elasticity of demand rises so that price moves closer to marginal cost in the home good market, and closer to marginal cost plus tariff in the import market. Thus the prices of both local goods and imports will fall relative to the post-tariff, pre-entry stage, and the price of home goods will be less than under free trade.

The final equilibrium, as shown in the last column of Table 9.4 above, has the following characteristics:

(i) The degree of product differentiation and product variety is increased by the tariff, as in the symmetric case.

(ii) The price of the home good is pushed *down* as a result of protection. It may seem paradoxical that there are more firms selling at a lower price than before while profit per firm remains the same as before the tariff (zero). However, although the firms are closer together, their markets are actually wider because the foreign firms' market areas have been reduced by their relatively higher prices due to the tariff. In the model analysed, it can be shown that, although there are 29.2 per cent more firms, the output per firm is 14.5 per cent higher than before the tariff. The larger output means lower average cost and thus a lower price at which profit is zero.

Although tariffs could be used in the small country case to lower the price of local goods, the prices of imports necessarily rise. The rise in import prices is less than the tariff, however, since price is closer to marginal revenue than under free trade and marginal revenue in the import market has risen by only the amount of the tariff.[14] Thus, if the tariff revenues were returned to the purchasers of imports (in such a way as still left them treating the market price as the relevant decision variable), the purchasers of both home goods and imports would be better off as a result of the tariff. In addition, there is a gain due to the increased product variety.

Thus a small country which is powerless to gain from tariffs under conditions of perfect competition, can gain from protection under monopolistic competition. This gain occurs only if the imports are closely related to the home goods, as in the assumed interleaved relationship above. Had the relationship between imports and home goods been like the split case studied earlier, there would be no interactions and no gains from the tariff.

HOW GENERAL ARE THE RESULTS?

The analysis which has been given has consisted of plausible stories backed up by the results generated for a specific (if highly representative) model. To obtain some idea of the extent to which these results can be generalized, it is necessary to look at the formal comparative statics, commencing with the symmetric case. Starting from a zero-profit equilibrium, increased profit per firm will lead to new entry and decreased profit to exits, so it is sufficient to fix the number of firms and examine the effect of the tariff on profit levels — the rest of the story then follows.

Define $NR(P, P')$ as the 'net revenue' or revenue less assigned variable cost from home market sales, and $NR'(P', P)$ as the net revenue from export sales, given by:

$$NR(P, P') = (P - m)Q(P, P') \qquad (9.9a)$$

$$NR'(P', P) = (P' - m - t)Q'(P', P). \qquad (9.9b)$$

Since the firms will choose P to maximize NR and P' to maximize NR', the first order conditions for maximization will take the form

$$NR_1 = Q + (P - m)Q_1 \qquad (9.10a)$$

$$NR'_1 = Q' + (P' - m - t)Q'_1 \qquad (9.10b)$$

where subscript 1 indicates the partial derivative with respect to the own price. Subscript 2, used below, will indicate cross-price derivatives. The effect of a small tariff change on the equilibrium position will be:

$$\frac{dP}{dt} = -\frac{Q'_1 NR_{12}}{NR_{11}NR'_{11} - NR_{12}NR'_{12}} \qquad (9.11a)$$

$$\frac{dP'}{dt} = \frac{Q'_1 NR_{11}}{NR_{11}NR'_{11} - NR_{12}NR'_{12}}. \qquad (9.11b)$$

The denominator in (9.11a) and (9.11b) is positive if the direct effects outweigh the cross effects, a standard condition for stability of equilibrium which will be assumed to hold here. Since $NR_{11} < 0$ is also a stability condition and Q'_1 is essentially negative, we have $dP'/dt > 0$ unambiguously — the unsurprising result that the consumer price of the imported good will rise as a result of the tariff.

The effect of the tariff on the equilibrium price of the home good is less certain, since it depends on the sign of the cross effect NR_{12}. Noting that $NR = (P - m)Q(P, P')$, we have

$$NR_{12} = Q_2 + (P - m)Q_{12}, \qquad (9.12)$$

where $Q_2 \geq 0$ and, in general, $Q_{12} < 0$, so that NR_{12} may have any sign, as may dP/dt in consequence. If the cross effects vanish, then $dP/dt = 0$, of course.

With the number of firms fixed, the profit per firm is the sum of the net revenues from the home and foreign markets less the fixed cost:

$$\Pi(P, P') = NR(P, P') + NR'(P', P) - FC$$

so that

$$\frac{d\Pi}{dt} = NR_1 \frac{dP}{dt} + NR_2 \frac{dP'}{dt} + NR'_1 \frac{dP'}{dt} + NR'_2 \frac{dP}{dt} + \frac{\partial NR'}{\partial t}$$

$$= NR_2 \frac{dP'}{dt} + NR'_2 \frac{dP}{dt} - Q' \qquad (9.13)$$

since NR_1, $NR'_1 = 0$ (P, P' being the net revenue maximizing prices in the home and foreign markets) and $\partial NR'/\partial t = -Q'$.

If the cross effects are zero, so that NR_2, NR'_2 vanish, then profits necessarily fall when the tariff is increased, so that the new final equilibrium will have fewer firms than before the tariff rose. This corresponds to the 'split case' of the previous discussions. If the cross effects are not zero, however, then the effect of the tariff on profit is no longer unambiguous since NR_2, NR'_2, dP'/dt are all positive, $-Q'$ is negative, and dP/dt can be positive or negative.

Thus, although the result given previously, that profits initially rise from the effect of the tariff in the 'interleaved' case, is certainly true for the specific model analysed, and the model itself has features that would be generally accepted as representative, the result cannot be regarded as truly general. It seems possible that tariffs might reduce the degree of product variety for some functional forms and some parameter values.

In the asymmetric case, the circumstances set out had certain special features, an important one of which was that the home-produced goods were not sold abroad. As a result, the increased monopoly power in the home market due to the tariff on imports gave a relatively large increase in profits. The larger the proportion of the home good sold abroad, the smaller the effect on profits due to this effect and thus the less the increase in the degree of product differentiation. Thus the no-export assumption gives a much stronger effect than when there are exports, and might thus be regarded as a special case.

CONCLUSIONS

It has been shown in this paper that, when there is monopolistic competition and a product-differentiated industry which operates in both trading partners, the degree of product differentiation (number of different products produced by the home industry) and the degree of product variety (number of different products available to the home consumers) are both affected by the existence and level of intra-industry trade, and both will, in general, be changed by protection.

Although trade increases the degree of product variety, trade restrictions do not necessarily reduce it. On the contrary, in both the large-country case (symmetric trade between two identical countries) and the small-country case (where the rest of the world does not react), the degree of product variety is *increased* as a result of the imposition of tariffs, at least for the specific model studied.

The reason for this result is basically the same in both the small- and large-country cases. With intra-industry trade in a monopolistic competition setting, imports are close but imperfect substitutes for home goods. Tariffs lower their competitiveness, so that the local firms have more monopoly power (lower elasticity of demand) and their profits rise. But excess profits then induce entry and thus more firms and more products.

Because of the inter-active but imperfectly competitive markets for home products and imports, a small country which imports goods in the same product-differentiated group as it makes locally can *gain* by imposing a tariff, something impossible with perfectly competitive markets. This possibility exists only when there are imports which are relatively close substitutes for local goods.

APPENDIX

This appendix sets out the features and properties of the special model on which the numerical solutions given in the text are based. The model conforms in all respects to the general model analysed in Lancaster (1979), but has specific functional forms for the compensating function of the consumer and the cost functions of firms, as well as specific numerical values for the system parameters. The compensating function has the specific form:

$$h(v) = 1 + v^2. \tag{9.A1}$$

On the basis of this compensating function, a consumer whose most preferred good is at distance u from the available good will be indifferent between buying that good and the adjacent available good (at distance D from the first available good) when the price of the target good (P) and that of the adjacent good (P') are related as follows:

$$P = P' \frac{1 + (D - u)^2}{1 + u^2}. \tag{9.A2}$$

For the above compensating function and the assumed value of the elasticity of substitution ($\sigma = 2$), the demand function for the individual at distance v from the available good has the form:

$$q(P, v) = \frac{1}{P[1 + AP(1 + v^2)]}, \tag{9.A3}$$

where A is a constant expressing the importance of the group good in the total utility function. The value $A = 4$ will be assumed for all the succeeding analysis, a convenient number that implies expenditure on the product differentiated group is 20 per cent of total expenditure when $P = 1$, that is, when the price of the group good is equal to that of the homogeneous outside good used as numeraire. It is convenient to write (9.A3) in the form:

$$q(P, v) = \frac{k}{4P^2(a^2 + v^2)}, \tag{9.A4}$$

where $a^2 = (1 + 4P)/4P$ and is a function of P but not of v.

Note: q as used above is the per capita demand for an individual with unit income. It is also used for the total demand at a point, and for other income levels. In these cases, the basic q is multiplied by a factor k representing the population density and/or per capita income.

For a uniform density k, aggregate demand for a half-market of width u is given by:

$$Q(P, u) = k \int_0^u q(P, v)\, dv$$

$$= \frac{k}{4P^2} \int_0^u \frac{dv}{a^2 + v^2}$$

$$= \frac{k}{4P^2} \arctan \frac{u}{a}. \tag{9.A5}$$

Solving for u as a function of P, P', and D in (9.A2), we can obtain an explicit expression for Q as a function of P, P', and D. This expression (9.A5′) is reproduced in the main text as equation (9.5):

$$Q(P, P', D) = \frac{k}{4P^2} \arctan \frac{2P^{1/2}[P'(PP'D^2 - (P-P')^2)^{1/2} - P'D]}{(P-P')(1 + 4P)^{1/2}} \tag{9.A5′}$$

To determine the elasticity of demand E, we note that

$$\frac{dQ}{dP} = q(P, u) \frac{du}{dP} + \int_0^u \frac{\partial q(P, v)}{\partial P}\, dv. \tag{9.A6}$$

From the dividing condition (9.A2), the effect of P on u, given D and P', can be shown to be

$$\frac{du}{dP} = -\frac{1}{2} \frac{1 + u^2}{(P-P')u + P'D}. \tag{9.A7}$$

For an equilibrium configuration in the uniform case, goods are uniformly spaced along the spectrum and have the same prices, so that $P' = P$. Since adjacent goods have equal prices, the dividing consumer is at the midpoint between adjacent goods, so that $u = D/2$ and (9.A7) becomes

$$\frac{du}{dP} = -\frac{1}{P} \frac{D^2 + 4}{8D}. \tag{9.A8}$$

Differentiation of $q(P, v)$ from (9.A3) with respect to P gives:

$$\frac{\partial q}{\partial P} = -\frac{2k}{P^2} \frac{b^2 + v^2}{(a^2 + v^2)^2}, \tag{9.A9}$$

where $b^2 = 1 + 8P/8P$.

By direction integration of (9.A9) with respect to v we obtain

$$\int_0^u \frac{\partial q}{\partial P}\, dv = -\frac{1}{a^2 P^2} \left[\frac{(b^2 - a^2)u}{a^2 + u^2} + \frac{b^2 + a^2}{2a^3} \arctan \frac{u}{a} \right]. \tag{9.A10}$$

The elasticity $E(P, P', D) = -P\,dQ/Q\,dP$ can be obtained as an explicit but complicated expression by combining (9.A3), (9.A5′), (9.A6), (9.A7), and (9.A10). The elasticity properties given in the main text can be shown to hold by investigating these various components of E taken separately.

The numerical solutions used to illustrate the scenarios described in the text were based on the above demand model with k (the population–income density) put equal to 50 and a cost function for all firms with a marginal cost of 0.5

and a fixed cost of 3.0. The actual numerical solution values for key variables at different equilibrium configurations are given in the following tabulation:

Variable	Autarchy	Free trade	Symmetrical protection	Asymmetrical protection
P	0.625	0.573	0.59	0.61
P'	n.a.	0.573	0.632	0.654
D	0.535	0.394	0.35	0.414
Q_L	12.0	10.4	13.8	13.8
Q_I	–	10.4	3.2	5.0

where Q_L is the quantity of the home good sold on the local market, and Q_I is the quantity of imports sold locally – in the symmetric case, this is also equal to the export sales of the home firms.

NOTES

*The research incorporated in this paper was supported by the National Science Foundation, Grants SES 8025048 and SES 8208915.
1. Lancaster (1979, 1980).
2. The monopolistic competition equilibrium is stable only if $\sigma > 1$.
3. Dixit and Stiglitz (1977), for example.
4. The general quadratic form $1 + bv^2$ satisfies all the requirements of the compensating function, as shown in Lancaster (1979), Appendix A. The choice of b (= 1 here) sets the scale on the spectrum. When a good is at unit distance from the consumer's most preferred good, it is valued half as much as a unit of most-preferred good. This 'psychic' measure is valid in this model because of the assumption that consumers' preferences are identical in every way except for their choice of most-preferred good.
5. Preliminary studies by the author suggest that the analysis of monopolistic competition with non-uniform preference distributions may differ considerably from the analysis of the uniform case.
6. There are, of course, many scenarios for the process of attaining equilibrium. The one set out here is simple and illustrates the forces operating.
7. In the uniform density case with uniform preferences, increasing the density by a factor of k merely changes the marginal and average quantities by k, leaving all elasticity relationships unchanged.
8. There are, of course, many other arrangements, including many other symmetrical ones. The two chosen represent the most and the least inter-active structures.
9. It would be possible to devise some index of product variety that gives less weight to goods consumed in smaller quantities, and which converges to the autarchy level as the tariff reaches the prohibitive rate.
10. See, for example, Eaton and Lipsey (1976), Prescott and Visscher (1977).
11. Lancaster (1982).

12.   This is a gold standard world.
13.   There may be, in addition, a very large range of imported product differentiates which are on a portion of the spectrum where no home goods are produced – this is what we might expect when this is a very small country. It will be assumed that our interest is confined to the region in which home goods compete, and that tariffs are imposed only on goods in this region.
14.   The argument here would not hold completely if the marginal-cost curve were rising.

REFERENCES

Dixit, A. K. and Norman, V. (1980), *Theory of International Trade* (Cambridge, England: Cambridge University Press).

Dixit, A. K. and Stiglitz, J. E. (1977), 'Monopolistic Competition and Optimum Product Diversity', *American Economic Review*, 67, 297–308.

Eaton, B. C. and Lipsey, R. G. (1976), 'The Non-uniqueness of Equilibrium in the Loschian Location Model', *American Economic Review*, 66, 77–93.

Helpman, E. (1981), 'International Trade in the Presence of Product Differentiation, Economies of Scale and Monopolistic Competition: A Chamberlin-Heckscher-Ohlin Approach', *Journal of International Economics*, 11, 305–40.

Krugman, P. R. (1979), 'Increasing Returns, Monopolistic Competition, and International Trade', *Journal of International Economics*, 9, 858–64.

Krugman, P. R. (1980), 'Scale Economies, Product Differentiation, and the Pattern of Trade', *American Economic Review*, 70, 151–75.

Lancaster, K. (1979), *Variety, Equity and Efficiency* (New York: Columbia University Press).

Lancaster, K. (1980), 'Intra-Industry Trade under Perfect Monopolistic Competition', *Journal of International Economics*, 10, 151–75.

Lancaster, K. (1982), 'Innovative Entry: Profit Hidden beneath the Zero', *Journal of Industrial Economics*, 31, 41–56.

Prescott, E. C. and Visscher, M. (1977), 'Sequential Location among Firms with Foresight', *Bell Journal of Economics*, 8, 378–93.

10

The Pattern of International Trade in Differentiated Products: an Incentive for the Existence of Multinational Firms

Bruce R. Lyons

1. INTRODUCTION

Recent models of monopolistic competition have been able to establish why there may be a substantial amount of international, intra-industry trade between identical countries. These monopolistic models assume either that it is costless to alter product specifications,[1] or that all products in a market are equally good substitutes for one another.[2] Consequently, products enter until there are no pure (excess) profits. We relax both assumptions to find that profits can continue even in long-run equilibrium,[3] and suggest that this provides a rationale for the existence of multi-national firm (MNFs).

The incentive for MNFs derives from the fact that long-run profits are maximized only by producing a given range of products in more than one country. The pricing and specification of such products must also be co-ordinated, and this is best facilitated by internal organization, rather than external collusion. Whilst the empirical association between intra-industry trade and MNFs has often been noticed, it is sometimes implied that it is the practices of MNFs that 'cause' the increased trade. The argument of this paper is that, to the contrary, cost and demand factors can create the conditions for intra-industry trade, and that these conditions 'cause' MNFs to exist.

The basic structure of the model is as follows. Consumers are assumed to have differing tastes, which can be represented by a position along a line. A section of this *spectrum* of tastes, which follows in the tradition of Hotelling (1929) and Lancaster (1979), is shown in Fig. 10.1. For instance, consumers who favour sweet things may be best catered for by products to the left of the spectrum, whilst those who prefer bitter foods may be better satisfied towards the right. Product A is *geographically* located in country 1, and may sell to customers in country 2 only by paying positive *trading costs*, such as transport and tariffs. Products A and B are *psychically* separated by a distance Δ (as well as their production bases being geographically separated). A large Δ implies that A and B are very different, and a small Δ implies that they are

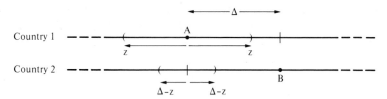

Fig. 10.1. The spectrum of tastes

Note: a dot —•— refers to the geographical location and the specification of a product; a straight dash —+— refers to a specification that is manufactured in another country; and curved brackets —(—•—)— represent the extent of a product's market area in each country.

similar. Thus, for a given length of spectrum, the smaller is Δ (the closer A and B are psychically spaced) the greater the degree of *product differentiation* in the industry, and the more variety is available to consumers.[4] Product spacing and product differentiation are thus inverse measures of the same thing, and will be used interchangeably. If product A attracts all consumers who lie within a psychic distance z on either side of its specification, it is said to have a *market area* (or width) of $2z$. It will be useful to refer to z as the *half-market area*.

Not every specification can be made because there are economies of scale in the production of each product. The equilibrium degree of product differentiation is shown to depend on the pricing behaviour of firms and the conditions faced by potential entrants. This paper concentrates on co-operative pricing since this may be expected to apply within MNFs.[5] If excess profits were to attract new entry, there would be little point in setting a co-operative price. However, if dies must be struck, tools set up, and/or a consumer image projected, it becomes costly to alter product specifications. It will be argued that the commitment of existing firms to such sunk costs is sufficient to deter entry, even by those who have access to the same cost curve as incumbents. Thus profits may persist in the long run and, along with trading costs, this provides the motivation for the existence of MNFs.

Section 2 sets out the assumptions of the model in greater detail, and Section 3 develops the autarky equilibrium. The equilibria for two (and many) countries are summarized in Section 4 and detailed in the Appendix. Section 5 investigates the conditions favouring the existence of MNFs. Following an analysis of international differences in size, tastes, tariffs, and efficiency, the conclusion includes a brief discussion of some welfare considerations.

2. ASSUMPTIONS OF THE MODEL

2.1. Demand

The differing blends of characteristics that a product may contain are represented by a line of infinite length,[6] along which consumers are evenly distributed with density, y per unit distance. Individuals have to consider both the price of a product, p, and the 'distance', x, it lies from their 'ideal' specification (combination of characteristics). All consumers are identical in that they have the same individual demand function,

$$q = f(p, x) \tag{10.1}$$

with $f_1 < 0$ and $f_2 < 0$.[7] Of course x, and therefore quantity demanded, varies between individuals unless all possible products are available. Consumers buy only that product whose price–distance combination yields the greatest utility. A consumer lying z away from a product priced p, and $\Delta - z$ away from a product priced $\hat{p}$, is indifferent between buying either product if and only if,

$$g(p, z) = g(\hat{p}, \Delta - z), \tag{10.2}$$

where, $g_1 > 0$ and $g_2 > 0$. $g(\ )$ is a more general form of what spatial economists often term the 'delivered price', $p + t(z)$. Lancaster (1979, p. 50) suggests $g = ph(z)$, where $h'(z) > 0$, $h''(z) > 0$, (e.g. $h(z) = 1 + z^2$) and h is termed the 'compensating function'.

2.2. Technology

There are economies of scale in the production of any one product, the total cost function being

$$C = cQ + K, \tag{10.3}$$

where Q = total output, and c and K are positive parameters. All existing firms and potential entrants have identical cost functions. Following Lancaster (1979, p. 33) 'quantities of different [products] will receive the same measure if and only if the embodied characteristics collections . . . require the same resources'.

2.3. Behaviour of Firms

All firms (including potential entrants) are rational present value maximizers with perfect foresight.[8] Price is a flexible instrument which may be altered without cost, but price discrimination between customers at different psychic distances is not feasible. Product specification and geographical location may be freely chosen prior to entry. Having commenced production, further entry may or may not induce existing firms to alter their specifications. The conditions under which each possibility is seen to be the rational expectation for potential entrants are considered in Section 5. Products enter the market sequentially and rapidly until an equilibrium is reached when further entry would be unprofitable.

2.4. International Trade

There are two (or more) identical countries which each have the same demand, technological and behavioural characteristics. In order to sell to consumers in another country, trading costs must be incurred on each unit sold. These costs are borne by the firm, which can discriminate in price internationally, though limits are set by arbitrage. Trading costs may include transport, tariffs, language, customs, bureaucracy, and any other socio-legal costs associated with selling in a foreign environment. The marginal cost of exports (and imports) is given by $\hat{c} > c$.

3. AUTARKY EQUILIBRIUM

Each firm has two decision variables at its disposal — price and product specification. In making each decision, the reactions of its nearest neighbour on each side, including potential neighbours, must be taken into consideration. Since all firms face similar cost and demand conditions and are perfect foresight profit maximizers, we search for a *symmetric, co-operative equilibrium*. Three different conditions of entry will be considered. These may be seen as corresponding to Bain's (1956) (i) blockaded entry (there exists no constraining entry threat), (ii) effectively impeded entry (the behaviour of incumbent firms prevents entry), and (iii) free entry (incumbents cannot prevent entry if price exceeds cost). We differ from Bain in that it is product proliferation, and not limit pricing, that deters entry in the second case.

First consider Q, the total demand for each product. A product which attracts all potential customers with tastes within a distance z on either side of its location, has a demand curve consisting of two identical half-markets of consumer density, y. Some consumers buy their ideal ($x = 0$) whilst others are marginal to the product ($x = z$). Thus,

$$Q = 2y \int_0^z f(p, x)\, dx = 2yF(p, z), \qquad (10.4)$$

where, $F_1 < 0$ and $F_2 = f(p, z) \geqslant 0$.

Given that price is a flexible instrument, and that other firms can be expected to act in a similar manner, firms maximize profits for each product,

$$\pi = [p - c]Q - K \qquad (10.5)$$

by setting *price*, p^* such that $\partial \pi / \partial p = 0$. Thus,

$$F(p^*, z) + [p^* - c]F_1(p^*, z) = 0 \qquad (10.6)$$

with $\partial^2 \pi / \partial p^2 < 0$, so $2F_1(p^*, z) + [p^* - c]F_{11}(p^*, z) < 0$.

Co-operative pricing ensures that price-cutting is expected to raise only the volume of purchases by existing consumers, and not to extend market area. Symmetry suggests that prices will be uniform. From equation (10.2), the behaviour of the consumer marginal to two neighbouring products ensures that $z = \Delta/2$, where Δ is the distance between the two products.

We now turn to the determination of product spacing, Δ. This is seen to depend on the condition of entry.

(i) *If there is no threat of entry,*[9] a firm will wish to fill a given length of the spectrum[10] such that it maximizes profit per product *times* the number of products, n. It must therefore choose to differentiate its product (set $\bar{\Delta}$) such that

$$\frac{\partial n\pi}{\partial \Delta} = n[p^* - c]yf(p^*, \tfrac{1}{2}\bar{\Delta}) + \frac{\partial n}{\partial \Delta}\{[p^* - c]\,2yF(p^*, \tfrac{1}{2}\bar{\Delta}) - K\} = 0. \quad (10.7)$$

Effectively a firm considering the introduction of an extra product must weigh the losses due to narrower markets for each product in its range, against the extra profit on the marginal product $(\partial n/\partial \Delta < 0)$.[11] Optimal price is found by substituting $z = \tfrac{1}{2}\bar{\Delta}$ into equation (10.6).

(ii) *If the above product spacing would leave profitable gaps in the market, but potential entrants expect existing products to maintain their specifications in the face of entry*, sustainable profits are maximized by maximizing the spacing that deters entry, Δ^*. ($n\pi$ is increasing in Δ for all $\Delta < \bar{\Delta}$). Consider the location of product B in Fig. 10.2, given that A already exists. B notes that a potential entrant between A and B can expect to capture at most only a *half* of the market area between them; then he locates such that this potential entrant can anticipate no profits, even though optimal pricing is expected to be followed. The maximum entry-deterring market width, Δ^*, is thus given by,

$$[p^e - c]\,2yF(p^e, \Delta^*/4) - K = 0, \quad (10.8)$$

where the entrant's expected price, p^e, is found from

$$F(p^e, \Delta^*/4) + [p^e - c]F_1(p^e, \Delta^*/4) = 0. \quad (10.9)$$

If potential entrants do not expect co-operative pricing, p^e will be lower than in (10.9) and product spacing can be wider. Further products locate symmetrically along the line until there are no more profitable gaps in the

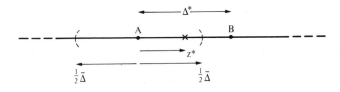

Fig. 10.2

market.[12] Optimal price is now found by substituting $z = \frac{1}{2}\Delta^*$ into equation (10.6).

Note that positive profits are earned even with potential entry by firms facing identical cost conditions. Such profits cease to attract further entry because entrants can expect only half the market size of existing firms. This large discrete jump in demand, and consequently localized competition, is one of the most distinctive features of the Hotelling–Lancaster model, in contrast to either the homogeneous product case, or the more traditional monpolistic competition models.[13] As Archibald and Rosenbluth (1975) argue, it also makes the idea of a non-cooperative equilibrium much less likely to pertain if rivals can have such a severe effect.

(iii) *If potential entrants expect existing products to alter their specifications in the face of entry*, new products will enter the market whenever profits are earned, and the eventual equilibrium will be characterized by zero profits. Since product differentiation in the fixed location model is just sufficient to deter entry, if products were spaced only a little further apart, this would induce entry between every existing product. The number of products would double, and no profits would be earned. Thus the free relocation co-operative equilibrium product spacing is a fraction wider than $\frac{1}{2}\Delta^*$, and price is given by substituting $z = \frac{1}{4}\Delta^*$ into equation (10.6) (i.e. p^e in equation (10.9)).

Although this model contains no entry barriers in the conventional sense (that potential entrants are at some cost disadvantage), the expected fixity of specifications is sufficient to permit profits to persist in the long run. We defer until Section 5 the important consideration of the conditions under which rational entrants will expect fixed specifications, and complete this section with a brief discussion of non-cooperative pricing.

There is no particular reason why firms should take the trouble to price co-operatively if, as when location is freely flexible, this does not lead to any eventual gain in profits. On the other hand, the case for any other pricing rule is not much stronger, and the co-operative solution does have the advantage of providing a limiting result. No price higher *or* lower than p^e can give positive profits at spacing $\frac{1}{2}\Delta^*$. Any other pricing rule must therefore lead to *less* product differentiation. In general, without co-operation, price-cutting is expected to widen a product's market area, as well as to increase sales to existing customers. Formally, $z = z(p, p', \Delta)$ where p' is the price of the nearest rival, conjectured $dp'/dp \neq 1$, $z_1 < 0$, $z_2 > 0$ and $z_3 > 0$. The expected demand elasticity is increased and prices will be cut below p^*.[14]

To complete the taxonomy of possibilities, firms may pursue non-cooperative pricing, yet still have effectively fixed locations for their products. Rivals would then be in a situation of playing a differentiated duopoly pricing game, with spacing anything between a minimum of the zero-profit equilibrium (as with flexible location), and something greater than the co-operative fixed location equilibrium. Greater spacing than Δ^* is possible because entrants can no longer expect such a favourable price in this more competitive atmosphere. Between these limits, it is difficult to conceive of an appropriate location rule for firms which are not sophisticated enough to co-operate over price.

In summary, for any given pricing rule, fixed location reduces the degree of product differentiation below the free relocation level. Non-cooperative pricing must lead to less product differentiation if relocation is free; but relative to co-operative pricing, it may raise or reduce variety if product specifications are fixed on entry. The remainder of this paper considers the effects of international trade on such markets. Only co-operative pricing equilibria are analysed (but see Lancaster (1984) for the Bertrard–Nash case with flexible relocation), and the emphasis will be on fixed specification entry-deterrence since this represents the most interesting case for multinational firms.

4. EQUILIBRIUM WITH TWO COUNTRIES

If there are zero trading costs between two identical countries, demand conditions differ from autarky simply by a doubling of the density of consumers to $2y$. This increases the equilibrium degree of product differentiation in each of our three conditions of entry: no entry threat, fixed location entry deterrence, and free relocation.[15] Intuitively, in the latter two cases, since profit per unit market width rises with y, there must be more products if new entry is not to be profitable. With blockaded entry, a rise in y can be seen as a fall in relative fixed costs, K, which increases the attractiveness of adding another product to the range. Thus, *international trade increases the variety of products available to consumers in each country.* Furthermore, it is easily shown that the elasticity of market area with respect to y is less than minus one in the two cases where entry is a constraining factor.[16] Thus, *the introduction of a second country more than doubles the number of products available.* This is because following a simple doubling, each consumer is provided with a product nearer his or her ideal. The marginal consumer is therefore willing to pay more for and purchase more of the chosen product. The potential profitability of the industry is raised and more variety is necessary to exclude further entry. The welfare effects of this increase in product differentiation are discussed briefly in the final section. Meanwhile, in order to discuss the role of multinational firms in this model, it is necessary to introduce trading costs.

Consider the pattern of specialization as a new product range is developed in two identical open economies between which there are trading costs. Apart from prices and product specifications, firms must now also choose the geographical location of production. Two symmetric equilibria are shown in Fig. 10.3. Figure 10.3(a) shows the 'split' case where each country concentrates on one particular section of the spectrum. Figure 10.3(b) shows the 'interleaved' case where each country produces along the entire spectrum, with each supplying every alternate product.[17] *It is the basic proposition of*

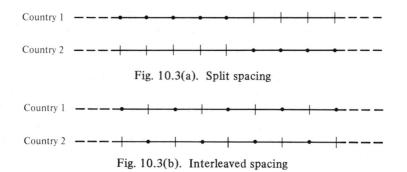

Fig. 10.3(a). Split spacing

Fig. 10.3(b). Interleaved spacing

this section that in a co-operative equilibrium it is the interleaved case that will develop.

The detailed proof is left to the Appendix, but an outline is given here. The argument may be simply stated in terms of Fig. 10.4. The NR curves relate net revenue (profits gross of fixed costs) in a domestic (NR_D) or foreign (NR_F) half-market to the radius of that market. Pricing is given as in equation (10.6). It is easily shown that for a given z, both the height and slope of the domestic curve exceed that for exports because of trading costs.

Now if a product is surrounded by local neighbours, as in the *split* case, the single-country equilibrium applies in each country. Each half market width is $\frac{1}{2}\Delta$, and total profit is $\pi_s = 2NR_{DS} + 2NR_{FS} - K$. However, the slope of NR_D at $\frac{1}{2}\Delta$ exceeds that of NR_F and it would pay to be able to obtain a wider domestic market at the expense of a smaller foreign market. *Interleaved* firms are able to do this because the optimal domestic price is greater than that for neighbouring imports. This can be seen in Fig. 10.1. If A and B price identically, charging more for their products in the foreign market, they each end up with

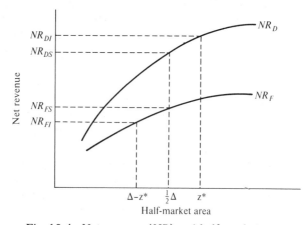

Fig. 10.4. Net revenue (NR) and half-market areas

a domestic half-market area $z > \frac{1}{2}\Delta$, and export area of $\Delta - z$. Thus, $\pi_I = 2NR_{DI} + 2NR_{FI} - K > \pi_S$. Furthermore, it can be shown that interleaving permits a wider entry-deterring spacing of products, which facilitates even greater profits.

If more than two countries are involved in trade, interleaving need only take place between *pairs* of countries. It is possible that only two countries will supply the entire spectrum of products, or that pairs of countries will concentrate on producing for different segments of the market, e.g. France and Germany provide strong but slow varieties, whilst Britain and Italy provide fast but unreliable products.

It is interesting to consider some comparative statics at this equilibrium. In particular, what happens if trading costs are higher, perhaps due to a symmetric tariff, when the market is formed? At the no-tariff spacing, the export price is higher, and export profits lower, than without the tariff. To set against this, the domestic market area is larger as are domestic profits. However, it is not possible for the net effect to be an increase in profits because if this was so, the new set of prices would have been chosen before. This contrasts with Lancaster's (1984) finding that domestic profits *can* rise more than the fall abroad if a tariff is imposed. The difference is due to the fact that the tariff permits greater monopoly power in Lancaster's domestic market, whilst this is already fully exploited in our co-operative equilibrium.

If a tariff reduces profits at a given spacing, it will also reduce the variety of products available in equilibrium. As we move from free trade and introduce a tariff, the total number of products in the world declines. As the tariff becomes large, imports (and exports) become very small, so when it becomes prohibitive, this has no substantial effect on production in each country. Throughout this continuous relationship, fewer products are being made in each country. This confirms the zero trading costs result that with co-operative pricing, *each country provides fewer products under autarky* than it does when there is international trade. Trade thus gives access both to foreign varieties *and* more that are home produced. Once again this contrasts with Lancaster (1984) who finds that non-cooperative pricing leads to *more* products being produced in each country under autarky, though trade still gives access to greater variety through imports. In Lancaster's model, trade raises competition, pushing price down and reducing the number of sustainable products. In our model, trade provides each consumer with a product nearer to his ideal, raising per capita demand and thus profit per product: more product differentiation is required if further entry is to be unprofitable.

Thus far, it has always been assumed that the market is formed when trading costs are given. What difference does it make if trading costs change *after* product specifications have been chosen? If location is freely flexible or if it is fixed, but the change in costs is fully anticipated or if there is no threat of entry, all existing results hold. With fixed location entry-deterrence, an unanticipated rise in trading costs raises import prices and reduces the amount of trade and profits as before; but product differentiation is unaltered unless losses are made. However, an unanticipated fall in trading costs can have a much more significant effect. A small reduction is sufficient to attract new entry throughout the product range, doubling the variety available and reducing profits to zero. If even a small probability is attached to such an event, expected profit maximizers will locate their products much closer than in the equilibrium outlined earlier, sacrificing current profits for greater security. Nevertheless, *the freeing of trade in an economy characterized by fixed specifications and entry-deterrence is potentially a dramatic event.*

5. MULTINATIONAL FIRMS (MNFs)

The incentive for the existence of multinational firms rests on their ability to extract more profits from the market than could domestic firms alone. Internal organization within an MNF permits the exploitation of three advantages of co-operative behaviour. These derive from the ability to (i) set the optimal price for each product in each market, (ii) differentiate products optimally — to maximize product spacing whilst deterring entry, and (iii) geographically locate production optimally — such that there is 'paired interleaving'. Direct ownership minimizes the legal, logistic, and economic problems associated with international collusion.

The fixity of specification, economies of scale, and differences in consumer tastes combine to create conditions suitable for exploitation by multi-product firms. The factor providing the additional incentive for multinationalism is the existence of trading costs. Without these, or the fear of them (as may be the case with tariffs), there is no reason in our model for a firm to transcend national boundaries. The feasibility of multi-nationalism is greatly enhanced by the probable need only to operate in two countries in order to derive the full benefits of optimal geographical location.

The expected fixity of product specification is critical, since without it, there are no excess profits to be earned. Products would still be produced in each country, but the incentive for common ownership would vanish. It is therefore important to investigate the conditions under which fixity may be rationally expected by potential entrants.[18] Assume δK fixed costs must be sunk (non-recoverably) in a specification before production starts and $(1 - \delta)K$ are fully recoverable if production ceases $(0 \leqslant \delta \leqslant 1)$. Costs may be sunk because dies are struck, tools set up, specific operations learned, and/or a consumer image projected. Start from a situation of the fixed location entry-deterring equilibrium we have described, and consider the relative returns to an existing product sticking with, or altering its specification if entry actually takes place.[19]

If $\delta = 1$, it is never rational to alter the specification of an existing product as long as price remains above marginal cost (and if it does not, it never pays to enter anyway). All fixed costs are bygones and there is nothing to be gained by vacating a 'free' product slot.

If $\delta = 0$, it is apparently rational to alter an existing product as long as this leads to a wider market area (which it must, since other products will also be induced to change until symmetry of spacing returns). Existing firms have no commitment advantage over entrants.

If $0 < \delta < 1$, the choice is not clear cut. However, it is possible that specification changes are rational for a firm that owns a single product, but not for one that owns a number of neighbouring products. If entry in the middle of the multi-product firm's range requires it to adjust the position of n of its products (on either side of the entrant) in order to reach a new optimum spacing, it is not rational for it to move if $n\delta \geqslant 1$. This is because the sum of sunk cost losses exceeds K, and it is in the same position as the single-product firm with $\delta = 1$. The vulnerability of a multi-product firm to costly readjustment means that it is cheaper to effectively sink (write off) fixed costs in the specifications nearest the entrant. In a perfect foresight model, this is sufficient for entrants to anticipate no change in specifications.

Finally, multi-product firms may wish to maintain their product range even when it is *apparently* rational for them to alter it. Such action (or rather inaction) may be a useful device to prevent an invasion of the market. This argument may even apply when $\delta = 0$. A similar strategy would be for existing firms to price competitively against entrants, so reducing their expected profits. Stubborn refusal to alter specifications, however, has the political advantage of appearing less predatory to the regulatory authorities.

Thus, the range of circumstances for which location is expected to be fixed may be quite wide, particularly if there are substantial sunk costs.

Looking beyond the immediate framework of our model, MNFs may have further advantages, such as a more effective bargaining position against monopolistic inputs.[20] Monopsony power is enhanced by the threat to switch supply to foreign-produced close substitutes, and this may reduce costs in both countries if inputs are not internationally organized. An apparent disadvantage of MNFs is if there are complementarities in the production of different products. However, this does not alter our conclusions unless such complementarities require *both* geographic *and* very close product links, e.g. a factory can be shared, but only between two neighbouring products on the spectrum. Even in that case interleaving between groups of products might be expected to result.

The number of firms, as opposed to the number of products, is not determined within the present model. It has been argued that the co-ordination of pricing, product differentiation, and geographical location favours internal organization within one firm. On the other hand, Prescott and Visscher (1977) point out that financial, managerial, and training costs may increase either with the size of firm or the speed with which it sets up new products. Such factors may limit any tendency towards complete monopoly, but a substantial concentration of MNFs, with each producing a number of differentiated products along a segment of the spectrum, is still expected to develop in the type of market under consideration.

6. INTERNATIONAL DIFFERENCES IN SIZE, TASTES, EFFICIENCY, AND TARIFFS

In this section, we hold the total number of products constant and investigate the effects of relative differences between two trading countries. It is assumed throughout that the differences we consider arise *before* the pattern of specialization and trade originally develops.

(a) Size

Recall that for countries of equal size, the domestic market is more profitable than any foreign market: both the difference between price and marginal cost, and total demand are higher. Now consider a *small* rise in the density of consumers in country 1 compared with that in country 2 ($y_1 > y_2$). It can be shown that this does not alter the market share of each product in each country because optimal price is independent of consumer density.[21] However, there are two changes arising from country 1's larger home market. First, products located in country 1 are more profitable because they sell more at a lower cost.[22] Second, an equal market share implies a greater volume of exports by country 2 than it imports. Imports as a share of domestic demand are the same everywhere, but exports as a share of output differ. Thus products located in the large country are more profitable and have larger sales, but the industry as a whole imports more than it exports. This simply results from two countries each producing the same number of products, but selling to different-sized markets. In the MNF context, if we term the larger country as the 'parent' and products based abroad as 'subsidiaries', the model predicts that subsidiaries will have lower profit rates, but higher export to output ratios than their parents.[23] If the market size difference is *large*, the advantages of a large domestic market will outweigh the benefits of interleaving, so that country 1 becomes the dominant location for the entire spectrum of products.[24]

(b) Tastes

Tastes may not be distributed evenly over the spectrum (y may vary). If high-density areas arise in the same place in each country, nothing important changes though more products will be crowded into these areas than elsewhere (see Hay, 1976). If there is a *national* element in the taste distribution, the situation is exactly analogous to our discussion of different-sized countries; each country is 'large' for part of the spectrum, but 'small' elsewhere. Once more, if the differences are *small*, interleaving continues. Exports as a share of domestic output are large where domestic tastes are slack, and small where domestic tastes are more intense. This contrasts sharply with the Linder (1961) hypothesis that countries *always* export intensively those products which cater for predominant domestic tastes and import for those with peripheral palates. Of course, as the differences become more acute our model agrees with Linder, and international specialization takes place according to national preferences.

(c) Efficiency

If one country has lower *fixed costs* than another ($K_1 < K_2$), a *small* difference again does not affect the equilibrium. Country 1 is more profitable (and provides the most likely potential entrant) but product specifications, geographical location and, this time, trade propensities are unaltered. *Large* differences result in cost savings from location in country 1 that exceed the benefits of interleaving. The efficient country will dominate the spectrum. *Small* differences in *marginal costs* ($c_1 < c_2$; $\hat{c}_1 < \hat{c}_2$), are more complex since optimal prices are affected. Products from the low-cost country will have larger market areas in each country, exporting more and importing less. The same would be true of a *devaluation* by country 1. *Larger* cost differences will lead to complete domination by the low-cost country.

(d) Tariffs

The effect of changing the general level of tariffs is given in Section 4. Here we consider the effect of a differing relative tariff ($c_1 = c_2$; $\hat{c}_1 < \hat{c}_2$), such that product spacing is unaltered. The high-tariff country 1 has both a larger home and a larger export market than has country 2. This is because the relative price of country 1's products is cheaper. Country 1 is therefore the more profitable, as well as exporting relatively more and importing less than country 2. A sufficiently big difference in tariff rates will make country 1 dominant in all products.

In each case discussed in this Section, domination of all product lines by the larger, more efficient, or more protected country is more likely to happen if trading costs are low, since this minimizes the benefits of interleaving. On the other hand, domination would be much less likely if the differences were to arise *after* the establishment of an equilibrium, because sunk costs protect existing positions.

7. CONCLUSIONS AND SOME WELFARE IMPLICATIONS

This paper has set up a co-operative model of an industry characterized by differentiated products and sunk costs. Positive profits can be earned in long-run equilibrium even when potential entrants are at no apparent cost disadvantage (nor is there any consumer loyalty). With two or more countries trading together, it is shown that the most profitable configuration of products is one of 'interleaving' with each country providing alternate, rather than neighbouring, products along the spectrum of tastes.[25] In contrast to non-cooperative pricing, higher trading costs (including symmetric tariffs) must reduce profits and thus the variety of products available.

It is argued that MNFs may be necessary if maximum profits are to be attained because pricing, the degree of product differentiation and geographical location each require co-ordination. The preconditions for the benefits of multinational operation in this model are that there is an underlying demand for variety, there are economies of scale and sunk costs, and there are significant but not prohibitive trading costs. Casual empiricism tends to support this characterization of the industries in which MNFs are found to operate. For instance, steel, computer programming, and bricks might fail on one or other of these preconditions, but some engineering industries, chemicals, or consumer durable goods might plausibly qualify. It is worth emphasizing that the model clearly associates intra-industry trade with intra-firm trade by multinationals.[26] Intra-industry trade would exist without the multinationals, but this paper has indicated some additional conditions that provide a sufficient incentive for multinational ownership.

Should the empirical relevance of a model predicting intra-firm trade in finished products by MNFs be doubted, Helleiner (1979) has collated the following statistics. After discussing why the figures are likely to under-estimate the extent of the phenomenon, he concludes: 'It seems thoroughly safe to say that US intra-firm transactions make up more than half of total US imports' (ibid., p. 165). US export data appear to exhibit a similar degree of intra-firm trade. Figures for other countries are harder to come by, but one set of estimates suggests 'that 29% of Swedish exports in 1975 and 30% of U.K. exports in 1973 were transmitted on an intra-firm basis' (ibid., p. 162). Particularly relevant from the point of view of this paper is that much of this trade is not in intermediate inputs or capital equipment, but is in products ready for direct sale. 'Substantial proportions of exports from US parent firms to their majority-owned affiliates (40% for manufacturing firms, 49% in total) were for resale without further manufacture or for lease or rental abroad according to the 1970 survey by the US Department of Commerce . . . A survey of 27 major German transnational firms indicated that fully two-thirds of intra-group exports by parent companies were for resale by their foreign affiliates . . . A recent survey of 100 US firms by Business International found that finished goods made up 59% of their intra-firm exports and imports (both showed the same percentage) in 1975' (ibid., p. 167). As a rough order of magnitude, then, intra-firm trade in finished products accounts for about a quarter of all US trade in manufactures, and this average figure will mask some considerable inter-industry differences. There is no evidence to suggest that other developed countries are substantially different. Undoubtedly part of this trade is simply with 'sales-only' subsidiaries, but an unknown proportion 'is reciprocal among specialised subsidiaries' (ibid., p. 167).

The purpose of this paper has been purely positive: to establish the patterns of trade, specialization, and ownership that are expected to prevail under given conditions. A full analysis of the welfare implications must await another paper,[27] but we conclude by making a few basic observations. First, note that more variety does not necessarily mean higher welfare, because the entry of a new product implies an externality in reducing the demand for substitutes, whilst raising industry average costs (the number of overheads).[28] Nor does a free market necessarily provide sufficient variety from the social point of view because new products cannot capture as profit the full extent of the consumer surplus they introduce. Welfare is *not* a monotonic function of variety. Against this background, if free trade increases the number of products produced in each country, welfare may conceivably fall.

The welfare role of MNFs is equally ambiguous. In as much as they facilitate the co-operative entry-deterring equilibrium, they raise price for any given product variety (and reduce variety at any given price). However, although it must be better to provide the same variety at a lower price, this outcome cannot be guaranteed simply by outlawing co-operation (or the multi-nationals). For instance, price competition in a market economy may reduce vareity below the social optimum. Two policy objectives, price and variety, require two policy instruments (e.g. a subsidy and enforced marginal cost pricing) if the social optimum is to be approached.

The existence of monopoly profits provides another reservation to the full benefits of free trade, particularly if a country does not manufacture any of the products in the range. The absence of capacity may be because the country is small, or inefficient, or a late developer (of the capacity to enter the industry efficiently), or just because it is one of many identical countries which missed out when the industry first emerged. In the last two cases, there is no inherent disadvantage other than a quirk of history. In the first case, the problem of size may be overcome by joining a free trade area, as long as this reduces trading costs sufficiently. Failing that, and in the other cases, the *opposite* policy *may* prove beneficial. A tariff can be used to extract monopoly rents in the short run, and to encourage the emergence of a domestic industry in the longer term. Either way, monopoly profits are kept at home, which is a gain to be set against the loss of variety that may ensue. Note that in contrast to the usual monopoly tariff argument, even a *prohibitive* tariff may be beneficial if it permits the existence of an otherwise deterred domestic industry.

APPENDIX

1. THE PATTERN OF SPECIALIZATION BETWEEN TWO COUNTRIES

Consider the geographical location of products as in Fig. 10.A1. Each product is separated by the same psychic distance Δ.

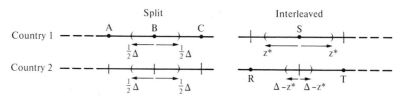

Fig. 10.A1. Market areas

In the *split* equilibrium, both domestic and foreign markets are shared equally between neighbouring products. Each market is similar to the single-country equilibrium described in the text. Price in the foreign market is no less than in the domestic market because of trading costs. (Proof: differentiate equation (10.6) with respect to p^* and c, and invoke the second-order conditions.) Note, however, that the marginal return to a slight widening of the domestic market area exceeds that for exports.

Proof: Differentiating equation (10.5) to get the marginal return

$$\partial\pi/\partial z = [p^* - c]\, 2yf(p^*, z) > 0, \tag{10.A1}$$

$$\partial^2\pi/\partial z\,\partial c = 2y\left\{[p^* - c]f_1(p^*, z)\frac{dp^*}{dc} + f(p^*, z)\left[\frac{dp^*}{dc} - 1\right]\right\} < 0. \tag{10.A2}$$

The RHS of (10.A2) is negative since, $f_1 < 0$, $dp^*/dc \geqslant 0$ (see earlier proof), and $dp^*/dc \leqslant 1$ (in this range because of the arbitrage constraint).[29] Thus, higher costs imply a lower marginal return at any given z, including $z = \frac{1}{2}\Delta$.

At the *interleaved* equilibrium, the prices of domestic, p, and foreign produced, $\hat{p}$, products must again be chosen. Sophisticated firms, however, will not be content to follow the pricing rule of equation (10.6), because the marginal profits in each market area may not be equalized.

The relative market areas of domestic products and imports are decided by the behaviour of the marginal consumer as in equation (10.2), and firms may wish to adjust relative prices so as to bring marginal returns for each product closer to equality. Written formally, the problem for product S in co-operation with R and T, is to maximize L with respect to p, $\hat{p}$, z and the Lagrangean multiplier, λ. where

$$L = [p - c]\, 2yF(p, z) + [\hat{p} - \hat{c}]\, 2yF(\hat{p}, \Delta - z) - K - 2y\lambda[g(p, z)$$

$$- g(\hat{p}, \Delta - z)].$$

Denoting maximized values by a (*), the first-order conditions may be written as

$$F(p^*, z^*) + [p^* - c] F_1(p^*, z^*) - \lambda g_1(p^*, z^*) = 0. \qquad (10.\text{A}3)$$

$$F(\hat{p}^*, \Delta - z^*) + [\hat{p}^* - \hat{c}] F_1(\hat{p}^*, \Delta - z^*) + \lambda g_1(\hat{p}^*, \Delta - z^*) = 0. \qquad (10.\text{A}4)$$

$$[p^* - c]f(p^*, z^*) - [\hat{p}^* - \hat{c}]f(\hat{p}^*, \Delta - z^*) - \lambda[g_2(p^*, z^*)$$
$$+ g_2(\hat{p}^*, \Delta - z^*)] = 0. \qquad (10.\text{A}5)$$

$$g(p^*, z^*) - g(\hat{p}^*, \Delta - z^*) = 0. \qquad (10.\text{A}6)$$

These conditions may be interpreted as follows. Unsophisticated firms might ignore (10.A5) and set $\lambda = 0$. If sophisticated firms observe that the marginal return to increasing the market area of domestic products exceeds that of imports, (10.A5) suggests $\lambda > 0$ (since $g_2 > 0$). From (10.A3) and (10.A4), they therefore reduce domestic price and raise import price in order to take advantage of the situation. (10.A6) is what Lancaster (1979) calls the dividing condition, and it states the constraint that consumers decide which product they wish to buy.

If the marginal return in the domestic market at z^* is no less than that for imports at $\Delta - z^*$, it is straightforward to show that interleaving is more profitable than split spacing. (*Proof:* This follows directly from the concavity of the profits function in z, and inequality (10.A2)). This is illustrated for unsophisticated firms by Fig. 10.4 in the text ($NR_{DI} + NR_{FI} > NR_{DS} + NR_{FS}$); and sophisticated firms can only do better.

Most demand specifications verify the assertion that the domestic market is no less profitable at z^* than are imports at $\Delta - z^*$. If $f(p, z) = f(g(p, z))$, as in all partial equilibrium models of spatial demand, the 'delivered price', g, is relevant for both the choice of product and the quantity demanded. Thus, $f(p^*, z^*) = f(\hat{p}^*, \Delta - z^*)$ and since $[p^* - c] \geqslant [\hat{p}^* - \hat{c}]$ (arbitrage constraint), from (10.A5), $\lambda > 0$. Lancaster (1979) adds an outside good and a budget constraint in his model, the effect of which is to raise the quantity demanded of lower priced products at the same 'delivered price'. This reinforces the acceptability of our assertion by further raising domestic profitability. Similarly, a consumer with a fixed budget for the product must buy more of the low-priced good, and raise marginal domestic profitability.

If demand conditions contravene this property, it is just conceivable that split spacing may be superior. This would involve the following requirements: (i) $f(p^*, z^*) < f(\hat{p}^*, \Delta - z^*)$, e.g. honey is more expensive than marmalade but nearer to my ideal tastes, and I am at the margin in (10.A6); if I decide to buy honey, I will eat a great deal and buy less beer, but if I choose marmalade, I will eat less and drink more beer (either option gives me equal satisfaction); *and* (ii) the wider domestic price–cost margin is insufficient to cancel this quantity effect; *and* (iii) this domestic loss at the margin is enough to cancel the initial gain due to a wider domestic market (as shown by (10.A2)). Such a chain of conditions is unlikely to have much empirical content and is ruled out throughout this paper. Interleaving is superior with a sufficient condition being that

$$f(p, z) = f(g(p, z)).$$

So far, we have proved only that interleaving is superior at a given Δ. If product location is freely adjustable, this is also sufficient to prove that interleaving will be the eventual equilibrium since any split spacing is vulnerable to entry. Lancaster (1984) calls this the 'minimum entropy' property. With no threat of entry, the above proof is again sufficient because firms are free to differentiate exactly as they wish, and any product range is more profitable if it is interleaved. It remains to be shown that interleaved entry-deterrence permits a wider product spacing than the split case (wider spacing saves fixed costs and raises potential profits).

In the split case, potential entry will clearly be at E in Fig. 10.A2 since we have just shown that this is more profitable than the same specification made in country 1. In the interleaved case, potential entrants are indifferent between countries (but say country 2 is chosen). We must pose the question: for a given product spacing, could U ever be more profitable than E?

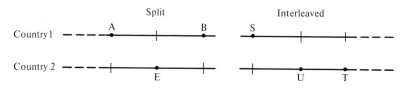

Fig. 10.A2. Potential entry

First consider the case where E and U both locate midway between their rivals (this can be shown to be E's best position). Unlike E, U has a low-cost producer, T, as a near neighbour and so cannot expect such a wide domestic market area. Abroad, U cannot benefit by having wider foreign and narrower domestic markets. Furthermore, U is unable to price optimally in each half-market since each varies in length, and price discrimination is not possible except internationally. If U locates other than midway between S and T, say further from T, it is open to E to also locate further from B. By the same argument as before, E must do better.

Since E is more profitable than U, the entry-deterring spacing of A and B must be closer than for S and T. Thus, not only does interleaving provide greater profits at an equal spacing of products, but is also provides a wider equilibrium spacing of products. Co-operative, foresighted firms will therefore select this profit-maximizing pattern of production. Note also that a similar proof can be applied to demonstrate that interleaving is superior to *any* alternative pattern of specialization.

2. THE PATTERN OF SPECIALIZATION WITH MANY COUNTRIES

Section 1 of this Appendix proves that interleaving is superior to a split pattern of specialization in the two-country case. The purpose of this section is to investigate how this might generalize with many identical countries. Two possible patterns suggest themselves. The pattern in Fig. 10.A3(a) will be termed 'pairing'

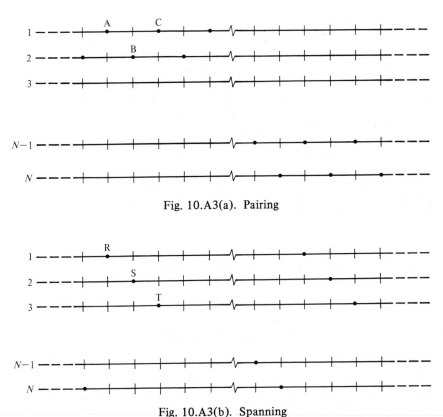

Fig. 10.A3(a). Pairing

Fig. 10.A3(b). Spanning

since interleaving is exhibited for pairs of countries only. Figure 10.A3(b) will be termed 'spanning' since each of the N countries produces every N'th product along the entire span of the spectrum.

With *pairing*, each country has two home and two foreign half-markets, just as in the two-country case, plus $(2N-4)$ foreign half-markets shared with other similar exporters.

With *spanning*, matters are not so straightforward because of asymmetries. Recall that for the two-country case it was profitable to lower domestic price below, and raise export price above the single-country optimum rule (given by equation (10.6)). Whilst paired products A, B, and C can apply this rule symmetrically, if R and S apply the same rule in country 1, product S will find it has a smaller market area on its eastern side than does T on its west. This implies that S might benefit from a slightly lower price to maximize profits between S and T in country 1. There will be further knock-on effects to the east of T. The net effect, however, is that R has a smaller domestic market area than does A in a co-operative profit-maximizing equilibrium. Concavity of the net revenue functions, together with the fact that profits at the margin of the interleaved domestic market area are no less than at the foreign margin. ensures that wider foreign markets cannot compensate for the loss of domestic area compared with pairing.

The problem with spanning is that it is not possible to set the optimum price in each half-market. The lack of symmetry and the impossibility of price discrimination within a country necessitates costly compromises. Note that potential entrants could locate in positions of similar potential profitability with either configuration, so the entry-deterring spacing is the same.

Since any configuration of products (other than the split case which has already been proved inferior) can be interpreted as a combination of pairing and spanning, pairing is expected to develop in a co-operative equilibrium. Although interleaving may be a substantial improvement on split markets, perhaps rather less can be said for this conjecture about pairing. It rests on a very sophisticated approach to pricing, and if N is large and trading costs are small, the domestic market might become of relatively little importance. Nevertheless, it remains of interest to state the conclusion weakly. Each identical country need not produce over the entire spectrum, as long as it is interleaved with another in the range of products it does produce.

Finally note that there is no reason in this model why every country should produce some of the range of products. Any two countries may supply the rest of the world with all their requirements, and reap the monopoly profits for themselves. Lancaster (1980) however suggests some general equilibrium and stability reasons why the total number of products might be divided equally between the N countries.

NOTES

1.   E.g. Lancaster (1980).
2.   E.g. Krugman (1980), and Dixit and Norman (1980).
3.   See Hay (1976), Prescott and Visscher (1977), and Easton and Lipsey (1978) for specific, single-country models based on a similar solution concept.
4.   This paper does not make the distinction between product differentiation and variety made in Lancaster (1984).
5.   Lancaster (1984) has studied non-cooperative pricing. Furthermore, within the present model any one product has at most only two *direct* rivals, one on each side, and it is implausible to expect such limited competition to continue for long without a co-operative solution being sought. See Archibald and Rosenbluth (1975).
6.   Alternatively the line may be a circle; or of finite length, but with the ends having modified properties. See note 12. In such cases, we must assume there are many products in equilibrium in order to avoid an integer problem.
7.   Subscripts denote partial derivatives with respect to the ith argument e.g. $f_2 = \partial f/\partial x$.
8.   This exceedingly strong assumption is imposed in order to focus clearly on the possibility of monopoly profits, even in the absence of imperfect information or differing costs for potential entrants.

9. In the sense that new entry is unprofitable at the unconstrained profit-maximizing equilibrium.

10. If any profits are earned, it will also wish to maximize the length of the market over which it operates: see Section 5.

11. We ignore the integer problem involved in differentiating a discrete number, and consider only firms that make many products. Thus, if $n = L/\Delta$, where L is the length of market over which the firm operates, $\partial n/\partial\Delta = -L/\Delta^2$.

12. See Prescott and Visscher (1977) and Hay (1976) for a full derivation of such an equilibrium. Our assumption regarding the line of infinite length is to ensure that there is no special advantage in locating at the end of the line. With a finite line, location Δ^* from the end does not attract entry, so end-products benefit from a larger market. While this loss of symmetry does not lead to Hotelling's instability problem (because specifications are fixed), it does alter the end firm's optimal price (unless $dp^*/dz = 0$). This has knock-on price effects all along the spectrum. To avoid this problem of 'the tail wagging the dog', either the finite line assumption must be abandoned, or we could follow Lancaster (1979) in assuming special demand characteristics for consumers at the end. Alternatively, we could incorporate such differential price effects. This would greatly add to the complexity of the analysis, whilst adding little insight.

13. E.g., Chamberlin (1933), Dixit and Stiglitz (1977).

14. Lancaster (1979) provides an example of Nash–Bertrard pricing ($dp'/dp = 0$), with flexible location. Salop (1979) suggests a model where such pricing may lead to a kinked equilibrium with $p = p^*$.

15. *Proof:* Depending on the entry condition, totally differentiate equation (10.7), (10.8) or (10.5) (set equal to zero) with respect to y and Δ, (and invoke the second-order condition that (10.7) provides a maximum.)

16. For instance, in the entry-deterrence case, $[y/\Delta^*] d\Delta^*/dy = -4F(p^*, \Delta^*/4)/\Delta^*f(p^*, \Delta^*/4)$. Now since the total demand for a product, $2yF(p^*, \Delta^*/4)$ clearly exceeds the demand that would pertain if all consumers were marginal, $\frac{1}{2}y\Delta^*f(p^*, \Delta^*/4)$, the elasticity must be less than minus one.

17. The terms 'split' and 'interleaved' are due to Lancaster (1984), though this paper was first drafted before I had sight of that paper.

18. Eaton and Lipsey (1978) provide a detailed analysis for single-product firms.

19. I.e. in Fig. 10.A2, if U enters, should S and/or T move?

20. Negotiated government subsidies also fall into this category as a negative input cost.

21. The Lagrangean function in the Appendix can be formed for each country separately (e.g. y_1 replaces y), and y does not enter equations (10.A3)–(10.A6).

22. The least-disadvantaged potential entrants also live in country 1 for the same reason. Thus an unanticipated fall in trading costs, or growth in demand, would induce entry in the larger country first.

23. If parents are based in the small country, the opposite is obviously expected to prevail.

24. In the extreme, as y_2 approaches zero and net revenues in country 2 approach zero, the chioce is between supplying country 1 from both low- and high-cost sources, or from only the low-cost source. The latter must dominate.

25. In comparison, non-spatial models, such as Krugman (1980), cannot predict a *pattern* of trade, beyond the number of products and size of overall trade flows.

26.   As such it differs from Hymer's theory (see Kindleberger, 1969) based on the necessity of local production to exploit local conditions (tastes). The latter gives no obvious rationale for extensive intra-firm trade in final products.
27.   See Lyons (1983) for a more detailed discussion of the points made in these paragraphs.
28.   An extreme example is given by a homogeneous product with a collusively set price. New entry does not reduce price, yet it adds to average costs.
29.   The arbitrage constraint is sufficient, not necessary. If binding however, domestic and export prices are no longer independent. For simplicity only, this complication is set aside in what follows.

REFERENCES

Archibald, G. C. and Rosenbluth, G. (1975), 'The "New" Theory of Consumer Demand and Monopolistic Competition', *Quarterly Journal of Economics*, 89, 569–90.

Bain, J. (1956), *Barriers to New Competition* (Cambridge, Mass.: Harvard University Press).

Chamberlin, E. H. (1933), *The Theory of Monopolistic Competition*. (Cambridge, Mass: Harvard University Press).

Dixit, A. K. and Norman, V. (1980), *Theory of International Trade* (Cambridge, England: Cambridge University Press).

Dixit, A. K. and Stiglitz, J. E. (1977), 'Monopolistic Competition and Optimum Product Diversity', *American Economic Review*, 67, 297–308.

Eaton, B. C. and Lipsey, R. G. (1978), 'Freedom of Entry and the Existence of Pure Profit', *The Economic Journal*, 88, 455–69.

Hay, D. A. (1976), 'Sequential Entry and Entry Deterring Strategies in Spatial Competition', *Oxford Economic Papers*, 28, 240–57.

Helleiner, G. K. (1979), 'Transnational Corporations and Trade Structure: the Role of Intra-firm Trade', in H. Giersch (ed.), *On the economics of intra-industry trade* (Tübingen: J. C. B. Mohr), 159–81.

Hotelling, H. (1929), 'Stability in Competition', *Economic Journal*, 34, 41–57.

Kindleberger, C. P. (1969), *American Business Abroad* (New Haven and London: Yale University Press).

Krugman, P. (1980), 'Scale Economies, Product Differentiation and the Pattern of Trade', *American Economic Review*, 70, 950–9.

Lancaster, K. J. (1979), *Variety, Equity and Efficiency* (Oxford: Basil Blackwell).

Lancaster, K. J. (1980), 'Intra-industry Trade under Pefect Monopolistic Competition', *Journal of International Economics*, 10, 151–75.

Lancaster, K. J. (1984), 'Protection and Product Differentiation', This volume.

Linder, S. B. (1961), *An Essay on Trade and Transformation* (New York: Wiley).

Lyons, B. R. (1983), 'Immiserizing Trade in Differentiated Products', *in preparation*.

Prescott, E. C. and Visscher, M. (1977), 'Sequential Location among Firms with Foresight', *Bell Journal of Economics*, 8, 378–93.

Salop, S. C. (1979), 'Monopolistic Competition with Outside Goods', *Bell Journal of Economics*, 10, 141–56.

11

Import Protection as Export Promotion: International Competition in the Presence of Oligopoly and Economics of Scale

Paul Krugman

1. INTRODUCTION

When businessmen try to explain the success of Japanese firms in export markets, they often mention the advantage of a protected home market. Firms with a secure home market, the argument runs, have a number of advantages: they are assured of the economies of large-scale production, of selling enough over time to move down the learning curve, of earning enough to recover the costs of R & D. While charging high prices in the domestic market, they can 'incrementally price' and flood foreign markets with low-cost products.

No doubt the argument that import protection is export promotion is often a self-serving position of those who would like protection themselves. Still, there is an undeniable persuasiveness to the argument. Yet it is an argument which economists schooled in standard trade theory tend to find incomprehensible. In a world of perfect competition and constant returns to scale, protecting a product can never cause it to be exported. It may cause some other good which is complementary in production to be exported — but this is hardly what the businessmen seem to have in mind.

The purpose of this paper is to show that there is a class of models in which the businessman's view of import protection as export promotion makes sense. There are two basic ingredients in these models. First, markets are both oligopolistic and segmented: firms are aware that their actions affect the price they receive, and are able to charge different prices in different markets. As Brander (1981) has shown, and as Brander and Krugman (1981) elaborated, models of this type allow countries to be both importers and exporters within an industry, because firms will engage in 'reciprocal dumping' into each others' home markets.

The second ingredient is some kind of economies of scale. These may take several forms. The simplest would be static economies of scale, i.e. a declining marginal cost curve. It is also possible, however, for more subtle forms of scale economies to produce the same results· for example, dynamic scale economies of the 'learning curve' type, or competition in R & D. As the paper will stress, the end result is very similar. It is the distinction between increasing and decreasing costs, not the distinction between statics and dynamics, which usually sets the views of practical men and trade theorists apart.

In each case the basic story of protection as promotion remains the same. By giving a domestic firm a privileged position in some one market, a country gives it an advantage in scale over foreign rivals. This scale advantage translates into lower marginal costs and higher market share even in unprotected markets.

The paper is in six sections. Section 2 presents the basic, static model of competition, and Section 3 shows how protectionism can promote expansion in all markets. Section 4 develops an alternative model where there are no static economies of scale, but where R & D plays a similar role. In Section 5 neither of these effects operates, but learning by doing is shown to produce similar effects. Finally, Section 6 summarizes the results and suggests some conclusions.

2. MODEL I: STATIC ECONOMIES OF SCALE

There are two firms, home and foreign. Each firm produces a single product, which it sells in a number of markets in competition with the other firm. The firms' products may but need not be perfect substitutes. The segmented markets in which they compete may be divided by transport costs, border taxes, or type of purchaser; they may include markets in each firm's home country and also markets in third countries.

I will adopt an abbreviated way of representing demand conditions in the different markets; following Spencer and Brander (1982), I will skip the writing of demand functions and go directly to the revenue functions of the firms. In market i $(i = 1, \ldots, r)$ the revenue function of the home firm is:

$$R_i = R_i(x_i, x_i^*), \tag{11.1}$$

where x_i, x_i^* are deliveries to the ith market by the home and foreign firms respectively. Similarly, the foreign firm's revenue function is:

$$R_i^* = R_i^*(x_i, x_i^*). \tag{11.2}$$

I will assume that each firm's marginal revenue is decreasing in the other firms's output:

$$\partial^2 R_i / \partial x_i \, \partial x_i^* < 0 \tag{11.3}$$

$$\partial^2 R_i^* / \partial x_i^* \, \partial x_i < 0. \tag{11.4}$$

Another condition will also be assumed:

$$\Delta = \frac{\partial^2 R_i}{\partial x_i^2} \cdot \frac{\partial^2 R_i^*}{\partial x_i^{*2}} - \frac{\partial^2 R_i}{\partial x_i \, \partial x_i^*} \frac{\partial^2 R_i^*}{\partial x_i \, \partial x_i^*} > 0. \tag{11.5}$$

The usefulness of this condition will become obvious below; it amounts to saying that 'own' effects on marginal revenue are greater than 'cross' effects.

On the cost side, each firm will face both production costs and transport costs: thus total costs for each firm will be:

$$TC = \Sigma\, t_i\, x_i + C\,(\Sigma\, x_i) \tag{11.6}$$

$$TC^* = \Sigma\, t_i^*\, x_i^* + C^*\,(\Sigma\, x_i^*), \tag{11.7}$$

where we assume declining marginal cost of production: $C'', C^{*''} < 0$. Notice that transport costs need not be the same for the two firms. For the home firm's domestic market, presumably $t_i < t_i^*$; for the foreign firm's domestic makets, we expect $t_i^* > t_i$; there may also be third country markets to which either may have lower transport cost.

How do these firms compete? Each firm must choose a vector of deliveries, i.e. it must choose x_i or x_i^* for each market. The simplest assumption to make about competition is that each firm takes the other firm's deliveries as given in each market. The result is a multi-market Cournot model, where the firms' decision problems are:

$$\max_{\{x_i\}} \Pi = \Sigma\, R_i(x_i, x_i^*) - \Sigma\, t_i x_i - C(\Sigma\, x_i) \tag{11.8}$$

$$\max_{\{x_i^*\}} \Pi^* = \Sigma\, R_i^*(x_i, x_i^*) - \Sigma\, t_i^* x_i^* - C^*(\Sigma\, x_i^*). \tag{11.9}$$

The first-order conditions which determine equilibrium are

$$\frac{\partial R_i}{\partial x_i} - t_i - \mu = 0 \quad i = 1, \ldots, n \tag{11.10}$$

$$\frac{\partial R_i^*}{\partial x_i^*} - t_i^* - \mu^* = 0 \quad i = 1, \ldots, n \tag{11.11}$$

where μ, μ^* are marginal production costs. In each market, firms set their marginal revenue equal to marginal cost.

To interpret this equilibrium, it is useful to think in terms of an imaginary iterative process by which we might compute the solution. Specifying this process is purely an expositional device, with no implications for the outcome; but it does help to make clear the underlying logic of the model.

Suppose, then, that we use the following procedure. We begin by making a guess about the firms' marginal cost, and play a Cournot game in each market on the basis of that guess. We then sum the chosen levels of deliveries to get total output and compute the implied marginal cost. This estimate of marginal cost is then used for a second round and so on until convergence. The stages of this computation can be represented by the geometric apparatus presented in Figs. 11.1, 11.2, and 11.3.

Figure 11.1 shows the competition in a representative market for given estimates of marginal cost μ, μ^*. The curves FF and F^*F^* are the reaction functions of the domestic and foreign firm respectively. Their slopes are:

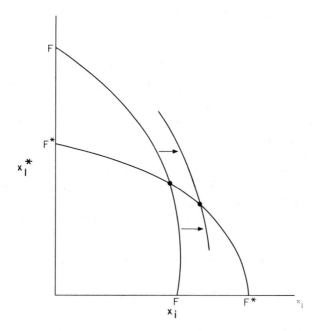

Fig. 11.1

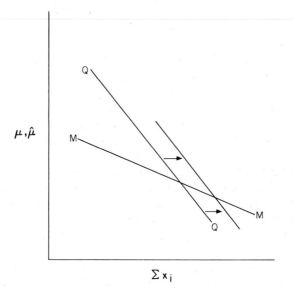

Fig. 11.2

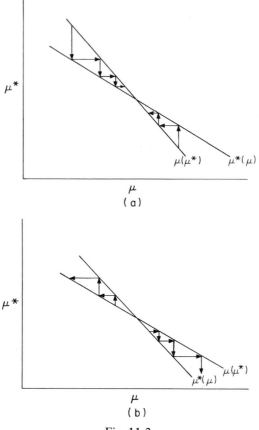

Fig. 11.3

$$\frac{-\partial^2 R_i/\partial x_i^2}{\partial^2 R_i/\partial x_i \partial x_i^*} \quad \text{and} \quad \frac{-\partial^2 R_i^*/\partial x_i \partial x_i^*}{\partial^2 R_i^*/\partial x_i^{*2}} \; ,$$

both negative by (11.3) and (11.4); while by (11.5), *FF* is flatter than F^*F^*.

Suppose that we reduce μ, the home firm's estimate of marginal cost. The result will be to push *FF* out, as shown in the diagram; x_i will rise and x_i^* will fall. This will happen in *each* market in which the firms compete, so that total output of the home firm will rise and total output of the foreign firm will fall.

Figure 11.2 illustrates the next step. On one hand, the lower the firm's estimate of marginal cost, the larger its output. On the other hand, the larger the output, the lower its actual marginal cost. These relationships are indicated by the curves *QQ* and *MM*. The equilibrium for the firm — conditional on the *other* firm's estimate of marginal cost — is where *MM* and *QQ* cross. As drawn,

QQ is steeper than *MM*; this will be true if marginal costs do not fall too steeply, and we will assume that this is the case.

Suppose now that the foreign firm were to raise its estimated marginal cost, μ^*. This would imply a leftward shift of F^*F^* in each market. For a given μ, output of the home firm would rise, i.e. the *QQ* curve shifts right. The end result is that domestic marginal cost is decreasing in foreign marginal cost, and vice versa. This takes us to the final step in determining equilibrium illustrated in Fig. 11.3.

Domestic marginal cost is decreasing in foreign, foreign marginal cost is decreasing in domestic; an equilibrium is where the schedules $\mu\ (\mu^*)$ and $\mu^*\ (\mu)$ cross. The curve $\mu\ (\mu^*)$ may cut $\mu^*\ (\mu)$ from above, as in Fig. 11.3a, or from below, as in Fig. 11.3b. A simple stability analysis suggests that the latter situation will 'almost never' be observed. Suppose that the two firms revise their estimates of marginal cost alternately; then the dynamics will be those indicated by the arrows. If $\mu\ (\mu^*)$ is steeper than $\mu^*\ (\mu)$, that is, if 'own' effects are again stronger than 'cross' effects at this higher level, equilibrium is stable. If $\mu^*\ (\mu)$ is steeper, the equilibrium is unstable.

It is possible and even important that there may exist no stable equilibrium except where one firm or the other ceases production. For the rest of this chapter, however, we will assume that there is a unique stable equilibrium where both firms produce at positive levels.

We have now decribed the determination of equilibrium in this model. The essential feature is the circular causation from output to marginal cost to output. Our next step is to show how this circularity makes import protection an export promotion device.

3. EFFECTS OF PROTECTION

Suppose that the home government excludes the foreign firm from some market previously open to it. This market might be the whole domestic market, or it might be some piece, say procurement by government-owned firms. For simplicity we consider a complete exclusion of foreign product, although a quota or tariff would have much the same result.

To find the effects of this, we first hold μ constant. The effect under this assumption is solely to raise x_i and lower x_i^* in the newly protected market. This in turn, however, affects marginal cost; in terms of Fig. 11.2, the home firm's *QQ* curve shifts right, the corresponding foreign curve shifts left. That is, for a given level of foreign marginal cost domestic cost falls; for a given level of domestic marginal cost foreign cost rises. The curve $\mu\ (\mu^*)$ shifts left, $\mu^*\ (\mu)$ shifts right; as Fig. 11.4 shows, the result (assuming stability) is a fall in μ, a rise in μ^*.

It only remains to complete the circle. This is done in Fig. 11.5, which shows a representative market other than the protected one. The change in marginal

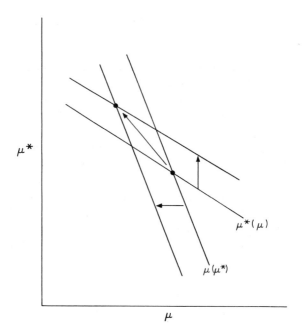

Fig. 11.4

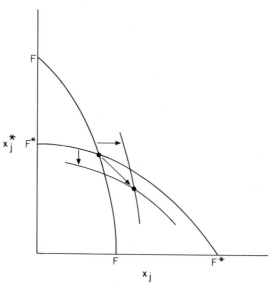

Fig. 11.5

cost cause *FF* to shift out, F^*F^* to shift in; x_j rises, x_j^* falls. *Protecting the domestic firm in one market increases domestic sales and lowers foreign sales in all markets.*

This is the businessman's view, and it should be clear why it is confirmed. There is a positive feedback from output to marginal cost to output. By protecting one market the government gives the domestic firm greater economies of scale, while reducing those of its foreign competitor. Thus decreasing costs are at the heart of the story.

Economists tend, however, to be sceptical of the importance of decreasing costs, at least for large industrial countries. Businessmen see more of a role for scale economies than economists do, but the empirical appeal of the protection-as-promotion argument lies in more subtle forms of decreasing cost. These are the dynamic economies of scale involved in the learning curve and in R & D. What I will do in the rest of this paper is show that these dynamic economies basically have the same implications as static decreasing cost, and that the protection-as-promotion argument remains valid.

4. MODEL II: COMPETITION IN R & D

In this section I assume that marginal costs are constant. Firms can, however, reduce their production costs by prior investment in R & D. This turns out to have effects very similar to those of static declining marginal cost.

There are again two firms, competing in a number of markets; demand looks the same as in Model I. Costs, however, look somewhat different. Marginal production cost is independent of the level of output, but decreasing in the amount of investment each firm does in R & D.

$$\mu = \mu\,(N) \tag{11.12}$$

$$\mu^* = \mu^*\,(N^*), \tag{11.13}$$

where

$$\frac{\partial \mu}{\partial N}, \frac{\partial \mu^*}{\partial N^*} < 0$$

$$\frac{\partial^2 \mu}{\partial N^2}, \frac{\partial^2 \mu^*}{\partial N^{*2}} < 0.$$

Profits of each firm are revenue, less production and transport costs, and also less R & D expense:

$$\Pi = \sum_i R_i\,(x_i, x_i^*) - \sum_i t_i\,x_i - \mu\,(N) \cdot \sum_i x_i - N \tag{11.14}$$

$$\Pi^* = \sum_i R_i^*\,(x_i^*, x_i) - \sum_i t_i^*\,x_i^* - \mu^*\,(N^*) \cdot \sum_i x_i^* - N^*. \tag{11.15}$$

In determining the outcome of a model like this, there is a question of the appropriate equilibrium concept. The issue is whether firms will adopt 'open-loop' strategies, taking the other firm's deliveries as given, or will make sophisticated 'closed-loop' calculations which take into account the effect of their own R & D decision on the other firm's subsequent actions. The issue has been repeatedly discussed; Spence (1981) is a recent example. I will opt for simplicity, and use the open-loop concept. This also has the advantage of making the parallel between R & D and static scale economies very transparent.

The first-order conditions for the home firm are:

$$\frac{\partial R_i}{\partial x_i} - t_i - \mu = 0 \tag{11.16}$$

$$\frac{\partial \mu}{\partial N} \cdot \sum_i x_i = 1, \tag{11.17}$$

where we neglect for simplicity the possibility of zero deliveries to some markets.

The import point to notice is that investment in R & D has an effect on profits which is proportional to expected sales. This is a form of increasing returns, and is the key to this model.

As in Model I, it is useful to think of calculating the equilibrium position iteratively. We first choose levels of R & D expenditure; use the implied marginal cost to compute outputs; recompute the optimal R & D using this; and so on to convergence. The crucial links are illustrated in Figs. 11.6 and 11.7. In Fig. 11.6 we show the determination of N given N^*. The higher is N, the lower will be marginal production cost, and thus the higher will be output; the curve QQ captures this relationship. On the other hand, the larger the output the greater the marginal profitability of R & D, so N is increasing in output along MM. As in Fig. 11.2, QQ is assumed steeper than MM.

If the foreign firm were to increase its own R & D, the effect would be to lower its marginal cost and reduce domestic output for any given N. Thus QQ would shift left and N fall. The result is that N is decreasing in N^* and vice versa; in Fig. 11.7 we show the 'stable' or 'own effects dominating' case which we assume to prevail.

The effect of reserving some market for the domestic firm is now obvious. At given N and N^* domestic output rises and foreign output falls. The QQ curve shifts out, its foreign counterpart shifts in. Thus $N(N^*)$ shifts right, $N^*(N)$ shifts down; N rises, N^* falls. Reduced marginal production costs for the home firm and higher marginal production costs for the foreign firm mean increased domestic sales in all markets.

The point here is that protection, by increasing the home firm's sales and reducing those of its foreign competitor, increases the incentive for domestic R & D at foreign expense. This in turn translates into a shift in relative

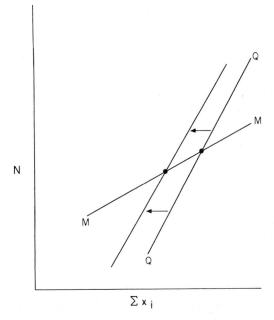

Fig. 11.6

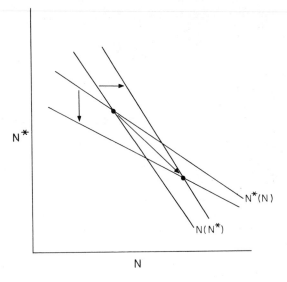

Fig. 11.7

production costs which leads to increased domestic sales even in unprotected markets. Even though there are no static scale economies, the result is exactly the same as in model I.

5. MODEL III: THE LEARNING CURVE

In this final model we consider yet another form of economies of scale. In this version there are neither static economies of scale nor explicit investment in R & D; instead, the increasing returns take a dynamic form: higher output now reduces the costs of production later. These learning-by-doing economies turn out to yield results very similar to those in the other models.

The model is a generalized version of one developed by Spence (1981). Again there are two firms, home and foreign. They compete in a number of markets, but now they compete over time as well as space. In each market the revenues of the two firms are:

$$R_i = R_i(x_i, x_i^*) \quad i = 1, \dots, n \tag{11.18}$$

$$R_i^* = R_i^*(x_i^*, x_i) \quad i = 1, \dots, n \tag{11.19}$$

where x_i, x_i^* now represent rates of delivery per unit time; otherwise they have the same properties we have been assuming all along.

On the cost side, each firm faces constant transport costs t_i, t_i^* to each market. At a point in time, production costs are characterized by constant marginal costs μ, μ^*. These marginal costs are, however, dependent on previous output. Let $Q = \Sigma x_i$, the home firm's rate of output at a point in time; the home firm's cumulative output to time t is then:

$$K(t) = \int_0^t Q \, dz. \tag{11.20}$$

The learning curve assumption is that marginal costs are a decreasing function of cumulative output to date:

$$\mu = \mu(K). \tag{11.21}$$

Now consider the firms' maximization problems. Following Spence, we will make the extremely useful assumption that firms maximize cumulative profits over a fixed horizon T *with no discounting*. Thus the home firm takes as its objective to maximize:

$$\Pi = \int_0^T \left\{ \sum_i [R_i(x_i, x_i) - t_i x_i - \mu(K)_i x] \right\} dt. \tag{11.22}$$

What does the optimum solution look like? By selling another unit in market i, the firm gains two things: the direct marginal revenue, and the indirect cost saving on future production costs. On the other hand, it incurs the direct costs of transportation and production. Thus the first-order condition at a point in time is:

$$\frac{\partial R_i}{\partial x_i} - t_i - \mu - \int_t^T \frac{\partial \mu}{\partial K} \cdot Q \, dz = 0. \tag{11.23}$$

If the left-hand side of (11.23) is zero at each point in time, it must also be constant over time. So we can differentiate with respect to time to get:

$$\frac{d}{dt}\left[\frac{\partial R}{\partial x_i} - \frac{d}{dt}\mu + \frac{\partial \mu}{\partial K} \cdot Q\right] = \frac{d}{dt}\frac{\partial R}{\partial x_i} - \frac{\partial \mu}{\partial K} \cdot Q + \frac{\partial \mu}{\partial K} \cdot Q$$

$$= \frac{d}{dt}\frac{\partial R}{\partial x_i} = 0. \tag{11.24}$$

The economic implication of this, as Spence points out, is that the firm sets output on the basis of a constant shadow marginal cost. The level of the shadow marginal cost is determined by the terminal condition: at time T, when the firm no longer considers the effect of current output on future cost, the shadow and actual marginal costs converge.

Again we can imagine an iterative procedure for calculating equilibrium. We can make a guess at the firms' terminal marginal costs μ_T, μ_T^*; find the cumulative output that results from these guesses, and the corresponding terminal marginal cost; and repeat the process. Without going into detail, it should be obvious that the result will be the same as in our first model. Each firm's terminal marginal cost will be decreasing in the other's; equilibrium is illustrated in Fig. 11.8, where we assume once again that 'own' effects predominate over 'cross' effects, so that μ_T (μ_T^*) is steeper than μ_T^* (μ_T).

The effect of protection is now exactly parallel to its effect in the case of static scale economies. Excluding the foreign firm from some market increases the cumulative output of the domestic firm and reduces the cumulative output of the foreign firm for given μ_T, μ_T^*. The result is that μ_T (μ_T^*) shifts left, μ_T^* (μ_T) shift up; μ_T falls, μ_T^* rises. This in turn means that x_i rises and x_i^* falls in all markets, whether they were directly protected or not.

6. SUMMARY AND CONCLUSIONS

The idea that a protected domestic market gives firms a base for successful exporting is one of those heterodox arguments, common in discussions of international trade, which are incomprehensible in terms of standard models yet seem persuasive to practical men. This paper has developed some simple models which make sense of the argument for protection-as-promotion. To get heterodox conclusions one needs heterodox assumptions: these models assume oligopoly instead of perfect competition, decreasing costs instead of constant returns. Interestingly, however, the economies of scale need not be simple static production economies but can take fairly subtle dynamic forms.

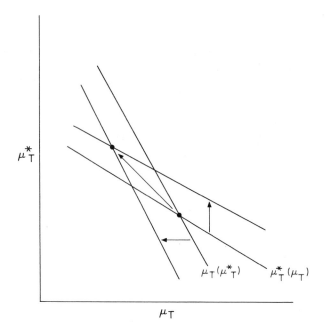

μ_T^*

$\mu_T(\mu_T^*)$ $\mu_T^*(\mu_T)$

μ_T

Fig. 11.8

What is the moral of this paper? Certainly not that the US should protect its manufacturers as a general strategy. For one thing, the paper contains no welfare analysis. The reason for this is that it is extremely complex. We are comparing second-best situations in any case; and if markets like the ones portrayed here are prevalent, we will not be able to use the standard tools of consumer and producer surplus.

Also, the difference between the conclusions of this paper and standard conclusions is one based on differences in assumptions; which view is more nearly true is an empirical matter. Showing that heterodox ideas are self-consistent does not show that they are right.

The moral of the paper, then, is a much more modest one: the things we are talking about here can be modelled. And it is important that we try. It may be that free trade and *laissez-faire* are good policies, and that most interventionist suggestions are self-serving, fallacious, or both. But the argument of trade theorists will remain unpersuasive unless their models begin to contain at least some of the features of the world which practical men accuse them of neglecting.

REFERENCES

Brander, J. A. (1981), 'Intra-industry Trade in Identical Commodities', *Journal of International Economics*, 11, 1–14.

Brander, J. A. and Krugman, P. (1981), 'A Reciprocal Dumping Model of International Trade', mimeo, M.I.T.

Spence, A. M. (1981), 'The Learning Curve and Competition', *Bell Journal of Economics*, 12, 49–70.

Spencer, B. J. and Brander, J. A. (1982), 'International R & D Rivalry and Industrial Strategy', mimeo, Boston College.

12

Tariff Protection
and Imperfect Competition

James Brander* and Barbara Spencer

1. INTRODUCTION

Experience with tariff negotiations yields the observation that most countries favour trade liberalization in principle, but are reluctant to undertake unilateral reduction of trade barriers. In return for reducing tariffs or quotas countries usually require compensation in the form of being allowed freer access to foreign markets. Thus, most recent trade liberalization has been multilateral in character rather than unilateral.

Many explanations of such behaviour could be advanced. Perhaps domestic political considerations make multilateral trade liberalization more feasible than unilateral liberalization, or perhaps most countries are large enough to pursue 'monopoly tariff' (or 'optimal tariff') policies. In this paper a rather simple contributing explanation, based on imperfect competition, is put forward. If imperfect competition is an important characteristic of some international markets, then firms in these markets may earn pure profits. Protection can shift some of this profit from foreign to domestic firms, and in addition, tariffs can transfer foreign rents to the domestic treasury in the form of tariff revenue. There is some cost in that markets are further distorted, but it is clear that, from a purely domestic point of view, protection is likely to be an attractive policy. A non-cooperative international equilibrium will involve such tariffs.

Simply shifting profit from one firm to another or from a firm to a government treasury is not beneficial to the world at large, so, from an international perspective, only the costs of protection remain. One country may benefit from protection, but the resulting losses to other countries usually more than offset this gain. Thus imperfect competition gives rise to beggar-thy-neighbour incentives for protective policies. The natural solution to this dilemma is through multilateral negotiation and trade liberalization, but unilateral tariff or quota reduction would not be expected.

This profit-shifting motive for protection suggests that a domestic firm would alway favour protection of its industry, regardless of whether the industry happened to be capital- or labour-intensive. If the industry involved were large, there might be factor price effects, but they would be small compared to the transfers of rent. Furthermore, if labour were also imperfectly competitive and could extract a portion of the extra rents accruing to the firm, labour in the industry would also favour protection.

The idea that imperfect competition might call for policy intervention has of course been recognized in the 'distortions' literature. (See, in particular, Bhagwati, Ramaswami, and Srinivasan, 1969; and Bhagwati, 1971.) Corden (1974) points out some second-best policy incentives that might arise under imperfect competition. Also the idea of using domestic policy to enhance the monopoly power of imperfectly competitive domestic firms has been considered. (See Basevi, 1979; Frenkel, 1971; and Auquier and Caves, 1979.) The setting in this paper, however, is quite different, as the central issue concerns shifting rent.

The possible use of protection to shift rents from imperfectly competitive foreign firms to domestic firms appears to have been largely ignored, which is surprising in view of the simplicity of the argument and its correspondence with actual perceptions in the business community. Katrak (1977) and Svedberg (1979) point out, using linear examples, that a tariff can be used to extract rent from a foreign monopoly, and De Meza (1979) suggests price controls. These papers do not, however, consider the role of domestic firms. Brander and Spencer (1981) consider the effects of a tariff in the case in which potential domestic entrants may be deterred from entering by a foreign monopolist.

Once it is recognized that both foreign and domestic firms are important, the question arises as to how firms interact with one another. There are many competing models of imperfect competition and the details of the analysis change according to which model is chosen. In this paper we first consider the case of simple foreign monopoly and then examine the simplest oligopoly model: Cournot duopoly with one foreign firm and one domestic firm. Even this simple Cournot model raises some interesting possibilities. From a purely positive perspective, intra-industry trade will normally arise, even if the firms produce identical products (as in Brander, 1981). On the normative side, a tariff will usually raise domestic welfare, although it is just possible that a subsidy could be the optimum policy.

We are also interested in the interaction between countries. What happens if other countries unilaterally set tariffs in response to the initial 'profit-shifting' tariff. We characterize the non-cooperative tariff equilibrium and contrast it with the co-operative equilibrium that would arise if countries could bargain and make binding agreements so as to maximize world welfare.

2. FOREIGN MONOPOLY AND THE TARIFF

The point that a tariff can be used to extract rent from foreign firms so as to increase domestic welfare can be made most simply in the case of foreign monopoly. The development in this section follows Brander and Spencer (1984). Taking the view that any one industry is small compared to the entire economy, we assume that domestic demand arises from a utility function that can be approximated by the form

$$U = u(X) + m, \tag{12.1}$$

where X is consumption of the good under consideration. In this section we use a partial equilibrium analysis so m is interpreted as expenditure on other goods. In later sections we embed the model in a simple general equilibrium framework where m is interpreted as consumption of a competitively produced numeraire good. Use of this utility function for both positive and normative analysis abstracts from a number of theoretical difficulties, including income effects, aggregation problems, and second-bast problems induced by other distortions in the economy and consequently allows us to focus on the pure rent-shifting incentives.

Since this utility function implies the marginal utility of income equals 1, inverse demand is just the derivative of u:

$$p = u'(X), \tag{12.2}$$

where p represents price. Also $u(X) - pX$ is equal to consumer surplus from X and is a consistent measure of the benefit to domestic consumers from consuming good X. Therefore, with tariff t, the net domestic gain, G, from imports of good X is

$$G(t) = u(X) - pX + tX. \tag{12.3}$$

Imports X depend on t, and the relationship $X = X(t)$ is determined by the behaviour of the foreign monopolist. Domestic welfare is maximized when $G_t \ (\equiv dG/dt)$ is equal to zero.

$$G_t = u'(X)X_t - Xp_t - pX_t + tX_t + X = 0, \tag{12.4}$$

where $p_t = p'X_t$. Using (12.2) and letting $\mu = -tX_t/X$, the elasticity of imports with respect to the tariff, (12.4) implies

$$G_t = -X(p_t + \mu - 1) = 0. \tag{12.5}$$

The effect of the tariff on price and the tariff elasticity of imports must sum to one. If the government placed no weight on consumer welfare and wished only to maximize tariff revenue, the condition would be $\mu = 1$. Equation (12.5) arises when tariff revenue and consumer surplus are given equal weight in the domestic objective function.

A useful rearrangement of (12.4) is

$$\hat{t} = X(p_t - 1)/X_t, \tag{12.6}$$

where $\hat{t}$ is the optimum tariff. Equation (12.6) indicates that $\hat{t}$ is positive if $p_t < 1$; that is, if an increase in the tariff causes price to rise by less than the tariff. On the other hand if $\hat{t}$ is negative a subsidy is appropriate. This arises if $p_t > 1$ so that an increase in the subsidy causes price to fall by more than the subsidy.

The comparative static effects p_t and X_t are therefore important in characterizing the optimal tariff. These are obtained by examination of the foreign firm's profit-maximization problem. Letting V be variable profit from the domestic market for the foreign firm and using k to denote (constant) marginal cost (including transport costs) we have

$$V(X) = Xp(X) - kX - tX. \tag{12.7}$$

The first and second-order conditions are

$$V_X = Xp' + p - (k + t) = 0 \tag{12.8}$$

$$V_{XX} = Xp'' + 2p' < 0. \tag{12.9}$$

The comparative-static effect X_t can be determined by differentiating $V_X = 0$ with respect to X and t which yields

$$X_t = 1/V_{XX} < 0. \tag{12.10}$$

X_t can be seen to depend on the relative convexity of demand. The appropriate measure of relative convexity is denoted by a variable R where

$$R = Xp''/p'. \tag{12.11}$$

From (12.11) and (12.9), $V_{XX} = p'(2 + R)$ so from (12.10) and $p_t = p'X_t$ we have,

$$p_t = 1/(R + 2). \tag{12.12}$$

Therefore p_t exceeds, equals, or falls short of one as R is less than, equals, or exceeds -1. We can also write (12.6) as

$$\hat{t} = -p'X(R + 1), \tag{12.13}$$

which leads to the following proposition.

Proposition 1

The optimum tariff is negative, zero, or positive as R is less than, equals, or exceeds minus one.

If R is less than minus one, the marginal revenue curve is less steeply sloped than demand. Therefore a decline in marginal cost due to a subsidy will cause price to fall by more than the subsidy and increase net domestic welfare. An example of a case in which a subsidy is optimal occurs if demand has constant elasticity. Denoting the constant elasticity by $\epsilon = -p/p'X$ yields $R = -1 - 1/\epsilon$ so $R < -1$ and $\hat{t} < 0$. Katrak (1977) and Svedberg (1979) consider the linear case. With linear demand $R = 0$ and $\hat{t}$ is positive. If one takes the view that demand is not likely to be highly convex, then it follows that positive tariffs will generally improve domestic welfare when the sole source of supply is an imperfectly competitive foreign industry.

3. DOMESTIC AND FOREIGN FIRMS

The main focus of this paper concerns the case in which there are both domestic and foreign firms. At this stage we also wish to make a few comments concerning embedding the industry of interest in a simple general equilibrium setting. Utility is assumed to arise from $U = u(X) + m^c$, where m^c is consumption of a competitively produced numeraire good, m, that can be produced in either the domestic country or the foreign country. Since the price of m is normalized to equal 1, domestic profit and government revenue are just added to $u(X)$ to obtain the domestic benefit function. (One extra dollar of profit or tariff revenue is used to buy one unit of m which produces one extra unit of utility.)

$$G(t) = u(X) - pX + tx + \pi, \tag{12.14}$$

where π is the profit of the domestic firm (which is assumed to be owned by domestic residents). Output in the domestic economy is produced using a single factor, which we refer to as labour, and good m has production function

$$L_m = m^p, \tag{12.15}$$

where L is the amount of labour used in the production of m and m^p is the amount of m produced domestically (which may differ from m^c, the amount of m consumed domestically).

There is a single domestic firm producing good X. Its production is denoted y, so that the total amount of X consumed domestically is $x + y$ where x is domestic sales by the foreign firm. The domestic production function for y is, in implicit form,

$$L_y = F + cy, \tag{12.16}$$

where F and c are measured in units of labour. Labour is supplied inelastically to the domestic economy in amount L so that $L_y + L_m = L$. The value of marginal product of labour in the competitive sector is one so the wage rate is one. The cost of producing y is then just $F + cy$ so the domestic firm has profit function

$$\pi = yp(X) - cy - F, \tag{12.17}$$

where F and c now represent dollar values. The variable c becomes marginal cost and F becomes fixed cost.

The foreign economy is similar, so the foreign firm has variable profit V from the domestic market where

$$V(x, y; t) = xp(X) - kx - tx, \tag{12.18}$$

where k is its (constant) marginal cost and t is the tariff.

This simple general equilibrium setting is, of course, equivalent to a partial equilibrium model in which profit functions (12.17) and (12.18) are specified directly. The point being made is that a partial equilibrium model can always be given the general equilibrium interpretation presented here. The essential question is not whether a model is partial or general equilibrium, but whether the industry in question is large enough to give rise to income effects, cross-substitution effects in demand and factor price effects. We have assumed that it is not so as to focus on the issue of central interest here: the rent-shifting aspect of a tariff under imperfect competition.

Maximizing G with respect to t yields first-order condition

$$G_t = -Xp_t + tx_t + x + (p-c)y_t + yp_t = 0, \qquad (12.19)$$

where subscripts denote derivatives. Rearrangement and substituting $\mu = -tx_t/x$ yields

$$G_t = -x(p_t - 1 + \mu) + (p-c)y_t = 0. \qquad (12.20)$$

The first term captures the change in consumer surplus and the change in tariff revenue arising from a change in imports from the foreign firm. Since $(p-c)y_t = \pi_t - yp_t$, the second term reflects the change in domestic profit and consumer surplus arising from the change in the price of the domestic output. More directly the second term is the marginal surplus, $p-c$, from domestic production times the change in domestic output. Solving (from (12.20)) for the optimal tariff, $\hat{t}$, yields

$$\hat{t} = -[(1-p_t)x + (p-c)y_t]/x_t. \qquad (12.21)$$

Comparison of expressions (12.6) and (12.21) is illustrative. With both domestic and foreign firms the optimal tariff is related to the effect of a tariff on domestic firms in addition to its effect on the foreign firm. The nature of the interaction between the two firms becomes important. Most reasonable representations of this interaction have the property that $y_t > 0$ and $x_t < 0$: a higher tariff decreases imports and increases sales of the domestic firm.

As before, the condition $p_t < 1$ is sufficient to insure that the optimum tariff is positive. However, even if $p_t > 1$ the optimum tariff may still be positive because the term $(p-c)y_t$ is positive.

Proposition 2

With both domestic and foreign firms, $p_t < 1$ is sufficient but not necessary for the optimal profit-shifting tariff to be positive. In particular (from (12.21)), a positive tariff is optimal if

$$p_t < 1 + (p-c)y_t/x. \qquad (12.22)$$

Proposition 2 is no surprise. In addition to capturing tariff revenue a domestic tariff now has the added feature that profits are shifted to the domestic firm.

An illustrative special case is the case in which the market rivalry between the two firms is resolved as a Cournot duopoly. In this case the domestic firm maximizes profit (given by equation (12.17)) with respect to its own output yielding first-order condition:

$$\pi_y \equiv yp' + p - c = 0. \qquad (12.23)$$

The first-order condition association with the profit-maximization problem faced by the foreign firm is (from (12.18))

$$V_x \equiv xp' + p - k - t = 0. \tag{12.24}$$

Equations (12.23) and (12.24) are the reaction functions of the two firms in implicit form. Each shows the 'best reply' output for the firm, given whatever level of output the other firm happens to be producing. The Cournot equilibrium occurs when both (12.23) and (12.24) are satisfied: neither firm can improve its profit given the output level of its rival.

Second-order conditions require $\pi_{yy} < 0$ and $V_{xx} < 0$. In addition, only stable equilibria are of interest. Stability can be insured by that rather weak requirement that each firm's perceived marginal revenue decline when the output of its rival rises. This means $\pi_{yx} < 0$ and $V_{xy} < 0$ and also implies that

$$D = \pi_{yy} V_{xx} - \pi_{yx} V_{xy} > 0. \tag{12.25}$$

((12.25) is necessary for stability but does not imply $\pi_{yx} < 0$ and $V_{xy} < 0$. Therefore stability is possible even if $\pi_{yx} > 0$ and $V_{xy} > 0$. This unusual possibility is not something we wish to examine here.)

It is then an easy comparative static exercise to show that y_t is positive and x_t is negative. Totally differentiating (12.23) and (12.24) with respect to y, x, and t yields comparative static matrix equation

$$\begin{bmatrix} \pi_{yy} & \pi_{yx} \\ V_{xy} & V_{xx} \end{bmatrix} \begin{bmatrix} y_t \\ x_t \end{bmatrix} = \begin{bmatrix} 0 \\ 1 \end{bmatrix}. \tag{12.26}$$

Then

$$y_t = -\pi_{yx}/D \tag{12.27}$$

$$x_t = \pi_{yy}/D. \tag{12.28}$$

Since $\pi_{yx}(\equiv yp'' + p')$ is negative and D is positive, y_t must be positive. Also with $\pi_{yy} < 0$ and $D > 0$, it follows that x_t is negative: an increase in the tariff increases output of the domestic firm and reduces imports. Furthermore, total domestic consumption tends to fall as the tariff is increased:

$$X_t = y_t + x_t = (\pi_{yy} - \pi_{yx})/D = p'/D < 0. \tag{12.29}$$

Proposition 3.

A tariff reduces domestic consumption.

The main point of this section is that, even though a tariff reduces domestic consumption, a country would normally perceive an incentive to impose a tariff since gains to domestic firms and increases in government revenue would more than offset losses to consumers.

4. TWO COUNTRIES

In considering a two-country world one important consideration is whether markets are unified or segmented (using the terminology of Helpman (1982)). Segmented markets arise when firms treat different countries as different markets in that they choose their strategy variables (in this case quantity) for each market separately. The segmented markets assumption corresponds to our perception of the way in which many firms operate: Toyota makes distinct decisions concerning how many cars to produce for domestic consumption and how many to export to the US; it does not bring its entire output to market in Tokyo and rely on arbitrage to distribute it throughout the world.

With segmented markets, imperfect competition gives rise to intra-industry trade. The causes and consequences of this type of intra-industry are described in Brander (1981) and Brander and Krugman (1983). The analytical point can be made by noting that the non-cooperative solution to the profit-maximizing problem faced by the firms involves intra-industry trade. Assuming that both countries charge tariffs and using asterisks to denote variables associated with foreign country, the domestic firm's total profit is

$$\pi = yp(X) + y^*p^*(X^*) - cy - c^*y^* - t^*y^* - F \qquad (12.30)$$

and the profit of the foreign firm is

$$\pi^* = xp(X) + x^*p^*(X^*) - kx - k^*x^* - tx - F^*. \qquad (12.31)$$

The coefficients c^* and k include transportation costs so $c^* > c$ and $k^* < k$. In any case, the first-order conditions are

$$\pi_y = 0; \quad \pi_x^* = 0; \quad \pi_{y*} = 0; \quad \pi_{x*}^* = 0. \qquad (12.32)$$

The first two equations, $\pi_y = 0$ and $\pi_x^* = 0$ are independent of x^* and y^* and their solution for the Cournot model is as presented in the previous section. Similarly $\pi_{y*} = 0$ and $\pi_{x*}^* = 0$ give rise to an equilibrium in the foreign country with both firms selling. Because of transportation costs, each firm will have a larger share of its home market than of its export market, but both firms will operate in both markets. Since firms set perceived marginal revenue equal to marginal cost in each market, and perceived marginal revenue is higher for the firm with the small market share, that firm can absorb transport costs and still find it profitable to be in the market. Helpman (1982) observes that the crucial element in firms' perceptions concerns market segmentation. Instead of perceiving only a single world market demand, each firm perceives distinct country-specific demands.

Our main focus here is on tariff policy. The domestic tariff t influences the market equilibrium in the domestic market and the foreign tariff t^* affects the foreign market. Each of these tariffs has an impact on the profits of both firms and therefore on the net welfare of both countries.

$$G = G(t; t^*) = u(X) - pX + tx + \pi \tag{12.33}$$

$$G^* = G^*(t^*; t) = u^*(X^*) - p^*X^* + t^*y^* + \pi^*. \tag{12.34}$$

Once again the 'best-reply' functions are defined by the first-order conditions:

$$dG/dt = 0; \quad dG^*/dt^* = 0. \tag{12.35}$$

If the profit functions are as written in expressions (12.30) and (12.31) the term 'best-reply' is rather misleading because the optimum tariff t is independent of t^*: what happens in the foreign market has no effect on the domestic market (and vice versa). If, however, marginal cost were not constant the two markets would interact and the tariff chosen by one country would depend on the tariff chosen by the other. Expression (12.35) is two equations in the two variables t and t^* whose solution characterizes the non-cooperative tariff equilibrium. This equilibrium is to be compared with the cooperative or world welfare-maximizing tariff levels.

The total world welfare is $G + G^*$. Since any one country's tariff revenue is a cost to the foreign firm, tariff revenue is irrelevant to world welfare. It is however possible that a positive tariff could increase welfare if transport costs were high. With constant marginal costs the domestic tariff does not affect sales x^* and y^* in the foreign country, so the total effect of a change in the domestic tariff on world welfare $G_t + G_t^* = G_t + V_t$ where V is the variable profit from the exports of the foreign firm. From (12.20),

$$G_t = -x(p_t - 1 + \mu) + (p - c)y_t$$

and from (12.5)

$$V_t = \frac{\partial V}{\partial x} x_t + \frac{\partial V}{\partial y} y_t + \frac{\partial V}{\partial t} = 0 + xp'y_t - x \quad \text{(assuming Cournot behaviour)}.$$

Adding these and using $\mu = -tx_t/x$ and $p_t = p'(y_t + x_t)$ yields

$$G_t + V_t = -xp'x_t + tx_t + (p - c)y_t.$$

Then noting that the first-order condition for profit maximization by the foreign firm implies $p + xp' = t + k$, the change in world welfare is

$$G_t + V_t = (p - k)x_t + (p - c)y_t. \tag{12.36}$$

Expression (12.36) requires very little interpretation. The effect of a change in the tariff on world welfare is just the marginal net benefit associated with x times the change in x plus the marginal net benefit of y times the change in y. Using the Cournot example developed in Section 3, we have $x_t < 0$ and $y_t > 0$. Since $p - k$ and $p - c$ are both positive, the two terms in (12.36) work in opposite directions. If k and c were roughly equal, x and y would also be roughly equal. Expressions (12.27), (12.28), and (12.29) then imply that y_t would be smaller in absolute value than x_t so $G_t + V_t$ would clearly be negative. However, if there are large transport costs k will exceed c and $G_t + V_t$ may be positive. The net benefit would be made possible by replacing high cost foreign production with low cost domestic production.

Proposition 4

If foreign marginal cost (including transport costs) is less than or equal to domestic marginal cost, an increase in the domestic tariff decreases world welfare.

From the international point of view higher tariffs have the effect of reducing intra-industry trade. This may be beneficial if there are high transport costs and, as a consequence, substantial waste. If transport costs are low, however, the pro-competitive effect of intra-industry trade offsets the waste due to transport costs and tariffs are inefficient. Tariffs are particularly undesirable if the domestic industry is 'weak' in the sense of having higher costs. Yet this is precisely the case in which unilateral pressures for tariffs are usually strongest.

Now we consider whether the non-cooperative solution involves a higher level of tariffs than the world welfare-maximizing solution. The world welfare-maximizing tariff requires that $G_t + V_t = 0$. Since $G_t = 0$ at the non-cooperatively chosen tariff but $V_t \neq 0$ the non-cooperative solution does not maximize world welfare. Since $V_t = xp'y_t - x < 0$, world welfare would increase if the tariff were reduced from the non-cooperative or unilaterally chosen level.

Proposition 5

The world welfare maximum may involve positive tariffs, but the non-cooperatively chosen tariffs exceed the world welfare-maximizing tariffs.

The important point is that the non-cooperative solution is generally inferior to the co-operative solution. Although each country perceives a unilateral incentive to impose a tariff, normally each would be better off if they could agree to have lower tariffs, hence the incentive for multilateral tariff reduction.

5. CONCLUDING REMARKS

An important aspect of world trade is that there is substantial trade in similar but not identical products. The greater variety of consumption made possible by international trade becomes an important source of gains from trade in addition to any pro-competitive effects of trade. Several authors have analysed such trade including Krugman (1979, 1980, 1981), Lancaster (1980), Helpman (1981), and Eaton and Kierzkowski (1984). Lancaster (1984) examines protection in such a context. The point we wish to make here is that the framework of this paper can be easily extended to include product variety, and gives rise to a different treatment of variety than the other papers just mentioned. If the output of the foreign firm sells for p and p^* in the domestic and foreign countries respectively, while the (slightly different) domestic output shells at prices q and q^*, then profit functions become

$$\pi = yq(x, y) + y^* q^*(x^*, y^*) - cy - (c^* + t^*)y^* - F \qquad (12.37)$$

$$\pi^* = xp(x, y) + x^* p^*(x^*, y^*) - (k + t)x - k^* x^* - F^*. \qquad (12.38)$$

As before, a non-cooperative equilibrium where $\pi_y = 0$, $\pi_{y*} = 0$, $\pi_x^* = 0$, and $\pi_{x*}^* = 0$ will normally involve intra-industry trade. As before, optimum tariffs can be calculated and similar results as for the homogeneous case follow. An economically interesting set of questions arise concerning how the degree of substitutability affects the extent of intra-industry trade and the structure of optimum tariffs, but serious analysis of these issues is beyond the scope of the present paper. The fact remains, however, that the central points of this paper are robust to the introduction of product differentiation.

The world described in the paper is one in which the rivalry of imperfectly competitive firms serves as an independent cause of international trade. In such a world firms tend to invade one another's home markets, which gives rise to intra-industry trade, even in homogeneous products. Yet such trade tends to be welfare-improving because of its pro-competitive effects. Only if transport costs are high will such trade be welfare-reducing.

The main objective of the paper is to use this imperfectly competitive setting to present a simple explanation of why a country might impose tariffs on foreign firms but be in favour of multilateral trade liberalization. The distinction is just the difference between a non-cooperative solution and a co-operative one.

We have used a simple Cournot model to demonstrate the main points. Similar insights would emerge in the more sophisticated imperfectly competitive environments described by Krugman (1984) and Shaked and Sutton (1984) since the nature of tariff incentives is based chiefly on the presence of pure profits. The principal role of the tariff is to shift profit from foreign firms to domestic firms and to the domestic treasury. Naturally each country would be reluctant to reduce such rent-generating tariffs, but might be persuaded to do so if domestically owned firms were to be allowed freer access to profitable markets.

We do not, of course, wish to suggest that policy-makers singlemindedly pursue welfare-maximizing policies of the sort described here, nor that policy-makers have access to all the relevant information required to formulate such policy. However, we would argue that if simple welfare-improving policies are available, some kind of incentive will be perceived, however imperfectly, by policy authorities.

Finally, it should be emphasized that our arguments should not be taken as support for using tariffs. The highly tariff-ridden world economy that would result from each country maximizing domestic welfare taking the policies of other countries as given would be a poor outcome. Our analysis is meant to contribute to an understanding of the motives that might underlie tariff policy, and provides support for the multilateral approach to trade liberalization.

ACKNOWLEDGEMENT

*   J. A. Brander would like to acknowledge gratefully the support of the
SSHRCC post-doctoral fellowship 456-81-3455.

REFERENCES

Auquier, A. and Caves, R. (1979), 'Monopolistic Export Industries, Trade,
    Taxes and Optimal Competition Policy', *Economic Journal*, 89, 559–81.
Basevi, G. (1970), 'Domestic Demand and the Ability to Export', *Journal of
    Political Economy*, 18, 330–7.
Bhagwati, J. (1971), 'The Generalized Theory of Distortions and Welfare', in
    J. Bhagwati *et al.* (eds.), *Trade, Growth and the Balance of Payments*,
    Essays in Honour of Gottfried Haberler (Chicago and Amsterdam): Rand-
    McNally and North-Holland).
Bhagwati, J., Ramaswami, V., and Srinivasan, T. N. (1969), 'Domestic Dis-
    tortions, Tariffs and the Theory of Optimum Subsidy: Some Further
    Results', *Journal of Political Economy*, 77, 1005–10.
Brander, J. (1981), 'Intra-industry Trade in Identical Commodities', *Journal of
    International Economics*, 11, 1–14.
Brander, J. and Krugman, P. (1983), 'A Reciprocal Dumping Model of Inter-
    national Trade', *Journal of International Economics* (in press).
Brander, J. and Spencer, B. (1981), 'Tariffs and the Extraction of Foreign
    Monopoly Rents under Potential Entry', *Canadian Journal of Economics*,
    14, 371–89.
Brander, J. and Spencer, B. (1984), 'Trade Warfare: Tariffs and Cartels', *Journal
    of International Economics* (forthcoming).
Cordon, W. M. (1974), *Trade Policy and Economic Welfare* (London: Oxford
    University Press).
De Meza, D. (1979), 'Commercial Policy Towards Multinational Monopolies –
    Reservations on Katrak', *Oxford Economic Papers*, 31, 334–7.
Eaton, J. and Kierzkowski, H. (1984), 'Oligopolistic Competition, Product
    Variety, and International Trade', this volume.
Frenkel, J. (1971), 'On Domestic Demand and Ability to Export', *Journal of
    Political Economy*, 79, 668–72.
Greenaway, D. (1984), 'The Measurement of Product Differentiation for Empiri-
    cal Analysis of Trade Flows', this volume.
Grubel, H. G. and Lloyd, P. J. (1975), *Intra-Industry Trade* (London: Macmillan).
Helpman, E. (1981), 'International Trade in the Presence of Product Differen-
    tiation, Economies of Scale and Monopolistic Competition: A Chamberlin-
    Heckscher-Ohlin Approach', *Journal of International Economics*, 11,
    305–40.
Helpman, E. (1982), 'Increasing Returns, Imperfect Markets and Trade Theory',
    Discussion Paper No. 18–82, Foerder Institute for Economic Research,
    Tel Aviv University.

Katrak, H. (1977), 'Multinational Monopolies and Commercial Policy', *Oxford Economic Papers*, 29, 283–91.

Krugman, P. (1979), 'Increasing Returns, Monopolistic Competition, and International Trade', *Journal of International Economics*, 9, 469–79.

Krugman, P. (1980), 'Scale Economies, Product Differentiation and the Pattern of Trade', *American Economic Review*, 70, 950–59.

Krugman, P. (1981), 'Intra-industry Specialization and the Gains from Trade', *Journal of Political Economy*, 89, 959–73.

Krugman, P. (1984), 'Import Protection as Export Promotion: International Competition in the Presence of Oligopoly and Economies of Scale', this volume.

Lancaster, K. (1980), 'Intra-Industry Trade under Perfect Monopolistic Competition', *Journal of International Economics*, 10, 151–75.

Lancaster, K. (1984), 'Protection and Product Differentiation', this volume.

Markusen, J. R. (1981), 'Trade and the Gains from Trade with Imperfect Competition', *Journal of International Economics*, 11, 531–52.

Pursell, G. and Snape, R. (1973), 'Economies of Scale, Price Discrimination and Exporting', *Journal of International Economics*, 3, 85–91.

Shaked, A. and Sutton, J. (1984), 'Natural Oligopolies and International Trade', this volume.

Svedberg, P. (1979), 'Optimal Tariff Policy on Imports from Multinationals', *Economic Record*, 55, 64–7.

13

A New Look at Economic Integration*

Wilfred Ethier and Henrik Horn

The literature on customs unions theory is gargantuan. Nevertheless it strikes us as inadequate, both in the theoretical cases it addresses and in the actual circumstances of the world economy to which it is commonly thought relevant. This paper aims to spell out the details of this inadequacy and to indicate some lines along which the theory ought to be developed.

Section 1 very briefly describes basic ideas in contemporary customs union theory, and Section 2 then discusses at some length necessary extensions. Two general propositions are advanced in the next section, and proved in Section 4. Section 5 develops a specific model incorporating the new features, and Section 6 then exhibits aspects of this model via some special comparative-statics exercises.

1. BASICS OF CUSTOMS UNION THEORY

There is a huge literature in this area for three distinct reasons: (i) the *institutional* fact that there are many types of discriminatory trade besides customs unions proper (preferential trading arrangements, free trade areas, common markets, economic unions, and so on), (ii) the subject demands disaggregation beyond two-country, two-commodity models, and therefore gives rise to *many conceivable combinations* of characteristics of countries, commodities, and trade flows, and (iii) the subject requires comparisons of *distorted* equilibria which, in particular in conjunction with the second point, increases the mathematical complexity of the analysis. In practice the latter two factors have proved decisive, with analysis concentrated disproportionately upon the case of a customs union proper (free internal trade combined with a common external tariff).

Two basic ideas stand out from the wealth of specific analysis. The first, which might be called the *Vinerian Description*, is the notion that the net effect of a customers union is dependent on the balance of trade creation and trade diversion. This idea is in truth the very core of customs union theory.

(A) *Vinerian Description*. Formation of a customs union produces trade creation between the partners, in response to the mutual elimination of tariffs on one another's goods, and trade diversion from third countries to the partners, in response to the tariff discrimination produced by the union.

Trade creation is by presumption beneficial and trade diversion harmful. Union formation is thus seen as a second-best exercise, with one distortion replaced by another. This, together with the need for at least some disaggregation, accounts for the multitude of separate possibilities. Other aspects of union formation have of course also received attention. Notable examples, to which we shall return, include changes in the terms of trade — both within the union and *vis-à-vis* the outside world — and also economies of scale and the degree of competition.

Mention of the terms of trade relative to the rest of the world brings us to the second basic idea, due to Kemp, Vanek, Ohyama, and Wan. Setting the external tariffs at appropriate levels can cause the member countries, in the aggregate, to trade with the rest of the world exactly the same collection and quantities of goods that, in the aggregate, they traded prior to the union. Then the union will have no effect at all on the rest of the world, and the members must in the aggregate benefit, because the only effect they experience is the freeing of mutual trade. In essence, manipulation of the external tariff schedule allows any customs union to eliminate all trade diversion and so consist only of trade creation. By allowing a small deterioriation in its external terms of trade, the union can ensure that also non-members benefit.

(B) *Kemp–Vanek–Ohyama–Wan.* By an appropriate choice of common external tariffs and of lump-sum transfers among members, any customs union can assure that no countries in the world lose, and that some gain, as a result of the formation of the union.

This proposition applies irrespective of initial conditions, and so establishes a sense in which the countries of the world always have incentives to form additional unions until global free trade is achieved.

2. DESIRABLE DEPARTURES

Although the two ideas discussed above hardly begin to do justice to the vastness of customs union theory,[1] they do indicate the distinguishing features of the subject and are its most important conclusions. Thus we take the pair as a benchmark from which to enquire in what direction contemporary problems mandate that the subject be further developed. We indicate four directions. The four have by no means been completely ignored by the literature; and in some cases have received formal treatment, but they do depart substantially from the core of received customs unions theory.

(i) *Trade Modification*

The basic element of the conventional theory is tariff discrimination: the *same* good that can be imported free of duty from a partner faces a tariff when it comes from a non-partner country. But partners also trade among themselves some goods which they do not import at all (either before or after the union) from outside countries. For want of a better term, we describe as *trade modification* the change in trade with outside countries due to the elimination of tariffs on goods traded only within the union.[2] Thus trade modification differs from its familiar sister concept of trade diversion in that it can be produced by tariff changes consistent with the Most Favoured Nation clause and with the GATT, that is, by economic integration resulting from the non-discriminatory elimination by the partners of tariffs on goods they import only from each other.

Suppose, as an example, that France and Germany form a customs union, with France eliminating its tariff on German automotive supplies, also initially imported from America. This discriminatory tariff change would presumably induce trade diversion, with imports of German automotive supplies replacing some or all of the imports from America. Now suppose in contrast that France initially imports small cars from Germany and large cars from America, and that the integration takes the form of a French abolition of the tariff on small cars. Such a non-discriminatory tariff change is not usually considered as within the domain of customs union theory, even though it is likely to deflect French demand from American to German automotive products in about the same way as the previous case. Next, suppose instead that there is a unified world automobile industry, with France importing engines from Germany and bodies from America, and that France abolishes its tariff on engines. This again causes trade modification, but now French imports of American bodies will likely rise along with French imports of German engines.

Trade modification differs from trade diversion in that it is not the result of geographical tariff *discrimination* but rather of the replacement of one set of tariffs by another, with the property that the tariffs which are changed apply directly to trade flows between a strict subset of countries. As the example makes clear, degrees of substitutability and complementarity between goods become crucial.

Extending the scope of the theory to encompass trade modification might well therefore open the gates to another flood of special cases — hardly welcome in this field especially. And the bulk of empirical work in the area cannot be interpreted as distinguishing trade diversion from trade modification. But there are good reasons why the theory should include both. First, of course, is that both are in principle part of the problem. More significant is the large volume of empirical work, by Kravis and Lipsey (1971) and many others, that in the last decade has revealed extensive international price discrimination at even quite disaggregated levels. As a result economists now tend, much more than before, to think of international trade as the exchange of differentiated products, rather than of homogeneous goods. This shift in perception calls for a shift in emphasis from trade diversion towards trade modification.

But the most important consideration is the range of phenomena to which the theory of economic integration ought to apply. Although many attempts at customs unions and free trade areas have been made since the Second World War, the only actual, substantially successful, instance to which the theory reflected in the Vinerian Description literally applies is western European integration. An important instance, to be sure, but past history. Customs union theory thus appears seldom to be used as a framework for thought about contemporary problems. But issues to which a theory of economic integration *ought* to apply are legion. As a glaring example, consider the dominant post-war exercise in global commercial policy: the cumulative tariff reductions produced by successive GATT rounds. As often emphasized by economists and men of affairs alike, these reductions have concentrated on trade in manufactures among the developed countries and have been much less relevant to the trade of LDCs. Thus we have experienced on an historical scale (and continue to do so as the Tokyo Round cuts are implemented) the very sort of nationally biased tariff reductions that are the very essence of the theory of economic integration. But our theory has not been thought relevant because those cuts, implemented under the Most Favoured Nation clause, directly conflict with the Vinerian Description. The incorporation of trade modification in addition to (or instead of) trade diversion is essential to the practical relevance of customs union theory.

(*ii*) *Intra-Industry Trade and Product Differentiation*

Related to the distinction between trade diversion and trade modification is the observation that customs union theory assumes trade in homogeneous products whereas product differentiation and intra-industry trade are pervasive in actual commerce. Theoretical models of these latter phenomena have been developed in recent years, and extension of these models to the theory of economic integration is obviously called for. Recall that our present widespread appreciation of the large and growing significance of intra-industry trade in the industrial world actually dates from studies of the effects of economic integration in Europe.

(*iii*) *Imperfect Competition and Scale Economies*

These phenomena have been considered in the light of customs union theory in the past. What is clearly called for now is the application of recently developed general equilibrium approaches.

(*iv*) *'Small' Tariff Changes*

Customs union theory has generally considered only 'large' tariff changes between partners: the complete elimination of internal trade barriers. Exceptions[3] have usually been accompanied by apologetic explanations of the convenience of marginal analysis. Large changes have been considered an essential aspect of the problem because theorists have often had in the backs of their minds the example of European integration, with free internal trade an objective from the start, and because the GATT rules permitting customs unions and free trade areas require the abolition of internal tariffs: mere reciprocal tariff preferences are ruled out. But the latter consideration is eliminated by our interest in trade modification. Furthermore, a concern with contemporary problems should redirect attention towards small changes, rendering marginal analysis of interest in its own right. The successive GATT rounds have, at each stage, constituted an incremental change toward free trade among the developed countries. If translated into tariff equivalents, the numerous voluntary export restraints of the 'new protectionism' of recent years likewise constitute incremental changes, though in the direction of economic disintegration. Another potentially important example is furnised by the codes of conduct regarding non-tariff barriers formulated during the Tokyo Round. These codes are not automatically binding on the GATT nations, or limited to them, but are to be individually acceded to by individual states. Thus each code seems likely to develop a circle of participating countries applying *vis-à-vis* one another the provisions of the code as regards the respective non-tariff barrier, but applying more restrictive prior standards toward non-participating countries. Thus the codes might well produce non-tariff equivalents of preferential trading areas.

It is easier to undertake by stages the departures recommended here. Therefore, in the following two sections we ignore imperfect competition and scale economies, but allow trade modification and enquire into the consequences of a small preferential change in tariffs, in a conventional context. Two general propositions, analogous to results well known in the theory of trade and domestic distortions, follow easily once attention is directed towards small tariff changes; these proportions are stated in Section 3, and are formally proved in Section 4. In the rest of the paper we consider also the remaining two suggested departures from the standard treatment of economic integration: product differentiation, and imperfect competition and scale economies. To highlight the impact of these additions, we construct in Section 5 a special formal model that incorporates all four departures, but that abstracts from some features already studied. In Section 6 we analyse properties of this model by means of comparative-statics experiments. Finally, some brief concluding remarks are given in Section 7.

3. TWO ADDITIONAL GENERAL PROPERTIES

Consider first an initial state of non-discriminatory (but tariff-ridden) world trade. Suppose that some subset of countries then initiates a marginal mutual reduction of tariffs on trade with one another. (Since the role of the external terms of trade is understood, suppose for simplicity that no change takes place in the terms at which these countries deal with the rest of the world.) Since trade is initially non-discriminatory, an additional unit of imports or exports by any country has the same effect on the welfare of residents of that country regardless of with whom the additional trade takes place. Thus the trade diversion and/or trade modification generated by the marginal preferential tariff reduction must have a zero first-order effect on welfare. But since trade is tariff-ridden, an additional unit of imports will cost any country less than that unit's contribution to welfare: any trade creation must have a positive first-order effect.

(C) *Preferential Trade is Better than Free Trade.* If tariffs are positive but non-discriminatory, any sub-group of countries can raise its joint welfare by means of marginal preferential tariff reductions that increase the gross value of their total trade (in the specific sense that the new trade flows yield the partners more tariff revenue than the old flows, at the initial tariffs and prices), if the prices of goods exchanged between those countries and the rest of the world do not change.

This proposition differs from the result of Kemp and Wan (1978), Ohyama (1972), and Vanek (1965) in that it is limited to small tariff changes, whose relevance we have just advocated. What this limitation buys us is a dispensation from the need to adjust external tariffs so as to eliminate trade diversion and trade modification: their welfare effects will be swamped by those of trade creation.

Now consider the opposite initial situation: a group of countries, in a tariff-ridden world, have formed a customs union with free internal trade. Suppose these countries stage a 'marginal retreat' from the union by imposing a small tariff on imports from one another. Free initial internal trade implies that a marginal import by any member from a partner yields a welfare increase equal to the welfare loss due to the exports required in payment. Thus the 'trade destruction' caused by the marginal internal tariff will entail a zero first-order effect on welfare. But any increased trade with the rest of the world produces a positive first-order effect since the initial external tariffs imply that an additional import increases welfare by more than the sacrifice required to pay for it.

(D) *Preferential Trade is Better than a Customs Union.* If any group of countries has free mutual trade in a tariff-ridden world, their joint welfare will be increased by a marginal tariff on one another's goods that raises total trade with the rest of the world (in the specific sense that the new volume of trade yields the partners jointly more revenue than the old, at the original tariffs and prices), if the prices at which the partners trade with external countries do not change.

In essence, the net benefits from 'undoing' some trade diversion and trade modification necessarily swamp the losses entailed by 'trade destruction', for a small retreat from a customs union. This partially undercuts the consistent motives for union formation that seem to be supplied by idea (B). Also (C) and (D) together imply a motivation for tariff preferences that fall short of complete union. This is quite consistent with the prominent contemporary issues that the previous section argued ought to be addressable by the theory of economic integration.

4. A FORMAL TREATMENT

4.1. The model

This section supplies explicit proofs of propositions (C) and (D) and discusses them further. Assume three countries: two partners (A and B) and the rest of the world (distinguished by an asterisk). There is a total of n traded goods, divided into the twelve groups described in Table 13.1. Groups 1 to 5 contain goods imported by country A, exportables are collected in groups 6–10, whereas country A does not trade in groups 11 and 12.

For each group i, Q_i denotes the n-vector with a zero in each component corresponding to a good not in group i, and with the country A domestic price of the respective good in each component that does so correspond. Thus $Q = \Sigma_{i=1}^{12} Q_i$ is the vector of country A domestic prices. Vectors P_i apply analogously to the partner country, so $P = \Sigma_{i=1}^{12} P_i$ denotes the vector of country-B domestic prices.

In like fashion, P_i^* denotes the vector of prices actually paid to the rest of the world, or received from the rest of the world, for goods in group i (with zeros in components corresponding to other goods). Let $R^A = P_1 + P_2^* + P_3^* + P_4^* + P_5^* + Q_6 + Q_7 + P_8^* + P_9^* + P_{10}^*$. Then R_A is the vector of prices at which country A actually transacts with foreigners, *except* possibly for those goods in group 5 that are imported from country B. In like manner, $R^B = P_1 + P_2^* + P_4^* + P_5 + Q_6 + P_7^* + P_9^* + P_{10}^* + P_{11}^* + P_{12}^*$ denotes B's actual international transaction prices, *except* possibly for goods in group 7 imported from A.

T_i^A, for $i = 1, \ldots, 4$, is the $n \times n$ diagonal matrix with *ad valorem* tariff rates of country A on goods in group i as the appropriate diagonal elements, and zeros elsewhere. T_{5B}^A and T_{5*}^A likewise denote tariff matrices of country A on goods in group 5 imported from B and from the rest of the world respectively. Country B tariff matrices T_4^B, T_6^B, T_{10}^B, T_{12}^B, T_{7A}^B, and T_{7*}^B are defined analogously. Let $T^A = T_1^A + T_2^A + T_3^A + T_4^A + T_{5*}^A$ and $T^B = T_4^B + T_6^B + T_{7*}^B + T_{10}^B + T_{12}^B$. Then

TABLE 13.1. *Description of the Commodity Groups*

Group	Commodity description
1	B exports only to A
2	B exports to A and to the rest of the world
3	the rest of the world exports only to A
4	the rest of the world exports to A and B
5	the rest of the world and B both export to A
6	A exports only to B
7	the rest of the world and A both export to B
8	A exports only to the rest of the world
9	A and B both export to the rest of the world
10	A exports to both B and the rest of the world
11	B exports only to the rest of the world
12	the rest of the world exports only to B

$$Q = (I + T^A) R^A,$$

$$P = (I + T^B) R^B.$$

Note also that $(I + T^A_{5B}) P_5 = (I + T^A_{5*}) P^*_5$ and $(I + T^B_{7A}) Q_7 = (I + T^B_{7*}) P^*_7$.

M^A_i is the n-vector of country A net imports of goods in group i (with zeros elsewhere), and $M^A = \Sigma^{10}_{i=1} M^A_i$. Also $M^A_5 = M^A_{5B} + M^A_{5*}$ and $M^A_{10} = M^A_{10B} + M^A_{10*}$ where the two vectors on the right in each case record trade with country B and the rest of the world respectively. Analogously for M^B_i, for $M^B = M^B_1 + M^B_2 + M^B_4 + M^B_5 + M^B_6 + M^B_7 + M^B_9 + M^B_{10} + M^B_{11} + M^B_{12}$, and for both $M^B_2 = M^B_{2A} + M^B_{2*}$ and $M^B_7 = M^B_{7A} + M^B_{7*}$. (Note that $M^A_1 = -M^B_1, M^A_2 = -M^B_{2A}, M^A_{5B} = -M^B_5, -M^A_6 = M^B_6, -M^A_7 = M^B_{7A}$ and $-M^A_{10B} = M^B_{10}$).

In country A, total expenditure – denoted by the national expenditure function $e^A(Q, u_A)$, where u_A denotes the vector of utilities of A residents – must equal income, composed of tariff revenue plus the value of national production, the latter given by the national product function $y^A(Q)$. Thus

$$e^A(Q, u_A) = y^A(Q) + T^A R^A [M^A - M^A_{5B}] + T^A_{5B} P^A_5 M^A_{5B}. \qquad (13.1)$$

Analogously for the partner country:

$$e^B(P, u_B) = y^B(P) + T^B R^B [M^B - M^B_{7A}] + T^B_{7A} Q_7 M^B_{7A}. \qquad (13.2)$$

4.2. A basic expression

Differentiating (13.1), noting that $\partial e^A / \partial Q - \partial y^A / \partial Q = M^A$ and that $dQ = dR^A + d(T^A R^A)$ gives

$$\frac{\partial e^A}{\partial u_A} du_A = -M^A dR^A - M^A_{5B} [d(T^A R^A) - d(T^A_{5B} P_5)] + T^A R^A d\bar{M}^A$$
$$+ T^A_{5B} P_5 dM^A_{5B}, \qquad (13.3)$$

where $\bar{M}^A \equiv M^A - M^A_{5B}$. In a like manner, we obtain for the partner country

$$\frac{\partial e^B}{\partial u_B} du_B = -M^B dR^B - M^B_{7A} [d(T^B R^B) - d(T^B_{7A} Q_7)] + T^B R^B d\bar{M}^B$$
$$+ T^B_{7A} Q_7 dM^B_{7A}. \qquad (13.4)$$

Equations (13.3) and (13.4) supply measures of the welfare effects on the partners of changes in commercial policy. The sources of these effects, spelled out on the right-hand sides of the equations, are analogous to the sources of welfare effects commonly discussed in conventional tariff theory.[4]

We measure the change in the joint welfare of the partner countries by $dW = (\partial e^A / \partial u_A) du_A + (\partial e^B / \partial u_B) du_B$. Remember that we suppose constancy in the prices at which A and B transact with the rest of the world, implying

$$M^A dR^A + M^B dR^B = -M^A_{5B} dP_5 - M^B_{7A} dQ_7.$$

With goods in group 5 (or group 7) being bought from the rest of the world at prices assumed to be unchanged, $d(T^A R^A) (d(T^B R^B))$ will have zero elements corresponding to positive entries in M^A_{5B} (or M^B_{7A}), and therefore

$$dW = M^A_{5B} [dP_5 + d(T^A_{5B} P_5)] + T^A_{5B} P_5 (dM^A - d\bar{M}^A) + T^A R^A \, d\bar{M}^A$$
$$+ M^B_{7A} [dQ_7 + d(T^B_{7A} Q_7)] + T^B_{7A} Q_7 (dM^B - d\bar{M}^B) + T^B R^B \, d\bar{M}^B,$$
(13.5)

where $T^A_{5B} P_5 (T^B_{7A} Q_7)$ has zeros corresponding to non-zero elements of $d\bar{M}^A$ $(d\bar{M}^B)$. Furthermore,

$$dP_5 + d(T^A_{5B} P_5) = d[(I + T^A_{5B})P_5] = d[(I + T^A_{5*})P^*_5] = P^*_5 \, dT^A_{5*},$$

$$dQ_7 + d(T^B_{7A} Q_7) = d[(I + T^B_{7A})Q_7] = d[(I + T^B_{7*})P^*_7] = P^*_7 \, dT^B_{7*}.$$

Since also M^A_{7A} (M^B_{7A}) has zero elements corresponding to non-zero elements in $P^*_5 \, dT^A_{5*}$ $(P^*_7 \, dT^B_{7*})$, our expression for the effect of tariff changes on the partners' joint welfare simplifies to

$$dW = (T^A_{5B} P_5) \, dM^A + (T^B_{7A} Q_7) \, dM^B + (T^A R^A) \, d\bar{M}^A + (T^B R^B) \, d\bar{M}^B.$$
(13.6)

This is our basic result. We now apply it to two special cases in order to derive propositions (C) and (D).

4.3. The propositions

Suppose first that all tariffs are initially non-discriminatory, so that $T^A_{5B} = T^A_{5*}$, $P_5 = P^*_5$, $T^B_{7A} = T^B_{7*}$, and $Q_7 = P^*_7$. Equation (13.6) then reduces to

$$dW = (T^A R^A) \, dM^A + (T^B R^B) \, dM^B.$$
(13.7)

Thus a small discriminatory tariff change (or any other small change) raises joint welfare if and only if the changes in trade volume would increase joint tariff revenues at the initial rates and prices, as was stated in proposition (C) above. Note in particular two aspects of this result.

First, the degree of trade diversion — reflected in the *composition* of dM^A_5 between dM^A_{5B} and dM^A_{5*} and in the composition of dM^B_7 between dM^B_{7A} and dM^B_{7*} — has no influence at all on dW. This is to be expected in the light of the previous section's informal discussion.

Second, trade modification — reflected in the magnitudes of dM^A_3, dM^A_4, dM^B_4, and dM^B_{12} — will add to or subtract from dW according as the goods involved are in this sense complementary to or substitutes for intra-union trade. This, again, is not surprising in view of the earlier discussion. Indeed, if the goods which countries A and B trade exclusively with the rest of the world are sufficiently strong substitutes for the goods they exchange with each other, they could have an incentive to form an 'anti-union', that is, to *add* a marginal discriminatory tariff on each others' goods. The two would have reason to seek separate preferential arrangements with the rest of the world, rather than with each other.

Suppose next that A and B initially have a full free trade area and impose marginal internal tariffs. Then $T_1^A = T_2^A = T_{5B}^A = T_6^B = T_{7A}^B = T_{10}^B = 0$ and (13.6) reduces to

$$dW = (T^A R^A) \, d\bar{M}^A + (T^B R^B) \, d\bar{M}^B. \tag{13.8}$$

Thus a marginal retreat from internal free trade will raise the partners' joint welfare if and only if it raises total tariff revenue collected on trade with the rest of the world, as stated above in proposition (D). It is instructive to decompose the right-hand side of (13.8) as follows:

$$dW = (T_5^A {}_* P_5^* \, dM_{5*}^A + T_{7*}^B P_7^* \, dM_{7*}^B) + (T_3^A P_3^* \, dM_3^A + T_4^A P_4^* \, dM_4^A$$
$$+ T_4^B P_4^* \, dM_4^B + T_{12}^B P_{12}^* \, dM_{12}^B). \tag{13.9}$$

Note that an 'undoing' of trade diversion — indicated by positive terms within the first set of parentheses on the right-hand side of (13.9) — must increase W regardless of how great the accompanying reduction in intra-union trade in the same goods happens to be. This is a consequence of the initial free internal trade, as discussed in the previous section.

The influence of trade modification is summarized by the second parenthesized term on the right-hand side of (13.9). Joint partner welfare is thereby raised or lowered according as this term is positive or negative, that is, according as the goods traded exclusively with the rest of the world are in this sense on balance substitutes for or complementary to intra-partner trade.

Trade diversion and trade modification are central in both exercises. The presumptive role of trade diversion is clear: it should cause both a marginal reduction of a discriminatory tariff and a marginal retreat from a free trade area to raise joint partner welfare. But the role of trade modification depends crucially upon whether the goods traded exclusively with the rest of the world are on balance substitutes for or complements to intra-union trade, in the sense that discrimination in favour of the latter reduces or increases the volume of the former, with the change in this volume measured by the net changes in partner tariff revenue it would generate at initial prices and tariffs.

Neither non-discrimination nor a free trade area would constitute an optimal policy — for A and B jointly, given tariffs on goods from the rest of the world — without a very special balancing of the various influences discussed above. If exclusively external trade is on balance neither strongly substitutable for, nor complementary to, internal trade, optimal policy for the partners will presumably entail tariff preferences that fall short of a full free trade area, so that both non-discrimination and customs unions should be unstable.

Significant net *substitutability* both reduces the gain from initial preferences and increases the gain to a retreat from a full union. Thus one expects it to cause optimal policy to feature a lower degree of preference. Sufficient substitutability should make optimal an 'anti-union' with the members actually discriminating against one another. Significant net *complementarity*, finally, increasing the gain from initial preferences and reducing that from a retreat, presumably causes the optimal policy to approximate more closely free internal trade. Large enough complementarity could cause the optimal policy to be a 'super union' with internal trade actually stimulated by subsidies finance by tariffs on external trade. Note that the European Community's Common Agricultural Policy — which does not naturally come to mind in a discussion of optimality — does in fact possess some of the characteristics of such a case.

5. SCALE ECONOMIES AND PRODUCT DIFFERENTIATION: A SPECIAL MODEL

The previous sections focused on trade modification as well as trade diversion and considered small tariff changes rather than large ones. But we said nothing about induced change in the *number* of distinct commodities (that is, in the degree of product differentiation), and, more prominently yet, imperfect competition and scale economies are foreign to the optimality conditions central to the logic of the propositions. Thus we have set off on some but not all of those departures from standard theory that we have argued for.

We have no wish to construct the awesome structure that would simply add our further suggested innovations to what we have already done in the previous section. Instead we now consider a special model that incorporates our four desired departures in as sharp a fashion as possible: by abstracting from other features. For better or worse, this is also the strategy used in the recent literature on international trade and scale economies, imperfect competition, and product differentiation.

We continue to suppose three countries: the partners (A and B) and the rest of the world, denoted by an asterisk. A and B can be thought of as DCs, the rest of the world as an LDC. A and B produce goods in two common sectors: manufactures and food. There are n and m different variants of manufactures produced in A and B, respectively. They are all (equally) imperfect substitutes to each other from the consumer's point of view, although they are produced with the same homothetic technology, characterized by internal, increasing returns to scale. Food, on the other hand, is produced in all three countries, under constant returns to scale.

We consider the following special trade pattern. A and B export their respective manufactures to each other and to the rest of the world, and both countries import food from the latter. We assume furthermore that A and B have formed a customs union with their internal tariff τ set at zero, and with a common external tariff t. The rest of the world imposes no trade restrictions.

It is clear that, with such a trade pattern, this customs union does not cause any trade *diversion*, since the non-member country exports a different good from that exported by the union countries. But the union will give rise to trade *creation* and trade *modification*.

Following, e.g., Dixit and Stiglitz (1977), we assume the preferences of each country's representative consumer to be given by

$$U^k = \left(\sum_{i=1}^{n} (X_i^k)^\beta + \sum_{j=1}^{m} (Y_j^k)^\beta \right)^{\alpha/\beta} (Z^k)^{1-\alpha}; \quad k = A, B, * \tag{13.10}$$

with $0 < \alpha < 1$, and $0 < \beta < 1$, and where X_i^k is the amount of the country A-produced manufacture i that is consumed in country k, Y_j^k is the amount of the country-B produced manufacture j that is consumed in k, and Z^k the consumed quantity of food in k.

Let us now turn to the production side. The production process for manufactures can be thought of as consisting of two stages: first primary factors are used to produce a (non-traded) intermediate input under constant returns to scale, in the amounts M^A and M^B in the two DCs. This input is transformed to final differentiated goods under increasing returns. Since the equilibrium under study is characterized by strong symmetry, in the sense that $X_i^k = X^k$, $\forall i$, and $Y_j^k = Y^k$, $\forall j$, each firm in the manufacturing sector in A employs M^A/n of the intermediate good, and correspondingly M^B/m in B. We assume that entry is free, so the condition for industry equilibrium is that profits are zero

$$PX = r^A \frac{M^A}{n}, \quad \text{and} \quad QY = r^B \frac{M^B}{m},$$

where P and Q are the prices received by producers of manufactured products in A and B, respectively, r is the price of the intermediate input, and where $X \equiv X^A + X^B + X^*$, and $Y \equiv Y^A + Y^B + Y^*$. The internal increasing returns to scale stem from a fixed cost a, coupled with a constant marginal cost b. We could therefore alternatively simply define

$$M^A \equiv n(a + bX), \quad \text{and} \quad M^B \equiv m(a + bY),$$

and consider r^A, and r^B, as the 'factor-price index' in the separable cost function.

The conditions for profit-maximization in the two manufacturing industries can be stated as

$$P\beta = r^A b, \quad \text{and} \quad Q\beta = r^B b. \tag{13.12}$$

To express the conditions in this form we use the fact that each firm will adjust its quantities in the three markets in such a way that it receives the same price everywhere.

Now, from (13.11) and (13.12) we immediately get that the total output volume of a firm in the manufacturing sectors is fixed.

$$X = Y = \frac{a}{b} \frac{\beta}{1 - \beta}.$$

This is in particular due to the homothetic technology. It then follows that

$$n = \frac{1-\beta}{\alpha} M^A, \quad \text{and} \quad m = \frac{1-\beta}{\alpha} M^B.$$

The union countries' respective output of food is given by the transformation functions $T(M^A)$ for A, and $S(M^B)$ for B. The domestic produce is sold at the same price as imported food: $P_F(1+t)$, where P_F denotes the price of food excluding the union's external tariff t. The price of the intermediate good must be the value of the alternative use of the resources devoted to the production of one unit of the good, or

$$r^A = -P_F(1+t)\, T'(M^A),$$
$$r^B = -P_F(1+t)\, S'(M^B).$$

(13.13)

The rest of the world is assumed to use one factor only, with the reward r^*, and with the fixed supply L^*. It takes one unit of this factor to produce one unit of food, and the condition for profit maximization (and industry equilibrium) is therefore simply

$$P_F = r^*.$$

Two variables that will be of interest in the comparative-statics exercises are the internal and external terms-of-trade, $q \equiv Q/P$, and $p \equiv P_F/P$, respectively. With the aid of (13.11) and (13.13), and recalling the definitions of M^A and M^B, the two variables may be expressed as

$$q = \frac{S'(M^B)}{T'(M^A)}$$

(13.14)

$$p = \frac{-\beta}{b P_F(1+t)\, T'(M^A)}.$$

(13.15)

Let us finally, before proceeding to the comparative-statics exercises, give the clearing conditions for the goods markets (the respective demand functions are given in the Appendix)

$$X = \frac{\alpha}{P}\left[\frac{I^A}{n+my_A^\beta} + \frac{I^B/(1+\tau)}{n+my_B^\beta} + \frac{I^*}{n+my_*^\beta}\right]$$

(13.16)

$$Y = \frac{\alpha}{Q}\left[\frac{I^A/(1+\tau)}{ny_A^{-\beta}+m} + \frac{I^B}{ny_B^{-\beta}+m} + \frac{I^*}{ny_*^{-\beta}+m}\right]$$

(13.17)

$$L^* + T(M^A) + S(M^B) = \frac{(1-\alpha)}{P_F}[I^A/(1+t) + I^B/(1+t) + I^*],$$

(13.18)

where τ denotes the union's internal tariff.

Comparative-statics exercises will be conducted to expose the basic nature of our model. To have a recognizable point of departure and standard of comparison, we shall conduct an exercise similar to that of proposition (D) discussed in Sections 3 and 4. Thus we start with internal free trade ($\tau = 0$), and with a common positive external tariff ($t > 0$). We first increase the common external tariff and then increase the common internal tariff. To facilitate matters we make the following assumption: the partners have a transfer scheme such that the relative changes in their incomes I^A and I^B are identical and equal to $\hat{I}$. This reflects our concern with the partners' *joint* experience, but is not without practical relevance: the Common Market is an example of a union with an internal transfer scheme.

The rest of this section presents the comparative-statics results. Discussions of these results are postponed to Section 6.

Since we use P_F as the numeraire, we have from (13.18):

$$\frac{\hat{I}}{(1-\alpha)} = -\frac{PnX}{I^A + I^B}\hat{M}^A - \frac{QmY}{I^A + I^B}\hat{M}^B + \hat{t}, \qquad (13.19)$$

where $\hat{t} \equiv dt/(1 + t)$.

The numbers of firms in the manufacturing sectors are proportional to the outputs of the two intermediate goods

$$\hat{n} = \hat{M}^A,$$

$$\hat{m} = \hat{M}^B.$$

The terms-of-trade changes are directly obtained from (13.14) and (13.15)

$$\hat{q} = \sigma^B \hat{m} - \sigma^A \hat{n}, \qquad (13.20)$$

$$\hat{p} = -\hat{t} - \sigma^A \hat{n}, \qquad (13.21)$$

where

$$\sigma^A \equiv \frac{M^A T''(M^A)}{T'(M^A)}, \quad \text{and} \quad \sigma^B \equiv \frac{M^B T''(M^B)}{T'(M^B)}.$$

The changes in trade and consumption patterns are given by

$$\hat{y}_A = (\sigma^B \hat{m} - \sigma^A \hat{n} + \hat{t})/(\beta - 1), \qquad (13.22)$$

$$\hat{y}_B = (\sigma^B \hat{m} - \sigma^A \hat{n} - \hat{t})/(\beta - 1), \qquad (13.23)$$

$$\hat{y}_* = (\sigma^B \hat{m} - \sigma^A \hat{n})/(\beta - 1), \qquad (13.24)$$

$$\hat{z}_A = \hat{n} + \frac{m}{n+m}\left(\frac{\beta}{1-\beta}\sigma^A - 1\right)(\hat{n} - \hat{m}) - \frac{m}{(n+m)}\frac{\beta}{(1-\beta)}\hat{t}, \qquad (13.25)$$

$$\hat{z}_B = \hat{n} + \frac{m}{n+m}\left(\frac{\beta}{1-\beta}\sigma^A - 1\right)(\hat{n} - \hat{m}) + \left(1 + \frac{m}{n+m}\frac{\beta}{1-\beta}\right)\hat{t}, \qquad (13.26)$$

$$\hat{z}_* = \hat{n} + \frac{m}{n+m}\left(\frac{\beta}{1-\beta}\sigma^A - 1\right)(\hat{n} - \hat{m}), \tag{13.27}$$

where $\hat{\tau} \equiv d\tau/(1 + \tau)$, and $z_k \equiv Z^k/X^k$ for $k = $ A, B, *.

The following two expressions are reduced forms of the market equilibrium conditions for X- and Y-goods, respectively, and they will be the starting point of the proceeding analysis:

$$-\theta^*\hat{\imath} - \left[\theta^B + (\theta^B - \theta^A)\frac{\beta}{(1-\beta)}\frac{m}{(n+m)}\right]\hat{\tau} = \left[\sigma^A + \frac{1}{1-\alpha}\right]\hat{n}$$

$$+ \frac{m}{n+m}\left[\frac{\beta}{1-\beta}\sigma^A - \frac{1}{1-\alpha}\right](\hat{n} - \hat{m})$$

$$+ \frac{m}{(n+m)}\frac{\beta}{(1-\beta)}(\sigma^A - \sigma^B)\hat{m}, \tag{13.28}$$

$$-\theta^*\hat{\imath} - \left[\theta^A - (\theta^B - \theta^A)\frac{\beta}{(1-\beta)}\frac{n}{(n+m)}\right]\hat{\tau} = \left[\sigma^B + \frac{1}{1-\alpha}\right]\hat{m}$$

$$- \frac{n}{n+m}\left[\frac{\beta}{1-\beta}\sigma^B - \frac{1}{1-\alpha}\right](\hat{n} - \hat{m})$$

$$- \frac{n}{(n+m)}\frac{\beta}{(1-\beta)}(\sigma^A - \sigma^B)\hat{n}, \tag{13.29}$$

where θ^k is the share of world income for country k.

We subsequently make the special assumption that $\sigma^A = \sigma^B \equiv \sigma$, i.e. that the elasticities of the slopes of the transformation curves are the same at the equilibrium point, in the two union countries. This has the merit, aside from increased analytical tractability, of highlighting aspects of particular interest: the importance of the degree of product differentiation and the importance of asymmetries between the member countries in the relative sizes of their manufacturing sectors and also in their relative incomes.

(13.28) and (13.20) give the following solution for relative changes in the number of variants in the member countries:

$$\hat{n} = -\frac{\theta^*}{\Delta}\hat{\imath} - \left[\theta^B + (\theta^B - \theta^A)\frac{1}{(1-\alpha)\sigma(n+m)}\frac{m}{\Delta}\right]\frac{1}{\Delta}\hat{\tau} \tag{13.30}$$

$$\hat{m} = -\frac{\theta^*}{\Delta}\hat{\imath} - \left[\theta^A - (\theta^B - \theta^A)\frac{1}{(1-\alpha)\sigma(n+m)}\frac{n}{\Delta}\right]\frac{1}{\Delta}\hat{\tau} \tag{13.31}$$

$$\hat{n} - \hat{m} = \frac{(\theta^A - \theta^B)}{\sigma}\hat{\tau} \tag{13.32}$$

and

$$\hat{N} = -\frac{\theta^*}{\Delta}\hat{t} - \frac{\Gamma}{\Delta}\hat{\tau},$$

(13.33)

where

$$N \equiv n + m,$$

$$\Delta \equiv \sigma + \frac{1}{1-\alpha} > 0$$

and

$$\Gamma \equiv \theta^A \frac{n}{n+m} + \theta^B \frac{m}{n+m} > 0.$$

The Appendix gives some intermediate steps in the derivation of the following two expressions for the relative changes in the indirect utilities V^A and V^*:

$$\hat{V}^A = \alpha \frac{\theta^*}{\Delta} \Lambda \hat{t} + \alpha \left(\frac{\Gamma}{\Delta} \Lambda - \frac{m}{n+m} \right) \hat{\tau}$$

(13.34)

$$\hat{V}^* = \alpha \left(\left(\sigma - \frac{1-\beta}{\beta} \right) \frac{\theta^*}{\Delta} - 1 \right) \hat{t} + \alpha \left(\sigma - \frac{1-\beta}{\beta} \right) \frac{\Gamma}{\Delta} \hat{\tau},$$

(13.35)

where

$$\Lambda \equiv \sigma - \frac{1-\beta}{\beta} + \frac{1}{\theta^A + \theta^B} \cdot \frac{1}{1-\alpha} \overset{>}{\underset{<}{=}} 0.$$

6. TARIFF CHANGES

Our comparative statics experiments incorporate the two types of changes in union commercial policy that are of interest: changes $\hat{t}$ in the common external tariff on imports of food, and the marginal imposition $\hat{\tau}$ of a mutual internal tariff on the exchange of differentiated manufactured goods. Consider each in turn.

6.1. An Increase in the Common External Tariff

Let us first examine the implication of an increase in the already positive common external tariff t. From (13.30) and (13.31):

$$\hat{n} = \hat{m} < 0.$$

The numbers of varieties of both types of differentiated goods fall as, in each partner country, resources are pulled from manufacturing into the now more highly protected agricultural sector. The contraction of manufacturing is entirely a reduction in the number of product varieties; each produced variety experiences no change in its level of production. With a common external tariff on food, (13.20) implies that $\hat{q} = \sigma(\hat{m} - \hat{n}) = 0$, so that no substitution between product varieties is induced.[5]

Our assumption about the third country ensures that it continues to export αL^* units of food. The shift of demand in A and B away from food turns the terms of trade in favour of the union. We have $\hat{p} = -\hat{t} - \sigma\hat{n}$, and substitution of (13.30) into this expression reveals that the relative price p of food in terms of manufactures does indeed fall, though by less than the tariff increase. The member countries hence have a terms-of-trade gain to set against the welfare loss from less product variety. But there is, of course, an additional source of gain: the increase in income. This source is partly reflected by the third term of Λ in (13.34). The direction of change in a member country's welfare is therefore ambiguous. We see that the total effect is more likely to be positive (i) the more sensitive the terms of trade are to given changes in product variety (higher σ), (ii) the less the evaluation of this variety (higher β), and (iii) the larger the share of the rest of the world in world income (smaller $\theta^A + \theta^B$).

The rest of the world has to face both a detrimental terms of trade effect and a reduction of product variety, and is therefore clearly worse off. Algebraically this is immediate from (13.35), noting that $(\sigma\theta^*/\Delta) - 1 < 0$.

6.2. A Marginal Internal Barrier

Now turn at last to the exercise treated by proposition (D) and suppose that $\hat{i} = 0$ but $\hat{\tau} > 0$. As a starting point, assume that the partners have equal national incomes: $\theta^A = \theta^B$. Then again the numbers of varieties produced in the two member countries decline by a common amount, so that $\hat{q} = \sigma(\hat{m} - \hat{n}) = 0$.

Each partner attempts to protect manufacturing, but with resources shifting over to the agricultural sector the result is just the opposite! The reason is as follows. The tariff causes each union member to divert spending from the manufactures of its partner to its own manufactures, and the fact that $\hat{q} = 0$ means that the outside country has no reason to substitute between X goods and Y goods. Thus from (13.22)–(13.24) we see that $\hat{y}_A = -\hat{\tau}/(1-\beta) < 0$, $\hat{y}_B = \hat{\tau}/(1-\beta) > 0$, and $\hat{y}_* = 0$. As the partners are of equal size, these effects just cancel.

The higher price of the partner's manufactures reduces demand, so that with constant output volumes of individual firms there is downward pressure on the number of firms. This is reinforced by the fact that the proportion $(1-\alpha)$ of the tariff revenue raised in the manufacturing sector is channelled into the agricultural sector. Thus the net effect is to protect food, not manufacturing. From (13.22)–(13.26) we have that $\hat{y}_A - \hat{z}_A < 0$ and $\hat{y}_B - \hat{z}_B > 0$, that is, a 'reversal' of trade modification.

It is instructive to compare the discussion in Sections 3 and 4 of proposition (D) with behaviour in the altered context of the present model. First, recall that in the earlier context gains actually resulted when the reversal of trade modification caused the union to import more from the rest of the world. The structure of the present model allows us to concentrate on what is new by ensuring that such gains shrink to zero: our assumptions about the third country imply that it exports an unchanged quantity of food to the union. Exclusively external trade is neither a substitute for nor complement to internal trade, to use our earlier terminology, and there is also now no trade diversion to 'undo'. Second, the terms of external trade were assumed fixed in proposition (D), but now the shift of demand toward food turns the terms of trade in the outside world's favour. From (13.15), $\hat{p} = -\sigma\hat{n} > 0$. This could of course be neutralized by an appropriate increase $\hat{t}$ in the common external tariff. But the most significant difference follows from the role of imperfect competition, scale economies, and the endogenous number of product varieties. As in the conventional analysis, zero first-order welfare effects are caused by shifts in union expenditure between existing X goods and Y goods. But in our model the output levels of all product varieties which continue to be produced are unchanged, and instead the number of varieties of manufactures falls. This is deleterious. The total effect on the welfare of country A or B is ambiguous, as can be seen from (13.34). There is now one additional term, compared to the case with the external tariff, which influences the direction of change in welfare: the relative sizes of the manufacturing sectors. The larger the partner's share of total manufacturing output, the larger the share that will be hit by the tariff, and the more likely it is that the internal tariff will actually reduce welfare, and that a 'super-union' will be optimal.

The external country is affected in an ambiguous way. Its terms of trade improve, so that it consumes more manufactures than before along with the same quantity of food. But, on the other hand, those manufactures possess less product diversity than before. In summary, it is possible that all countries lose from the internal tariff, or that all gain, with $\theta^A = \theta^B$. It is also possible that the member countries gain and the rest of the world loses. But, if the member countries lose, then so must the external country, rendering a 'super-union' beneficial to all!

Thus far we have supposed that $\theta^A = \theta^B$. The role of size disparities between partners is now easily exposed. (13.30)–(13.33) show that the internal tariff will still cause a decline in total output of manufactures, but that the smaller country will have to adjust its manufacturing sector more than proportionally: $\hat{n} > \hat{m} < 0$. There is hence a *reallocation* of manufacturing from the smaller (in terms of national income) partner to the larger. Intuitively, small-country-located firms will have a larger share of production hit by the tariff, inducing more exit to keep profits at zero. Indeed, it might possibly be the case that the larger partner's manufacturing output actually rises, if the difference in national income is sufficiently large. This reallocation of production might be one reason why customs unions tend to be formed by similar economies.

6.3. Intermediate goods

There is an alternative interpretation of our model. Assume only two consumption goods, food and a final manufacture, but many differentiated intermediate goods, or components, used to assemble the final manufacture. This interpretation is entirely consistent with our formulation if we let the CES part of the utility function (13.10) be the assembly function for the final manufacture, X_i^k and Y_j^k represent the inputs of components i and j, and the parameter β reflect the degree of substitutability between different components. The technology is then such that each single producer of an intermediate good faces internal increasing returns to scale available when the production process is geographically concentrated: an example of 'national' economies of scale.[6] Assembly of the final manufacture is costless, and exhibits increasing returns to scale in the number of different components that are used. To see this, note that the CES assembly function gives an output of $n^{1/\beta}X$ in the symmetric version, and hence the output increases faster than the input nX. These economies of scale are 'international', since the size of the world market for the manufacture determines n, and they also reflect the benefits of an increased division of labour in the world economy; they are assumed to be external to individual assembly firms.

There is, in this interpretation, trade both in intermediate goods, and in the final good food. There is initially a tariff only on the latter good, which is exported by the external country. It is immaterial whether finished manufactures are assembled where consumed, or whether they are all assembled in one partner country and then exported. But in the latter case the interesting possibility of tariffs on final manufactures is not covered by our analysis, the components must be taxed the same whether imported directly or embodied in final manufactures, and exports of the latter must be allowed drawbacks of tariffs paid for imported components. The total impact on each country's welfare of tariff changes is, of course, the same irrespective of model interpretation. What differ are the sources of welfare changes. We saw above that an increase in either the internal or external tariff reduced both n and m unless the partners were too different in terms of their national incomes. Here this means that fewer components will be used in the production of manufactures, leading to a situation with less exploitation of international returns to scale. The main welfare-reducing effect of the tariffs is thus that they are detrimental to the division of labour by diminishing the world market for the final manufacture. But, there is no loss here stemming from reduced exploitation of the traditional, national returns to scale. The two developed countries are trying to protect their home industries, and manage in the sense that a higher proportion of inputs are locally made. But with both countries acting in a similar fashion no overall gain is ensured.

7. CONCLUDING REMARKS

We live in a multilateral world. Therefore any non-universal change in commercial policy — and they are all in fact non-universal — ought to fall within the domain of the theory of economic integration. But it has not been so, since that theory usually has been too narrowly conceived. We have argued for four extensions: trade modification, consideration of small changes in policy, scale economies, and product differentiation under imperfect competition.

Adding the first two of these suggested extensions to the conventional framework we derived two basic propositions, suggested by familiar second-best theory, that are central to the characterization of the optimal policy for a subset of countries considering some degree of integration in a tariff-ridden world. We then developed a special, but illustrative, model incorporating all four of our suggested extensions and put it through its paces. Such an exercise is no more than an uncertain first step. But it is in the direction that must be followed, we maintain, if the theory of economic integration is to achieve the relevance to contemporary issues that it long since ought to have possessed.

APPENDIX

1. THE DEMAND FUNCTIONS

$$PX^A = \frac{\alpha I^A}{n + m y_A^\beta}, \quad \text{where } y_A \equiv \frac{Y^A}{X^A}$$

$$Q(1+\tau)Y^A = \frac{\alpha I^A}{n y_A^{-\beta} + m}$$

$$P_F(1+t)Z^A = (1-\alpha)I^A$$

$$P(1+\tau)X^B = \frac{\alpha I^B}{n + m y_B^\beta}, \quad \text{where } y_B \equiv \frac{Y^B}{X^B}$$

$$QY^B = \frac{\alpha I^B}{n y_B^{-\beta} + m}$$

$$P_F(1+t)Z^B = (1-\alpha)I^B$$

$$PX^* = \frac{\alpha I^*}{n + m y_*^\beta}, \quad \text{where } y_* \equiv \frac{Y^*}{X^*}$$

$$QY^* = \frac{\alpha I^*}{n y_*^{-\beta} + m}$$

$$P_F Z^* = (1-\alpha)I^*.$$

2. THE RELATIVE CHANGE IN THE INDIRECT UTILITIES

The indirect utility function for country A is

$$V^A = \gamma(R^A)^{-\alpha}(1+t)^{-(1-\alpha)}I^A,$$

where

$$R^A \equiv (nP^\rho + m(1+\tau)^\rho Q^\rho)^{1/\rho} = p^{-1}(n + m(1+\tau)^\rho q^\rho)^{1/\rho}$$

and

$$\rho \equiv \frac{\beta}{\beta-1}$$

and for the third country

$$V^* = \gamma(R^*)^{-\alpha}I^*,$$

where

$$R^* = p^{-1}(n+mq^\rho)^{1/\rho}.$$

γ is a constant, and R^k is a price index defined over the differentiated goods. These expressions become, when differentiated logarithmically,

$$\hat{V}^A = -\alpha\hat{R}^A - (1-\alpha)\hat{t} + \hat{I}$$

and

$$\hat{V}^* = -\alpha\hat{R}^*,$$

where we use that $\hat{I}^A = \hat{I}^B \equiv \hat{I}$, and that $\hat{I}^* = 0$.

Concentrate for a moment on the change in the price index R^A. The relative change can be split up into two components:

$$\hat{R}^A = \left[\frac{m}{n+m}(\hat{q}+\hat{\tau}) - \hat{p}\right] - \frac{1-\beta}{\beta}\hat{N}. \tag{13.A1}$$

The second term is the effect on the index of a change in the number of varieties available to the consumer, at given relative prices. This term is of course not present in the traditional analysis of customs unions, but will prove to be of considerable importance here.

Returning to the change in utility we get by substitution

$$\hat{V}^A = -\left[\hat{t} + \alpha\frac{m}{n+m}\hat{\tau} + \alpha\sigma\hat{N}\right] + \hat{I} + \alpha\frac{1-\beta}{\beta}\hat{N}. \tag{13.A2}$$

By substituting (13.10) and (13.A1) into (13.A2) we arrive at expressions (13.34) and (13.35) in the text.

NOTES

* The authors received useful comments from Elhanan Helpman and from participants at a seminar at the Institute for International Economic Studies, University of Stockholm. Henrik Horn gratefully acknowledges financial support from Humanistisk-Samhällsvetenskapliga Forskningsrådet, Sweden.
1. For recent examples see Wonnacott and Wonnacott (1981) and Lloyd (1982).

2.   See Meade (1955, 1956) and Ethier (1983, ch. 12).

3.   The most notable exception is no doublt James Meade (1955, 1956), who was criticized in this regard. For example Lipsey (1968, p. 271) refers to this 'very serious, possibly crippling, limitation'. The subsequent literature has largely avoided marginal analysis. See, however, Berglas (1979), Reizman (1979), McMillan and McCann (1981), and Lloyd (1982).

4.   For such a discussion, see section A.6 of Appendix I in Ethier (1983).

5.   In the more general case $\sigma^A \neq \sigma^B$ we would have $\sigma^A \hat{n} = \sigma^B \hat{m}$ so that manufacturing contracts relatively more in the country with the greater ease of substitution of food for the non-traded manufacturing intermediate good; the structure of such economies remains irrelevant. Also we would still have $0 = \hat{q} = \sigma^B \hat{m} - \sigma^A \hat{n}$.

6.   See Ethier (1979, 1982).

REFERENCES

Berglas, E. (1979), 'Preferential Trading Theory: The n Commodity Case', *Journal of Political Economy*, 87, 315–31.

Dixit, A. K. and Stiglitz, J. (1977), 'Monopolistic Competition and Optimum Product Diversity', *American Economic Review*, 67, 297–308.

Ethier, W. (1979), 'Internationally Decreasing Costs and World Trade', *Journal of International Economics*, 9, 1–24.

Ethier, W. J. (1982), National and International Returns to Scale in the Modern Theory of International Trade, *American Economic Review*, 72, 389–405.

Ethier, W. J. (1983), *Modern International Economics* (New York: W. W. Norton).

Kemp, M. C. (1964), *The Pure Theory of International Trade* (Englewood Cliffs: Prentice-Hall).

Kemp, M. C. and Wan, H. Y. (1976), 'An Elementary Proposition Concerning the Formation of Customs Unions', *Journal of International Economics*, 6, 95–8.

Kravis, I. B. and Lipsey, R. E. (1971), *Price Competitiveness in World Trade* (New York: National Bureau of Economic Research).

Kravis, I. B. and Lipsey, R. E. (1978), 'Price Behavior in the Light of Balance of Payments Theories', *Journal of International Economics*, 8, 193–246.

Lipsey, R. E. (1968), 'The Theory of Customs Unions: A General Survey', in R. E. Caves and H. G. Johnson (eds.), *Readings in International Economics* (Homewood: Richard D. Irwin).

Lloyd, P. (1982), '3 × 3 Theory of Customs Unions', *Journal of International Economics*, 12, 41–63.

McMillan, J. and McCann, E. (1981), 'Welfare Effects in Customs Unions', *Economic Journal*, 91, 697–703.

Meade, J. E. (1955), *Trade and Welfare* (London: Oxford University Press).

Meade, J. E. (1956), *The Theory of Customs Unions* (Amsterdam, North-Holland).

Ohyama, M. (1972), 'Trade and Welfare in General Equilibrium', *Keio Economic Studies*, 9, 37–73.

Reizman, R. (1979), 'A 3 × 3 Model of Customs Unions', *Journal of International Economics*, 9, 341–54.

Vanek, J. (1965), *General Equilibrium of International Discrimination* (Cambridge, Mass.: Harvard University Press).

Viner, J. (1950), *The Customs Union Issue* (New York: Carnegie Endowment for International Peace).

Wonnacot, P. and Wonnacot, R. (1981), 'Is Unilateral Tariff Reduction Preferable to a Customs Union? The Curious Case of the Missing Foreign Tariffs', *American Economic Review*, 71, 704–14.

14

The Measurement
of Produce Differentiation
in Empirical Studies of Trade Flows*

David Greenaway

At least since the discovery of Leontief's celebrated paradox a great deal of academic effort has been expended in exploring the determinants of the commodity composition of trade flows. Broadly speaking the bulk of this work has been directed at examining trade performance, through one or more of the following avenues:

(i) cross-section or time series investigations of the pattern of revealed comparative advantage;[1]

(ii) cross-section or time series investigations of import penetration and export sales ratios;[2]

(iii) cross-section investigations of the relative importance of inter- and intra-industry trade.[3]

One distinctive feature of this literature is the growing awareness of the potential influence of aspects of domestic market structure on the pattern of trade flows. This is of course no more than a formal recognition of the fact that trade flows cannot be monocausally explained by reference to relative factor proportions. Although this recognition certainly dates back at the very least to Ohlin, and possibly also to Smith, it is only recently that theoretical and empirical analysis of the links between market structure and trade flows have reached any degree of sophistication. Although a number of investigators in the 1960s were examining the link between market structure and international exchange (most notably Richard Caves), the impetus to recent work is undoubtedly due to the pioneering efforts of Balassa (1966) and Grubel and Lloyd (1975) in cataloguing the incidence of intra-industry trade and, more latterly to the efforts of Krugman (1979, 1980), Lancaster (1980), and others in theoretically modelling the two-way exchange of differentiated goods.

Now that it is widely recognized that the international exchange of differentiated goods can and does take place, the question of how one proxies product-differentiation inevitably assumes some importance. This follows from the need to subject specific analyses of the determinants of trade in differentiated goods to empirical scrutiny, and/or the need to establish the amount of trade in differentiated goods which actually occurs at a particular point in time, and how that volume change through time. Both avenues have been explored recently.

The purpose of this paper will be in part to survey this literature in order to respond to two questions. First, what measures have been used in cross-section studies to proxy product-differentiation and how useful are they? Second, to what extent can indexes of intra-industry trade accurately represent the volume of trade which takes place in differentiated goods on a cross-sectional basis.

The answer to these questions will permit us to proceed to a third issue: is there a more satisfactory method of dealing with product differentiation? In response to this the framework of a methodology for adjusting indexes of intra-industry trade will be sketched out which may form a basis for gauging more accurately the volume of trade in horizontally and vertically differentiated goods which takes place, again on a cross-section basis.

PRODUCT DIFFERENTIATION: A BRIEF TAXONOMY OF TERMS

For the purposes of this paper, three conceptually distinct forms of product differentiation will be identified, all of which can result in international exchange to a greater or lesser degree: (i) horizontal differentiation; (ii) vertical differentiation; and (iii) technological differentiation.

The distinction between these three types is important because their underlying determinants may differ. Although it may not always be possible to distinguish each in *practical* terms, they are conceptually separable and the meanings attached to each in this paper will be as follows:

Horizontal differentiation refers to differentiation by attribute or characteristics mix in the Lancaster sense. Within a given 'group' all products will share certain core characteristics. The manner in which these core characteristics are combined determines the product's specification and product differentiation can be identified by the presence of a variety of specifications in a particular group. Horizontal differentiation is often referred to as locational differentiation following the pioneering work of Hotelling (1929). Its existence depends on the presence of preference diversity and it is this form of differentiation which preoccupies Eaton and Kierzkowski, and Lancaster in the present volume. It is useful to distinguish horizontal differentiation from image differentiation, or what Lancaster (1979) refers to as pseudo-differentiation. This situation occurs when the core characteristics of all products in the group are identical (they have the same specification therefore), but they are differentiated by brand image.

Vertical differentiation refers to differences in the absolute amounts contained in different products. Thus if one product has x percent more of all characteristics than other products in the group, the products are vertically differentiated. As Lancaster (1979, p. 28) notes we can regard vertical differentiation as being broadly consistent with differences in 'quality'. Within a two-dimensional Lancastrian framework, vertical differentiation would be represented by changes in the scale of measurement on the axes. Thus, whereas horizontal differentiation refers to the availability of alternative specifications of a product in a given quality grade, vertical differentiation refers to the availability of alternative quality grades. In the absence of an income constraint, n consumers would strive to consume the 'best' quality of a given product, although they may nevertheless prefer n different varieties. Invariably therefore on associates vertical differentiation with the presence of different income groups in a given market. It is this form of differentiation which Sutton's 'natural oligopoly' is concerned with. It must, of course, be explicitly recognized that, in practical terms, it may be virtually impossible to separate horizontal from vertical differentiation, since, where indivisible products are concerned differentiation invariably takes the form of some hybrid of the two.

Technological differentiation occurs when one or more of the core characteristics of the group is/are technically altered. Thus either one of the axes bounding characteristics space is changed or an additional core characteristic may be added. Thus technological differentiation is associated with the introduction of certain characteristics or attributes which results in new, technically improved products which are considered superior to existing products by all consumers, in all quality grades. After some adjustment-lag all existing grades will therefore be made redundant. In much the same way as vertical differentiation merges into horizontal differentiation, technological differentiation may merge into vertical differentiation. Conceptually all three are distinct, although in practice the distinction may be somewhat opaque.[4]

The distinction between these various forms of product differentiation is important because their underlying determinants and the manner in which they affect international exchange may differ. Pure intra-industry trade *in the Lancaster–Krugman sense* unambiguously refers to the exchange of horizontally differentiated goods. Technologically differentiated goods will also be unambiguously associated with product cycle trade in the Vernon sense. Vertically differentiated goods are however more difficult to categorize — their exchange will certainly be recorded as intra-industry trade. Furthermore the relatively small volume of work which has examined intra-intdustry exchange on a 'case-study' basis indicates that vertical differentiation is an integral part of intra-industry specialization (see Adler, 1970, and Hocking, 1980). In addition, however, there may be overlap with the determinants of technological differentiation (viz., skill intensity, research intensity), especially if one accepts the Finger (1975a) neo-technology hypothesis.

It seems clear that most recent theoretical analyses of trade in differentiated goods have been concerned with explaining the exchange of horizontally differentiated goods.[5] The first question we might therefore address ourselves to is how well do those proxies employed in recent empirical analyses of trade in differentiated goods capture the essence of attribute differentiation.

PROXIES OF PRODUCT DIFFERENTIATION

In this section we shall provide a selective survey of recent approaches to proxying product differentiation. As well as identifying the principal proxies employed, we will seek to assess their usefulness for capturing horizontal differentiation.

Hufbauer Index

One of the most frequently used proxies for product differentiation is the index suggested by Hufbauer (1970), namely:

$$H = \frac{\sigma_{ij}}{M_{ij}}, \tag{14.1}$$

where σ_{ij} = standard deviation of export unit values for shipments of good i to country j, and M_{ij} = unweighted mean of those unit values. The index is therefore intended to proxy 'product differentiation' by reference to the coefficient of variation of export unit values, the implicit assumption being that these capture the effect of variations in export prices to different destinations.[6]

If the index successfully proxies the dispersion of export prices in a particular product group then it can certainly be viewed as a means of picking up vertical and perhaps technological differentiation, but *not* horizontal differentiation. Some analysts have recognized this and used the index as a proxy for vertical and technological differentiation. Caves (1981) use of the index is certainly consistent with this interpretation, as is that of Helleiner (1976). In other studies, however, its use is more equivocal. For example, Pagoulatos and Sorensen (1975) and McAleese (1979) appear to rely on it as a catch-all proxy for product differentiation.

Kravis and Lipsey (1971) and Gray and Martin (1980) have questioned whether an export unit value index can be regarded as a reliable proxy for an export price index, given its sensitivity to variations in the composition of trade within SITC categories. One might therefore observe the Hufbauer index changing simply as a result of variations in the mix of shipments among nations. Even if however, it does successfully measure the dispersion of export prices there remain a number of difficulties with its use. First, it presumes that trade in differentiated goods takes the form of exports of different varieties to different markets. This need not be the case. Two-way trade in differentiated goods could emerge with the home country producing and exporting one variety to several destinations yet importing a range of varieties (a phenomenon which Dreze commented on some years ago). Second, variations in export unit values can arise for reasons which have little if anything to do with product differentiation. Thus pricing policy may be geared to local market conditions in which case export prices would vary directly with the degree of market power exercised in each market — as well as being affected by the number of competing varieties, this will also be influenced by the degree of effective protection conferred on domestic producers in overseas markets.[7]

In summary, there might be a case for using the index to proxy vertical and technological differentiation, subject to the reservations made above, but it cannot be taken as a satisfactory proxy for horizontal differentiation. The index is one of the most widely used in empirical analyses of trade flows and its rather mixed 'performance' is at least in part related to ambiguity in what the index represents, (as well as the variety of ways in which it has actually been used, itself an interesting case of 'product differentiation').

Advertising Intensity

The use of advertising-intensity measures as proxies for product differentiation is relatively widespread in industrial organization studies. In this literature it is usual to distinguish between 'informative' and 'persuasive' advertising. Although the emphasis given to each may vary according to one's philisophical standpoint, it is possible to forge a link between product differentiation and advertising in both cases. Where informative advertising is concerned, some kind of differentiation would ordinarily be a prerequisite for advertising activity, whilst 'persuasive' messages will in general be directed at emphasizing (real or apparent) differences between varieties. It might therefore be argued that advertising expenditure proxies product differentiability directly. As Comanor and Wilson have contended, 'Although these product and market characteristics (*which constitute product differentiability*) are not easily measured, they are typically characterised by heavy advertising expenditures' (1974, p. 130, emphasis added).

This apparent link between advertising intensity and product differentiation has led a number of researchers to use inter-industry differences in advertising intensity (deflated by industry sales, net output, or apparent consumption) to proxy inter-industry differences in the extent of product differentiation in the study of trade flows. Thus Goodman and Ceyhun (1976), Helleiner (1976), Caves (1981), and Greenaway and Milner (1982) all use the ratio of advertising expenditures to sales in this way, whilst Tharakan *et al.* (1978) use the ratio of advertising expenditure to apparent consumption for the same purpose.

Assuming that some systematic relationship between advertising intensity and product differentiation existed, one might first of all enquire as to what aspect of product differentiation is being proxied by advertising intensity. Caves and Khalizadeh-Shirazi (1977), among others, have argued that advertising intensity tends to proxy horizontal differentiation in general, image differentiation (or pseudo-differentiation) in particular. If so, one might therefore expect advertising intensity to be more important in the case of 'convenience' goods than 'shopping' goods (Porter, 1976). If this is so, then advertising intensity is unlikely to be very helpful in the analysis of international trade flows. Since 'convenience' goods require many retail outlets, tend to have relatively low gross margins, and rely on repeat purchases, they are unlikely to figure prominently in international trade.

On the other hand, where specifications of goods differ, i.e. we have horizontal differentiation as opposed to image differentiation, there are clear incentives for firms to make the details of their specifications known through the medium of advertising. Once any one firm in the market makes the details of its specification known, others in the market have to follow. Following this line of reasoning leads one to conclude that the greater the number of varieties encompassed in the product spectrum the greater will advertising intensity be. Since theoretical analyses emphasize the importance of horizontal differentiation for intra-industry exchange we would expect such goods to figure prominently in trade. This uncertainty over whether any form of product differentiation is captured by advertising intensity is manifested in empirical studies. (Compare for example, the *a priori* expectations of Caves, 1981, and Greenaway and Milner, 1982.)

Even if it were clear that advertising intensity were unequivocally related to one particular form of product differentiation, there are further grounds for doubting whether inter-industry differences in advertising intensity are systematically related to inter-industry differences in product differentiation. Take for example the simple Dorfman–Steiner condition for optimal advertising expenditures:

$$\frac{AT}{PQ} = \frac{\eta a + \eta^* \eta ar}{|\eta|}, \tag{14.2}$$

where AT/PQ = advertising sales ratio, ηa = elasticity of demand with respect to advertising expenditures, η^* = elasticity of demand with respect to competitors' advertising expenditures, ηar = elasticity of response of competitors advertising with respect to 'own firms' advertising, and $|\eta|$ = price elasticity of demand.

It is clear from this that inter-firm and inter-industry differences in AT/PQ will result from variations in ηa. As Porter (1976) has demonstrated this elasticity will vary from advertising outlet to outlet such that inter-industry variations in AT/PQ may arise due to a differing relative dependence on high and low unit cost outlets. This in turn will be related to the nature of the product and/or the way in which legal and institutional rules impinge on the decision.

It is also clear from the Dorfman–Steiner condition that AT/PQ is affected by the conjectural variation term $\eta^* \eta ar$. The importance of this is that it may lead us to anticipate a systematic relationship between AT/PQ and market structure. Specifically it might be argued that even when there are a 'large' number of agents selling a differentiated product, optimal advertising will be relatively low. As however, the number of sellers is reduced, ηa rises and the incentive to advertise increases. As concentration rises so too does the term $\eta^* \eta ar$. Beyond some critically small number of sellers however, the gains from collusion and joint reductions in advertising expenditures are recognized and AT/PQ falls. The point is that advertising expenditure may be endogenous, rather than exogenously determined by preference diversity. Against this, recent work has emphasized that there are sound *a priori* grounds for anticipating an inverted 'U' relationship between market structure and product variety. Empirical analyses of advertising intensity and market structure are unfortunately inconclusive. Cable (1972), Greer (1971), and Sutton (1975) have found statistical support for the inverted 'U' hypothesis but this has been challenged by Reekie (1975). The point of importance for the present issue is that it may place a further question mark against the presence of a systematic relationship between product differentiation and advertising intensity.

In addition to these points, there are other influences which affect inter-industry patterns of advertising intensity but which have little obvious connection with product differentiation (such as different objective functions and different lag-structures). Enough has been said however, to highlight the potential shortcomings of the proxy.

Census Classification Proxies

An indication of the paucity of satisfactory proxies for product differentiation can be gauged from the fact that recently a number of researchers have sought to gain some guidance from the census classifications themselves. The procedure involved here is one of first deciding on a suitable level of aggregation at which to proxy an 'industry' then simply recording the number of categories classified at some lower level of disaggregation. Thus Loertscher and Wolter (1980) used the number of BTN tariff lines in each 3-digit SITC group; Caves (1981) used the number of 8-digit SITC product lines in each SITC 3-digit group; and Greenaway and Milner (1982) used the number of 8-digit SITC product lines in each 3-digit UK SIC group.

Clearly this is something of an *ad hoc* response to the problem. It presumes that the reference group has been defined in an manner which is consistent with an industry, or product group, and that the census disaggregation is consistent with the underlying notion of product differentiation. The extent to which these conditions are satisfied depends largely on the census classification used, and the way in which it is employed. Some minor adjustments can be made (such as the use of the BTN/SITC classifications by Loertscher and Wolter, and the SITC/UK SIC by Greenaway and Milner) to improve one's confidence in the 'methodology'. Ultimately however, the technique is relatively crude. Interpreting whether it does pick up product differentiation or not is really a matter of judgement and depends principally on the base and reference levels of aggregation chosen. For example, if one is working from the number of eight-digit listings in a three-digit group in so far as the index is capturing product differentiation it may be doing so in a hold-all fashion. If on the other hand, one were working with the number of eight-digit listings in a five-digit group the probability that one is capturing horizontal and possibly vertical differentiation principally and excluding technological differentiation is higher simply by dint of the lower level of aggregation. The great drawback with the method is however, that one might in fact be picking up categorial aggregation as Caves (1981) argued. Although this might be true, Greenaway and Milner (1982) offered some evidence to the effect that it may apply only in SITC product groups 0–4. Notwithstanding this the fact remains that a judgement has to be taken somewhere about the system of classification.

Hedonic Price Indices

In a recent note on product differentiation and international trade, Gray and Martin (1980) examine some of the shortcomings of the Hufbauer index then conclude: 'A more fruitful approach to product differentiation would be through the construction of "hedonic" price indices ... In this way the elusive concept of product differentiation can be better captured and used for analysis of trade in Chamberlinian goods' (p. 327).

The methods which we outlined above for proxying vertical and horizontal differentiation and the more common proxies for technological differentiation such as rate of product turnover, basically rely on quantifying the number of observed products consumed in a particular market, or by observing magnitudes which might be related to product variety (like advertising intensity or price dispersion). By contrast, hedonic price indices attempt to operationalize product differentiation in terms of a number of underlying characteristics. Rosen (1974) defines hedonic prices as: 'the implicit prices of attributes ... revealed to economic agents from observed prices of differentiated products and the specific amounts of characteristics associated with them' (p. 34).

The rationale behind the use of hedonic prices is that variations in product specifications manifest themselves in variations in product prices. Assuming that one can identify the relevant characteristics of a particular product regressing 'variety' prices against variety characteristics with a suitable functional form, allows one to interpret the estimated characteristic coefficients as implied prices of the attributes concerned.

The technique has been quite widely used in intertemporal price comparisons and in industrial economics studies. In the case of the former hedonic price indices are used in order to distinguish the 'quality' element in any price change. In the case of the latter they are used to identify those attributes which appear to be of particular interest to consumers (i.e. those with the highest regression coefficients, or implied prices). It is presumably this particular application which led to Gray and Martin's recommendation of greater reliance on the technique in studies of trade flows. Upon closer examination, however, one must question the usefulness of the technique for empirical analyses of trade flows. The methodology quite clearly relies on the presence of price differentials between alternative varieties. This, after all, is necessary for the estimation of 'implied price' for commodity characteristics. In this respect the technique may certainly be useful in the analysis of markets where vertical differentiation is important. This follows because those characteristics which are inherently measurable are invariably 'quality' based, and because relative quality differentials (on a cross-section basis) can be expected to be manifested in relative price differentials. Where, however, we are dealing with horizontal differentiation and an absence of relative price differentials across varieties the technique is clearly inappropriate. If Gray and Martin have in mind using the technique in connection with the study of trade in vertically differentiated goods then their conclusions are reasonable. But surely it is incorrect that the technique can better capture product differentiation 'for analysis of trade in Chamberlinian goods', i.e. horizontal differentiation?

Furthermore, even when the technique is used in connection with vertically differentiated products, two further points must be made. First, where price differentials do exist and coefficients can be estimated for all independent variables (i.e. product characteristics), the interpretation of the estimated coefficients may be far from unequivocal. For example 'implied price' in inter-country studies could be influenced by relative factor endowments as well as quality differences. Second, it goes without saying that all relevant characteristics should be included in the exercise. In practice only those which are cardinally measurable or can be captured by a dummy variable are included.

By way of concluding it can be said that the hedonic technique is useful in the study of vertically and horizontally/vertically differentiated products and when the analysis in question is constrained to a market specific investigation (as for example in Gregory and Tearle's 1973 study). It is self-evident that the methodology cannot normally be used in aggregate cross-section or time series studies, in the way that the other proxies discussed above can.

Summary on Proxies of Product Differentiation

To summarize the arguments so far: product differentiation has invariably been measured 'by proxy' and the relevant proxy entered as an independent variable in empirical analyses of trade performance. This has a number of drawbacks, especially when considered in connection with studies of intra-industry trade. Apart from the proxy specific shortcomings which we have already outlined there are two general problems. First, when a variety of independent variables are included, the nature of the exercise ensures that we are only really able to comment on the existence of a relationship or otherwise, rather than necessarily deducing much about the relative importance of various forces. Second, and leading from this first point, we are unable to comment on the relative importance and specific determinants of trade in horizontally and vertically differentiated goods.

PRODUCT DIFFERENTIATION AND INTRA-INDUSTRY TRADE

Clearly, if an index of intra-industry trade were available which accurately reflected the volume of trade which takes place in differentiated goods then the problem would all but disappear. An ideal index of intra-industry trade which measured the volume of trade in horizontally differentiated and vertically differentiated goods would obviously provide in itself an indication of the relative importance of trade in differentiated goods, and, more importantly could be used as a dependent variable for econometric study.

Some investigators have already equated trade in differentiated goods with recorded intra-industry trade at a particular digit of the SITC (or SIC), usually the third digit. There are, however, a number of well-known shortcomings associated with indices of intra-industry trade which inspire caution (to say the least) in such a practice. Broadly speaking the value of a given index of intra-industry trade will be determined by some combination of the following:

  (i) categorical aggregation,
  (ii) the two-way exchange of horizontally differentiated goods,
  (iii) the two-way exchange of vertically differentiated goods,
  (iv) the two-way exchange of technologically differentiated goods.

This being so, we are presented with two possibilities; either we could adjust our indices of intra-industry trade in a manner which allows us to interpret what remains as an index of the relative proportion of trade in (horizontally, vertically, and technologically) differentiated goods; or, more ambitiously we could adjust the crude index for categorical aggregation, and make some further adjustment to allow us to comment on the relative importance of horizontal, vertical, and technological differentiation.

Reducing the Impact of Categorical Aggregation

The recognition of the problem of categorical aggregation and the way in which it distorts measures of intra-industry trade dates at least from the pioneering work of Grubel and Lloyd (1971, 1975). Detailed examinations of the extent of categorical aggregation are relatively sparse, two notable exceptions being Finger's (1975b) work on the SITC and Rayment's (1976) work on the UK SIC.

The recognition that categorical aggregation is important has invariably been handled by the inclusion of a proxy intended to pick up categorical aggregation in cross-section work. Whilst this is a useful starting point in establishing that it is influential, it does not allow us to say anything about the relative importance of the phenomenon across industry groups.

Since categorical aggregation occurs when industrial categories are 'mis-classified' in some sense the first-best method of cleansing trade data of its influence might appear to be to regroup the basic data in a manner whereby the resultant categories conform more closely to a theoretical construct of an 'industry' and/or 'product group'. There are two principal difficulties with this option. First the absence of any unique criteria for regrouping — whether by reference to end-use or production characteristics. This is reflected in the two attempts at regrouping completed to date: Aquino (1978) reclassified data on the basis of 'technological intensity' whilst Balassa reclassified on the basis of 'substitutability in production'. Second, the problem of how one allocates trade in parts and components in any reclassified scheme. Despite the attractions of regrouping according to some systematic economic criterion the option remains problematic and as yet no wholescale attempt has been made.

An alternative is to examine the way in which categorical aggregation manifests itself and make *ad hoc* adjustments. As Gray (1979) recognized, categorical aggregation comprises two conceptually distinct components, an 'opposite sign effect' and a 'weighting effect'. Take the unadjusted Grubel and Lloyd index,

$$B_j = 1 - \frac{|\Sigma X_{ij} - \Sigma M_{ij}|}{\Sigma (X_{ij} + M_{ij})}. \tag{14.3}$$

If j is defined in such a manner that the i sub-groups have differing factor input ratios, i.e. we have categorical aggregation, then measured intra-industry trade at the jth level could be distorted by two influences. In the event that

$$|Xn - Mn| > 0 \quad \text{whilst} \quad |Xm - Mm| < 0$$

for any i, the value of Bj will be inflated by this opposite sign effect. Thus, where a category is mis-specified opposite signed trade imbalances at the $j - 1$ level of aggregation will unambiguously raise the level of intra-industry trade at the jth level. Secondly, since Bj may be a sum of the individual trade weighted sub-group indices, its value may be distorted relative to the measure for pure intra-industry trade depending on the relative importance of the component trade-weighted indices. The effect which this has on Bj is ambiguous; it could serve to inflate or deflate the index relative to its 'true' value.

The recognition of this is not new. The most frequent response however has been to seek reassurance in the behaviour of indices upon disaggregation (see for instance Grubel and Lloyd, 1975, and Gray, 1979). This is a legitimate *ad hoc* response. From the point of view of empirical analysis, however, it does not permit any systematic adjustments to be made to measured intra-industry trade at a given level of statistical aggregation.

One possible method for making some systematic adjustment would be to proceed from the assumption that categorical aggregation manifests itself in trade imbalance. Thus, if categorical aggregation results in a number of fourth-digit groups with differing factor ratios being combined, this will manifest itself in a pattern of offsetting imbalances at the fourth digit. When these imbalances are aggregated into a three-digit group the imbalances are in effect aggregated and the third-digit index is higher that it otherwise would be. To the extent that categorical aggregation is manifested in offsetting trade imbalance at the $j-1$ level of aggregation, it is possible to make some adjustment for its effects. Rather than measuring intra-trade by (14.3) one could apply the index

$$C_j = 1 - \frac{\Sigma\,|X_{ij} - M_{ij}|}{\Sigma\,(X_{ij} - M_{ij})} \tag{14.4}$$

$$C_j \leqslant B_j,$$

where $j = $ SITC 001–899 and $i = (001.1 \ldots 001.9)$–$(899.1 \ldots 899.9)$. Third-digit indices are thereby calculated from fourth-digit data. As one is summing individual imbalances at the fourth digit rather than aggregating them, the numerator in (14.4) must be equal to (in the case where all imbalances have the same sign), or greater than (in the case of offsetting imbalances) the numerator in (14.3).

This is a procedure which has been aplied by Greenaway (1982) to Swiss data and Greenaway and Milner (1982) to UK data. Two obvious points can be made about this procedure. First, one is no wiser about the appropriate level of aggregation for analysis. Logically one might argue that the procedure commends computation of C_j at the fifth digit, using eight-digit data. Second, categorical aggregation need not manifest itself in offsetting imbalances. Differing factor ratios at the fourth digit could be consistent with imbalances having the same sign. If, however, the Heckscher–Ohlin postulate (that specialization in accordance with relative factor endowments will determine the pattern of international exchanges) is accepted as a meaningful explanation of trade flows, then the assumption that categorical aggregation does influence the pattern of trade balances may not be entirely unreasonable. The problem is, of course, that offsetting imbalances may also be consistent with intra-industry specialization and ideal use of this procedure would entail its computation only for those activities where categorical aggregation is known to be a problem. In the absence of such information one simply has to make a judgment relating to the level of aggregation at which it is appropriate to study intra-industry trade and compute C_j. In the event that categorical aggregation inflates B_j, C_j will be a more appropriate measure. In the event that adjustment are made to categories where offsetting imbalance is the outcome of intra-industry specialization C_j will understate the extent of pure intra-industry trade.

The C_j index does have one further feature which recommends its use in preference to B_j, namely that it is an average of the trade-weighted sub-group indices.[8] This is especially useful when categories are misclassified (and categorical aggregation is therefore influential), since C_j is providing us with a weighted average of the sub-group indices. Thus the adjustment accommodates both the opposite sign and weighting effects.

One's judgement (based on experience of using C_j) is that it more appropriately measures the volume of trade which takes place in differentiated goods than B_j. The adjustments which it makes are in the right direction and this is especially useful in cross-section econometric analysis since frequently the independent varaibles used will be related to inter-industry trade, making any empirical results more difficult to interpret. Nevertheless, problems remain, most notably that in calculating C_j indiscriminately we may unknowingly be adjusting for categorical aggregation in activities where it is not a problem. Furthermore, if one wished to test specific hypotheses (such as the Lancaster model for example) on a cross-sectional basis, ideally one would wish to work with an' index on the left-hand side which accurately measured the exchange of horizontally differentiated goods only. This is a property which C_j clearly does not have.

It might be argued that it is for all practical purposes quite impossible to distinguish between alternative variants of product differentiation for cross-section study, in particular horizontal and vertical differentiation. Clearly, however, it would be of interest if one could establish the relative importance of each. By doing so it would be possible to test more directly for the forces which drive pure intra-industry exchange. By way of concluding this overview of alternative approaches to the examination of product differentiation one final approach will be sketched out.[9]

Residual Measurement of Pure Intra-industry Trade

This approach uses a methodology which has certain similarities with hedonic indices. In this context, however, we are interest in 'aggregation-adjusted' indices, i.e. indices of intra-industry trade which may be cleansed of categorical aggregation as well as being adjusted for certain types of differentiation. Suppose we write,

$$B_j = HD + VD + TD + CA + u, \qquad (14.5)$$

i.e. measured intra-industry trade in any category is made up of trade in horizontally (HD), vertically (VD) and technologically (TD) differentiated goods, and a certain volume of trade due to categorical aggregation (CA) then it is conceivable that what is essentially a stepwise procedure could be deployed to obtain an estimate of HD_j and/or VD_j. In the event that one wished to obtain an estimate of intra-industry trade associated with horizontally and vertically differentiated goods in a given cross-section one could estimate the equation

$$\hat{B}_j = \alpha_1 + \alpha_2 TD^* + \alpha_3 CA^* + u, \qquad (14.6)$$

where TD^* and CA^* are suitable and reliable proxies for technological differentiation and categorical aggregation respectively. If equation (14.6) is correctly defined (in the sense of including all relevant sources of variation in B_j apart from HD and VD) and if it has the appropriate functional form then $\alpha_1 \simeq 0$ and one could write

$$B_j - \hat{B}_j = D_j \simeq HD_j + VD_j. \qquad (14.7)$$

In other words, the residuals derived from the estimating equation could be regarded as an 'estimate' of the volume of trade which occurs in horizontally and vertically differentiated goods. *In principle*, one could in fact go further estimating

$$\hat{B}'_j = \alpha_1 + \alpha_2 TD^* + \alpha_3 CA^* + \alpha_4 VD^* + u. \qquad (14.8)$$

Again assuming that α is correctly defined such that $\alpha_1 \simeq 0$

$$B_j - \hat{B}'_j = D_j \simeq HD_j, \qquad (14.9)$$

i.e. we would use the residual as an estimate of trade in horizontally differentiated goods. D_j and/or D'_j could then be entered as dependent variables in empirical analysis.

If this procedure were accepted as legitimate it would have two clear advantages over orthodox measures of intra-industry trade:

1. D_j (or D'_j) could itself be a direct indication of the relative importance of trade in horizontally and vertically (or horizontally) differentiated goods. One would perhaps obtain a clearer indication of intra-industry trade than even regrouping would accomplish (since the latter might still pick up technological differentiation).

2. Entering D_j (or D'_j) as a dependent variable for econometric analysis allows one to obtain an altogether more meaningful indication of the role played by relevant explanatory factors (like decreasing costs or facets of market structure). This (as indeed with C_j) is the single most important justification for this type of approach. In existing cross-section analyses it is extremely difficult to extricate the influence of competing hypotheses.

These advantages alone recommend the procedure to serious consideration and some experimentation. As we have seen, no approach to the problem so far considered is without its practical and conceptual difficulties. This applies as much to this residual method as to others, and a number of the more obvious difficulties can be enumerated:

(i) If one were to employ D_j (D'_j) as a measure of relative importance of trade in differentiated goods in total trade there may be a measurement problem in that $D_j = \alpha_j HD$. If α_j can be assumed to be equal to 1 and constant across all j then it is permissible to use the corrected index. If, however, α varies across j then we have a further measurement problem to which there is no obvious solution. As with most other features of this methodology this is an empirical question. Even if this were a problem however, it would not preclude the use of D_j (D'_j) as a dependent variable in empirical analysis.

(ii) Whatever use we put D_j to, the validity of the exercise depends crucially on the specification of (14.6), in particular whether there are any omitted influences and whether there is any collinearity between the included variables.

Omitted variables in the strict sense are not a problem if (14.5) can in fact be treated as an identity. Collinearity might however be more problematic. Although the various notions of differentiation are conceptually distinct, in practical terms they are likely to overlap. (The importance of this problem would diminish if we were to adjust simply for categorical aggregation).

(iii) Much depends on the quality of the proxies itself. As we have already seen, there is no obvious candidate for categorical aggregation. Although Caves (1981) and Greenaway and Milner (1982) employed census classification proxies and indices of product specialization for this purpose neither is completely satisfactory. Similar comments apply to TD^* and VD^*. In the case of the former there is no shortage of candidates, e.g. research intensity (Caves, 1981; Greenaway and Milner, 1982), rate of product turnover (Finger and De Rosa, 1979), first trade date (Hufbauer, 1970; Finger and De Rosa, 1979) to name but a few. Anyone familiar with the literature on empirical analyses of innovation will be familiar with the caveats which often have to accompany the use of such proxies. For VD^*/TD^* we have argued that the Hufbauer index might be the most suitable proxy. There is no need to rehearse further our reservations about this proxy. The point is, if we are already using imperfect proxies on the right-hand side to obtain an estimate of D_j there is likely to be a good deal of 'noise' in the system.

(iv) One could summarize all of these points by arguing that in the same way as we did with estimates of the contribution of technical progress to growth, we are simply taking the residual as a hold-all.

Although this residual method is theoretically feasible, it is quite obvious that there are problems associated with its implementation. It is equally obvious, however, that there are problems with all the available alternatives (not least regrouping). What is at issue is whether the residual method offers more promise than the available alternatives. As with regrouping, an answer can only be given upon implementation and, perhaps more important, replication. The one major advantage it would have over regrouping is that it is likely to be more cost-effective and rather more flexible.

The extent to which these various difficulties exert an influence over the resultant measure will depend principally on the attempted adjustments. The most ambitious application would be to estimate (14.8) to derive an index of pure intra-industry trade. Any index which could accurately reflect the relative importance of the international exchange of horizontally differentiated goods would be of interest not only because it would facilitate direct examination of the forces which drive such trade, but also because it would help to illuminate the adjustment question.[10] One would imagine however that the difficulties of implementation adumbrated above would be at their most intractable. As an alternative therefore one could estimate (14.6). Given the overlap between horizontal and vertical differentiation, this may be regarded as a more realistic and more meaningful approach. If one can eliminate trade in product cycle goods, and categorical aggregation then what remains is an estimate of two-way trade in horizontally and vertically differentiated goods. This would certainly come closer to trade in Chamberlinian-type goods than an unadjusted measure.

CONCLUDING COMMENTS

The purpose of this paper has been to provide a critical review of the principal methods by which product differentiation is 'measured' in cross-section analyses of trade flows. The review has been deliberately selective in focusing on differentiation from an end-use perspective, and in focusing on those methods used most widely.[11] The review has deliberately emphasized shorcomings primarily in order to emphasize any gaps between theory and practice.

Two conceptually distinct, but related approaches have been followed. On the one hand a number of proxies for product differentiation have been included in econometric models of trade flows; on the other hand some researchers have attempted to measure the volume of trade in differentiated goods by equating this with measured 'trade overlap'. In the case of cross-section studies of intra-industry trade, the two approaches merge together.

The two approaches can be viewed as distinct in so far as they are applicable in different circumstances. Thus, if one wishes to relate product differentiation to import penetration or revealed comparative advantage (for whatever reason) then the inclusion of some appropriate proxy of product differentiation may be the most sensible way to proceed. To this end future research would be best directed at improving the quality of such proxies. If, however, one is interested in establishing the proportion of total trade in a given range of product groups which takes the form of the simultaneous exchange of differentiated goods, and more important perhaps, explaining this, then clearly the way forward lies with improved measures of intra-industry trade. In this respect little progress had been made since the important contribution of Grubel and Lloyd (1971). Aquino (1978) proposed an adjustment for trade imbalance which Greenaway and Milner (1981) called into question. Glejser *et al.* (1982) proposed a measure of intra-industry specialization which in fact appears to be a method for measuring relative import specialization and relative export specialization, but not intra-industry specialization. Anyway, these contributions have addressed other facets of the Grubel and Lloyd measure. The problem of cleansing it of categorical aggregation and product cycle influences remains. Until progress is made in this direction specific comment on the relative importance of pure intra-industry trade will remain problematic. Furthermore, it will mean that cross-section studies of intra-industry trade remain in effect sensitivity tests of a number of hypotheses.

We have addressed ourselves only to cross-section analyses. It is in fact likely that industry specific studies of the Adler–Hocking type will ultimately prove more fruitful. The point is however that given the constrained nature of economic research, a great deal of reliance is placed on cross-section work. More meaningful analysis of patterns of intra-industry trade is likely to follow when using C_j and D_j as outlined in the second half of this paper. Some encouraging results have already been generated with the former (Greenaway and Milner, 1982), whilst the latter has yet to be subjected to rigorous experimentation.

NOTES

*   This paper has benefitted from discussion at the Conference, and from specific comments from Chris Milner and David Sapsford.
1.   See for example Balassa (1965, 1977).
2.   See for example Turner (1980) and Connell (1973).
3.   See for example Loertscher and Wolter (1980), Caves (1981), and Greenaway and Milner (1982).
4.   If one were to think in terms of specific examples the presence of different coloured paints could be described as horizontal differentiation, and the availability of water-based and oil-based paints vertical differentiation. The introduction of non-drip (water-based and oil-based) paints could then be described as technological differentiation.
5.   Some recent models have been concerned with trade in functionally homogenous goods, see for example Brander (1981).
6.   Interestingly Hufbauer introduced the measure to test for product cycle influences. He calculated indices at the third digit of the SITC as averages of the underlying seven-digit values and used this to test the hypothesis that smaller, less-developed countries will produce and export standardized products whilst larger, developed countries will specialize in and export differentiated goods.
7.   An interesting case in point here is the impact which the provisions of the multifibre arrangements appear to have had on export prices of newly industrializing countries.
8.   Balassa (1979) used a similar index for this reason.
9.   It must be emphasized that this is at present a somewhat speculative approach with which the author is currently experimenting and initial results are little more than suggestive.
10.   There is scope for some confusion over terms here. Adjustment in this context refers to the resource reallocation implications of intra-industry exchange compared with inter-industry exchange, rather than the adjustment of indices which we have been discussing so far.
    This is another issue intimately related to the analysis of intra-industry trade, but it is an issue which has received little in the way of systematic study. An important exception is Krugman (1981). Greenaway (1982) comments on the issue in the context of the gains from intra-industry exchange.
11.   Other approaches have been suggested which, although theoretically more appropriate than some of those discussed, have yet to be tried and tested (like the residual method). Bernhardt and Mackenzie's (1968) entropy measure is an example, as is the possibility of getting at the concept through order backlogs, an approach with which the present author is also experimenting.

REFERENCES

Adler, M. (1970), 'Specialization in the European Coal and Steel Community', *Journal of Common Market Studies*, 8, 175–91.

Aquino, A. (1978), 'Intra-Industry Trade and Inter-Industry Specialisation as Concurrent Sources of International Trade in Manufactures', *Weltwirtschaftliches Archives*, 114, 275–95.

Balassa, B. (1965), 'Trade Liberalisation and "Revealed" Comparative Advantage', *Manchester School*, May, 99–123.

Balassa, B. (1966), 'Tariff Reductions and Trade in Manufactures among Industrial Countries', *American Economic Review*, 56, 466–73.

Balassa, B. (1977), 'Revealed Comparative Advantage Revisited: An Analysis of Relative Export Shares of the Industrial Countries 1953–71', *Manchester School*, 45, pp. 327–44.

Balassa, B. (1979), 'Intra-Industry Trade and the Integration of Developing Countries in the World Economy', in H. Giersch (ed.), *On the Economics of Intra-Industry Trade* (Tübingen: J. C. B. Nohr).

Bernhardt, T. and Mackenzie, K. (1968), 'Measuring Seller Unconcentration Segmentation and Product Differentiation', *Western Economic Journal*, 6, 395–403.

Brander, J. A. (1981), 'Intra-Industry Trade in Identical Commodities', *Journal of International Economics*, 11, 1–14.

Caves, R. E. (1981), 'Intra-Industry Trade and Market Structure in the Industrial Countries', *Oxford Economic Papers*, 33, 203–23.

Caves, R. and Khalizadeh-Shirazi (1977), 'International Trade and Industrial Organisation', in A. P. Jacquemin and H. W. De Jong (eds.), *Welfare Aspects of Industrial Markets* (Leiden: Nijhoff).

Cable, J. (1972), 'Market Structure, Advertising Policy and Inter-Market Differences in Advertising Intensity', in K. Cowling (ed.), *Market Structure and Corporate Behaviour* (London: Gray Mills).

Comanor, D. S. and Wilson, T. (1974), 'Advertising and Market Power' (Cambridge, Mass.: Harvard University Press).

Connell, D. (1979), 'The UK's Performance in Export Markets, Some Evidence from International Trade Data', Discussion Paper 6, NEDO, London.

Finger, J. M. (1975a), 'A New View of the Product Cycle Theory', *Weltwirtschaftliches Archiv*, 111, 79–99.

Finger, J. M. (1975b), Trade Overlap and Intra-Industry Trade', *Economic Inquiry*, 13, 581–9.

Finger, J. M. and De Rosa, D. (1979), 'Trade Overlap, Comparative Advantage and Protection', in H. Giersch (ed.), *On the Economics of Intra-Industry Trade* (Tübingen: J. C. B. Möhr), pp. 213–40.

Glejser, H., Goossens, K. and Vanden Eede, M. (1982), 'Intra-Industry versus Intra-Industry Specialization in Exports and Imports', *Journal of International Economics*, 12, 363–70.

Goodman, B. and Ceyham, F. (1976), U.S. Export Performance in Manufacturing Industries: An Empirical Investigation', *Weltwirtschaftliches Archiv*, 112, 525–55.

Gray, H. R. (1979), 'Intra-Industry Trade: The Effects of Different Levels of Data Aggregation', in H. Giersch (ed.), *On the Economics of Intra-Industry Trade* (Tübingen, J. C. B. Möhr), pp. 87–110.

Gray, H. Peter and Martin, J. P. (1980), 'The Meaning and Measurement of Product Differentiation in International Trade', *Weltwirtschaftliches Archiv*, 116, 322–9.

Greenaway, D. (1982), 'Identifying the Gains from Pure Intra-Industry Exchange', *Journal of Economic Studies*, 9, 40–54.

Greenaway, D. (1983), 'Patterns of Intra-Industry Trade in Switzerland, 1965–77', Weltwirtschaftliches Archiv, 119, 109–21.

Greenaway, D. and Milner, C. R. (1981), 'Trade Imbalance Effects in the Measurement of Intra-Industry Trade', *Weltwirtschaftliches Archiv*, 117, 756–62.

Greenaway, D. and Milner, C. R. (1982), 'Inter-Industry Patterns in Intra-Industry Trade: An Econometric Investigation', Discussion Paper No. 11, University College at Buckingham.

Greer, D. F. (1971), 'Advertising and Market Concentration', *Southern Economic Journal*, 38, 19–32.

Gregory, B and Tearle, D. (1973), 'Product Differentiation and International Trade Flows: An Application of the Hedonic Regression Technique', *Australian Economic Papers*, 12, 78–90.

Grubel, H. G. and Lloyd, P. J. (1971), 'The Empirical Measurement of Intra-Industry Trade', *Economic Record*, 47, 494–517.

Grubel, H. G. and Lloyd, P. J. (1975), *Intra-Industry Trade* (London: Macmillan).

Helleiner, G. K. (1976), 'Industry Characteristics and the Competitiveness of Manufactures from Less Developed Countries', *Weltwirtschaftliches Archiv*, 112, pp. 507–24.

Hocking, R. D. (1980), 'Trade in Motor Cars between the Major European Producers', *Economic Journal*, 90, 504–19.

Hotelling, H. (1929), 'Stability in Competition', *Economic Journal*, 34, 41–57.

Hufbauer, G. C. (1970), 'The Impact of National Characteristics and Technology on the Commodity Composition of Trade in Manufactured Goods', in R. Vernon (ed.), *The Technology Factor in International Trade*, (New York: NBER).

Kravis, R. and Lipsey, R. (1971), *Price Competitiveness in World Trade* (New York: Columbia University Press).

Krugman, P. R. (1979), 'Increasing Returns, Monopolistic Competition and International Trade', *Trade Journal of International Economics*, 9(4), 469–79.

Krugman, P. (1980), 'Scale Economies, Product Differentiation and the Pattern of Trade', *American Economic Review*, 70, 950–9.

Krugman, P. (1981), 'Intra-industry Specialisation and the Gains from Trade', *Journal of Political Economy*, 89, 959–73.

Lancaster, K. (1979), *Variety, Equity and Efficiency* (Oxford: Basil Blackwell).

Lancaster, K. (1980), 'Intra-Industry Trade Under Perfect Monopolistic Competition', *Journal of International Economics*, 10, 151–76.

Loertscher, R. and Wolter, F. (1980), 'Determinants of Intra-Industry Trade: Among Countries and Across Industries', *Weltwirtschaftliches Archiv*, 116, 280–93.

McAleese, D. (1979), 'Intra-Industry Trade, Level of Development and Market Size', in H. Giersch (ed.), *On the Economics of Intra-Industry Trade* (Tübingen: J. C. B. Möhr), 137–54.

Mann, H., Henning, J. A., and Meehan, J. W. (1973), 'Advertising and market Concentration: A Comment', *Southern Economic Journal*, 40.

Pagoulatos, E. and Sorensen, R. (1975), 'Two-way International Trade: An Econometric Analysis', *Weltwirtschaftliches Archiv*, 111, 454–65.

Porter, M. E. (1976), 'Interbrand Choice, Media Mix and Market Performance', *American Economic Review*, 66(2), 398–406.

Rayment, P. B. W. (1976), 'The Homogeneity of Manufacturing Industries with respect to Factor Intensity: The Case of the U.K.', *Oxford Bulletin of Economics and Statistics*, 38, 203–9.

Reekie, W. D. (1975), 'Advertising, Concentration and Competition: An Interchange', *Economic Journal*, 85, 156–64.

Rosen, S. (1974), 'Hedonic Prices and Implicit Markets: Product Differentiation in Pure Competition', *Journal of Political Economy*, 82, 34–55.

Scherer, F. M. (1980), *Industrial Market Structure and Economic Performance*, 2nd ed. (Chicago: Rand McNally).

Sutton, C. J. (1975), 'Advertising, Concentration and Competition', *Economic Journal*, 85, 173–6.

Tharakan, P. K. M., Soete, L. G., and Busschaert, J. A. (1978), 'Heckscher–Olin and Chamberlain Determinants of Comparative Advantage', *European Economic Review*, 11, 221–39.

Turner, P. (1980), 'Import Competition and Profitibility of UK Manufacturing Industry', *Journal of Industrial Economics*, 19, 155–66.

Author index

Subject index